3/27

CYNDI LAUPER: A MEMOIR

CYNDI

LAUPER

A Memoir

Cyndi Lauper

with Jancee Dunn

ATRIA BOOKS

NEW YORK LONDON TORONTO SYDNEY NEW DELHI

ATRIA BOOKS

A Division of Simon & Schuster, Inc.
1230 Avenue of the Americas
New York, NY 10020

First Atria Books hardcover edition September 2012

ATRIA BOOKS and colophon are trademarks of Simon & Schuster, Inc.

For information about special discounts for bulk purchases, please contact Simon
& Schuster Special Sales at 1-866-506-1949 or business@simonandschuster.com.

The Simon & Schuster Speakers Bureau can bring authors to your live event. For
more information or to book an event, contact the Simon & Schuster Speakers
Bureau at 1-866-248-3049 or visit our website at www.simonspeakers.com.

Designed by Dana Sloan

Manufactured in the United States of America

10   9   8   7   6   5   4   3   2   1

Library of Congress Cataloging-in-Publication Data

ISBN: 978-1-4391-4785-6
ISBN: 978-1-4391-7219-3 (ebook)

To David Thornton, my husband and best friend,
who always told me to write my story down.
Thank you for inspiring and helping me through every rough turn.
Thank you for lending your tremendous eye and ear to this book
and to nearly everything I've done since I met you.

THERE WERE SO many people who helped me throughout my career, too many to mention in this book. But I remember all the times these people worked tirelessly by my side without any accolades. We had a lot of laughs and good times together that I will always remember.

When I received my first gold record I sent it out to people who helped me, with an inscription that said, "You couldn't have done it without me." I'd like to make an adjustment now. I couldn't have done anything without all the help of everyone over all these years.

CHAPTER ONE

I LEFT HOME AT seventeen. I took a paper bag with a toothbrush, a change of underwear, an apple, and a copy of Yoko Ono's book *Grapefruit*. *Grapefruit* had become my window for viewing life through art. My plan was to take the train to the Long Island Rail Road and then a bus to Valley Stream. I had left dinner in the oven for my brother, Butch, who was five years younger than me. He was the reason I stayed so long. But things were just getting worse for me. This situation with my stepfather was impossible.

At the time, my mother worked as a waitress—five days a week, sometimes six, and it was a fourteen-hour day. My mom knew what was going on, but we got by; we had a system. I'd come home from school, go to my bedroom, and lock the door. She thought we could kind of live around my stepfather until she got on her feet a little more. My sister had left home already. She was living in Valley Stream with her friend Wha. She and I had always been sidestepping situations with my stepfather, but this time it was too creepy for me. I called my sister that day to tell her what had happened earlier in the bathroom.

The bathroom was in the back of the apartment, off a corridor that led to two bedrooms. I shared one of them with my sister most of our lives, and my younger brother's bedroom was right next to ours. The bathroom was rectangular, with a long, old-fashioned clawfoot tub. It ran the length of the right-hand wall past the toilet, which was by the door. The top of the tub curled over a bit so you could sit on its edge by the little sink on the back wall. As a child I used to watch my dad shave over that sink before he left for work. And I once saw my mom sit on the edge of the tub and sing the most beautiful rendition of Al Jolson's "Sonny Boy" to my little brother while he sat on her lap. It was one of the most haunting and heart-wrenching moments I'd ever witnessed.

One time my mom showed us how, if you attached a little hose to the faucet in the tub, you could clean yourself while you were on the toilet, like a bidet. This little task was all very civilized and very French. She loved everything French. At the time she would say that it was "chic," which she pronounced "chick." But whatever it was called, there was a drawback to this whole water-hose-connected-to-the-faucet-of-the-tub task. Because whatever water you ran in the tub you could hear through the pipes in the kitchen wall. So when I started experimenting with different kinds of water pressure that could be used while performing this task, she could hear the pipes jam in the kitchen. Of course, as a child, I didn't realize how unsettling something like that would be to my mother, who was washing the dishes. (And anything that had to do with my body would send her running for a thick anatomy book so she could explain about taking care of yourself, and what you should and shouldn't be doing "down there.")

The bathroom was an olive green. The middle of the wall that led to the sink had a heating vent in it. That always came in handy when I came in from the snow because it was butt-high. The bathroom door had four panes of frosted textured glass that looked like it had little pressed snowflakes in it. The glass allowed light through but provided some privacy. There was also a small window over the tub that looked out onto the alley. It was about two feet wide and three feet tall, and it had the same frosted snowflake glass as the door. If you stood in the tub, you could open the window a crack and steal a puff from a cigarette. But I was careful not to let my grandmother, whose kitchen window was right above, or Mrs. Schnur, who lived next door, catch me. From that window, I could also talk to someone sitting on the stoop in the alley. But all of those memories dissipated when the bathroom became a dangerous place.

It was late afternoon. I took a bath, thinking I was alone. There was a little hook latch on the bathroom door but the frosted glass now had a crack in it with a tiny hole. The hole was made by my mother's platinum wedding band the day my stepfather threw her against the bathroom door. I remember when she first got that ring and showed it to me. I said, "It's not gold." And she said proudly, "Platinum is more precious than gold and never wears down." Well, maybe the ring didn't wear down, but the ring wore *her* down. And the glass in the door was never repaired. It had been that way for a while. My stepdad wasn't good at fixing things. He worked and provided. That was the deal, I guess. And for a woman with three kids, that was a lot to ask. Anyway, because of that hole, I was always careful to use the bathroom when other people weren't around.

Even though I thought no one was home, I locked the door with the hook-and-eye latch anyway and filled the tub. I got in and leaned back. I put my legs up and sank into the water to rinse my hair off. But when I came up for air, I heard a creepy giggle and saw my stepfather's pear-shaped shadow against the frosted glass. I even saw his crazy eye looking through the hole. It was too much. It was worse than him beating the dog when she cried and making us keep her on a leash tied to the kitchen door. It was worse than him standing behind the furnace at night in his robe with that creepy giggle when I had to go into the basement to hang up the wet laundry. It was worse than him touching himself, right outside our bedroom window.

I knew the apathetic, cold look I needed to wear on my face to survive. But that day I just had to call my sister and tell her what happened. Elen said to get my ass out of there and come to her apartment, *now*. And all of a sudden I felt I could leave with someplace to go. So I cleaned up the kitchen for the last time, and made a round steak and a baked potato for supper and left it in the oven for my little brother. I knew I would be free but I would miss my little brother so much. I was worried about him. He was only eleven. But I didn't think he'd get hurt like I might have gotten hurt if I stayed. So I left. But I planned to come back for him one day.

My sis and I lived most of our lives dodging pedophiles and the crazy folks. Our big issues were with my stepfather—my mom's second husband—and, for me, my grandfather. My family always thought that my grandfather was off a little because of a stroke he had while watching a live wrestling match. But who knows when he actually did go "off"? It was ironic how wrestling would come back into my life and play such an important role in my career.

The day I finally left was at the end of fall. I had been watching the sky for months. There was a water tower that sat on top of the old Singer sewing machine factory, on the corner of our block in Ozone Park, Queens. I would watch the sun turn the little tower from dark sugar brown to golden orange, and then to a silhouette against a dusky sky. I watched birds fly over it when autumn came. I never tired of it. There was something I found profoundly beautiful about that industrial landscape. It had always been one of my escapes. And now I would walk past the old Singer factory and the abandoned Borden factory that stood farther down on Atlantic Avenue for the last time.

I made my way to the Jamaica Avenue El and caught the train to the Long Island Rail Road, which would take me to the bus that would get me to my sister's new apartment, in Valley Stream.

Funny thing is, I had been packing since I was fourteen to get away from that apartment in Ozone Park. My dad, who I saw once in a while, was a shipping clerk at the Bulova watch company. I used to think if I told my dad, he could help. But there was never the right time. My dad had become a bit of an elusive, tragic figure to me—tragic because he never looked happy anymore.

I remembered what he looked like when I was five. He seemed quiet but not as sad. I'd studied him closely as a child. I loved to follow him around. I remember my dad had a xylophone for a short time that he kept in what used to be the front porch but was now an open extension of my mom's and his bedroom. I remember seeing him play it a few times and being enamored with the sound. And I remember sitting under his xylophone when he wasn't around, trying to imagine what that sound would be like from inside the instrument. But it wasn't long before he switched the xylophone for a Hawaiian slide guitar. I would listen to him play that and look at the pictures of a land of palm trees and hula dancers that seemed to sway across the covers of his Hawaiian guitar songbooks.

But the one instrument that was more portable and the one he always seemed to have handy was the harmonica. He would always pull it out of his pocket and play something when times were dull and quiet, or if somebody said, "Hey, Freddy, play us a tune?" He would cup his hands over his mouth and start tapping his foot. Some of my favorite notes were those long and lonesome bended ones in between melodies that sounded to me like a cowboy by the campfire. And I liked to sit around a good make-believe campfire with him while he played, just like the ones photographed in my mother's *Life* magazines that sat on our TV set.

I loved pictures, especially ones I could imagine myself in. And lucky for me, my dad also loved taking them. He would take pictures of my sister and me with a special camera when we were small. It was a rectangle and had a little hood that came up and created a dark space, so you could see the frame of the picture he was about to take. All I had to do was step into it. But I used to cry if he snapped a picture of me when I wasn't ready. (Ya know, I don't cry if that's done to me now, but I do bitterly complain because I still hate a bad angle.) But at that time, to me, my dad had magic.

I watched my dad leave for work every day. I watched him walk off until he was so tiny I couldn't find him anymore on the horizon. I practiced recognizing him as he walked back out of the horizon toward me from blocks away, too. I must have been four and a half. I would pace in front of the two-family mother/daughter house we lived in, with shingles that looked almost like the color of Good & Plenty candy. I'd check to see if he was walking down from the Jamaica Avenue El train, which was around eight blocks away. I could always spot him. He was tall and thin with dark black hair. I could see him walking toward me even if in the distance he appeared only two inches tall.

He always wore a dark gray overcoat and a collared shirt with a narrow tie—but not so narrow that you couldn't see it when he crossed the corner of our street. And by the time he got there I'd already be running as fast as I could so that I could slam myself into the bottom of his overcoat and tell him how glad I was that he was home. Because when he came back, he brought an intriguing world with him—whether he brought his musical instruments or books on Chinese archaeology, or, like one late Saturday afternoon, he came into the house carrying a big yellow wood TV set that opened an even bigger world to me.

But it had been a long time since I sat on his lap as a child and begged him not to go. He and my mother had fought a lot back then. He said it was best. By the time I was ten, he'd either call from work and stay on the line until the dime ran out or put another nickel in, and I'd get tricked into thinking there was enough time to talk about something that might take more than five minutes. But when that nickel ran down, he would get off the phone. And that's when his being elusive became so prominent. He would meet us on the designated day of the weekend, at either an ice cream parlor or a candy shop by the train because he'd come in from the city. He took a room at the Washington Hotel in midtown Manhattan. I got to visit from time to time, but as I got older, he came to us more. We'd spend two or three hours together before he'd get back on the train and go to the city again. And like his phone calls, which were usually from work, the setting was never anyplace where we could talk about anything that was really serious.

I remember once trying to tell him something that happened while we were sitting together at the candy store counter. In those days, you could get food like french fries and a burger or an ice cream sundae or a root beer float, and sit on a stool at the counter. You used to be able to get different flavors of soda too, not just Coke or Pepsi. This is a piece of New York that has for the most part faded away.

I remember once toward the end of one of these visits with my dad, when we were sitting in that candy store next to the bakery on Liberty Avenue by the A train 104th Street stop, the guy at the counter slowly stopped wiping the ice cream cup he had just washed and widened his eyes as I got a few sentences into what was happening at home. And somehow it didn't seem to be a good time to bring it up, with this guy at the counter listening as closely as he was to what I wished could be more of a private conversation with my dad. So I just gave up.

And from time to time, I couldn't help but laugh when I'd get off of one of my dad's brief phone calls and hear my stepfather say, "Who was that on the phone—our father who art in New York?" And I'd say under my breath, "*Dominus* Nabisco." That was a joke my sister and I had with each other from when we were kids. We would reenact Sunday Mass. My sister was the priest and I was the faithful parishioner. She would hold up a white Necco candy wafer (of course, had they been shelling out those at church, I think a lot more kids would have gone to communion, even if confession was a little rough). Then she would piously say, "*Dominus vobiscum,*" and I would answer, "*Dominus Nabisco* to all." And even though my stepdad wasn't in on that joke, I said it to him anyway, because it made me laugh. My stepdad was funny. But that's what made him so tricky, because I thought he was psychotic too.

I never really told anyone about my home life. I had friends with parents who seemed worse off than mine, so I didn't think I had it so bad. It just seemed like life made some of the grown-ups go crazy. There were times, though, when I wished my dad had never left. I thought for some reason that an unmarried woman with two girls and a young boy was easy prey. So when my mom came home from work one day and said she was in love, we all were happy for her and thought it would be better. But unfortunately, she married a pedophile who beat her and bullied her. He'd threaten to beat her parents and rape her daughters while she was at work. And then he told her he would use the power of his family to crush her and her little family in court should she try to report his threats. There were times when my grandparents or perhaps Mrs. Schnur would have enough of the ruckus and call the police. But when the police came, they would say it was just domestic violence and leave. I wished I could go to my dad, but I never felt he was able to stick up for himself, let alone us.

I thought maybe life beat him down too. Survival seemed to be all anyone around me could handle. I survived by sleeping as much as I could in my bedroom with the door locked so that my stepfather could not follow through with his threats. Home life in that apartment was hard, and even though my mom told me to be a fighter and get through, it seemed a monumental task.

And for a time apathy set in, along with sinus headaches. I went to a doctor for them. I didn't think they might have been stress related. I thought they were just caused by allergies. The doctor gave me a prescription for phenobarbital. When I took the pills—wow, I felt good. But then for some reason the doctor thought I was scamming him and became angry at me, and said he would never refill the prescription.

There were some joyous, precious moments too, with my mom. My mom loved music and art and drama. I guess her love spilled over to me. She adored and craved the culture that life in that neighborhood denied her. She used to sing around the house, and sometimes she would paint by numbers. When she found a paint-by-numbers painting that she loved, she would set up the canvas very excitedly, like we were about to experience some culture just by having it up on the little easel it came with. Her favorite artists were the Impressionists: she loved Renoir, Monet, and the Postimpressionists Gauguin and van Gogh.

She also used to play Debussy, Tchaikovsky, and Satchmo on our new Philips stereo. And she loved Leonard Bernstein. So when she played us *Peter and the Wolf*, it was Bernstein's version. One day I remember we lay on her bed to listen to Debussy's "Afternoon of a Faun." It was so beautiful, I started to cry. I asked her if that's what music does sometimes, and she said yes.

I learned how to play guitar from a book by Mel Bay. God bless Mel. I'd play, sing, and write songs all the time. When I was nine, I got some Barbie dolls and two albums for Christmas. One was a Supremes album called *Meet the Supremes*, and the other was *Meet the Beatles*. I was glad to meet both of them. The Supremes sounded like they were my age, like they were my friends, and I would sing with them constantly. Their songs were memorable and easy to sing along to. And I guess that was the first call-and-response I ever sang. The Beatles, however, were intriguing in a different way because I had a crush on them. And because the media introduced them to us individually, and we were encouraged to pick our favorite Beatle, I picked Paul. My sister and I would dress up like the Beatles for our family, and perform with mops.

My sister, Elen, always wanted to be Paul, so I was John. Whatever my sister was doing, I wanted to be with her. My mom told me that I was born to be her friend, and I took that literally. Besides, I didn't mind being John, because he was married to someone named Cynthia. And that was really my name, not just Cindy. And I had a dream once that I was brushing my teeth with John Lennon and spitting in the same sink. (Later, I told that to Sean Lennon, but I think it scared him.)

By singing with my sister like that, and listening to John's voice, I learned harmony and the structure of songs. By the time I was eleven, I began writing with my sister. When Elen graduated from junior high school, she got an electric Fender guitar and amp, and I got her acoustic guitar when I was graduating from sixth grade. Our first song was called "Sitting by the Wayside." I guess if I heard my kid write that now I'd be worried, but we were living in the protest era.

Before that, I was always singing along to Barbra Streisand from my mother's record collection. I also performed for myself a lot with my mother's Broadway albums: *My Fair Lady, The King and I, South Pacific*. I was Ezio Pinza and Mary Martin. I was also Richard Harris in *Camelot*. At times when I sang I would act like my relatives, because they were always very dramatic. (They were Sicilian, after all.) But mostly I liked the way it felt to change my voice, and when I sang, I could imagine the leading man right in front of me. My interior life and my play life were so real to me that I could make up anything. I guess the saddest thing about being introduced to the Supremes and the Beatles, though, was that all of a sudden there was a difference between my mother's music collection and mine.

In high school I listened to Janis Joplin, Jimi Hendrix, Joni Mitchell, Sly and the Family Stone, the Chambers Brothers, the Four Tops, and Cream. Motown was king, and, of course, Beatles, Beatles, Beatles. When I got older, they came out with *The White Album*, and I put each of their pictures on the walls of my room. That's where I'd daydream, write poems, paint, write songs, or play other people's songs on my guitar. Sometimes I'd hear my mom call out to me to clean my room and I'd try to ignore her. Once I must have pushed her right over the edge because she finally came in and said, "I want you, and all your friends (pointing to the pictures on the walls), to clean this room up *right now.*" It was not easy for her.

I also liked to spend some time with my nana upstairs in her apartment. The air was a little lighter there, especially when Grandpa wasn't home. She'd tell me dramatic stories about her life in Sicily, while making very unusual sandwiches made of cottage cheese and peanut butter that she spread on toasted "light caloric" bread. She said that even though the sandwich might seem like an odd choice, it was very healthy and didn't taste bad either. Her stories seemed a little like Aesop's fables told in a thick Italian accent.

She once told me about a young man who would stand and wait in front of her window when she was a young girl just to catch a glimpse of her. As she told the story, she would act it out for me. She was very captivating, and as I looked through that window with her as she gazed down at her young suitor, I could understand why the guy felt that way about her. She described the length of her hair and swung gently around to show me how far it went down her back. I could almost see it move with her and feel how soft it was. Nana's hair was now short and cut to just under her ears, with a natural wave and gray highlights.

She told me how her father would not allow this courtship because the young man wore glasses; her father said, "What if when he gets older he loses his sight? What will you do then?" The smitten young man knew my grandmother liked to sew. So he gave her a little sewing kit, and therein lay the lesson: "Never give anything sharp or with a point on it to someone you love, because it will go straight to their heart," she would always say. And like Aesop's fables, my grandmother's stories had twists and turns in them, but with strange sad endings instead of happily ever after. I always felt bad that she didn't get to be happy in her young life. Her stories used to fill me with so many emotions. I would say things to her like, "Boy, Nana, if I was there with ya, I wouldn't let them hurt you. I'd give them such a hard time, they'd be sorry." But she would say, "You did what you were told in that time." And I'd come to realize that no matter how much I felt I was traveling back in time with her when she told these stories, I could never undo the wrong done to her because of a ridiculous mentality that kept women back.

As a kid, I heard a lot of sad stories about women. My mom loved art and music so much, but she wasn't allowed to accept a scholarship to a high school for voice, because my grandparents said, "Only whores go to school in Manhattan." This was another ridiculous belief that wore on me. In the end, my mom never graduated. She became sickly with gynecological issues and wound up dropping out of a local high school in Queens. She then went to work to help support her family. I knew she wanted it to be different for me.

There was another story I heard as a kid that started with, "You see Aunt Gracie? She was so beautiful when she was young, she could have been a model!" I always thought that when you heard a beginning like that, the story would be something upbeat. But no. This was another sad one that went like this: Aunt Gracie had a friend who took pictures of her and made a portfolio so that she could go to the modeling agencies. But my grandparents found the pictures and tore them up. I guess they were horrified to see their youngest daughter posing in a shorts set and smiling so pretty for the camera. I think they also tore up part of her spirit, because she never went back to the photographer to get other copies.

She still had a killer smile and a great joy in her, but it was coupled with big lows. Sometimes you just never knew what you did to set her off. And she didn't feel well a lot in her life. We thought, as it was said in the vernacular of my old neighborhood, that the sickness "was set in by unhappiness." But I do have her to thank for my cousins who I grew up with, Susie and Vinny. What a gift they are.

Around thirty-five years after I heard that story about Aunt Gracie as a kid, life brought those pictures to me. I was remaking "Disco Inferno" with Soul Solution. It was 1999. I was talking with Bobby, half of the Soul Solution team, and he told me his uncle took pictures of my aunt when she was young. He gave them to me and as I looked at them, I thought, "Ya know what? My mom was right. My aunt was very beautiful. She really could have modeled." And for the time, she was tall enough. She was five foot seven. She looked glamorous, like a young Polly Bergen. Aunt Gracie wore an artichoke hairdo in the picture, which was the rage in the fifties. (Natalie Wood wore the same style in *Rebel Without a Cause*.) There was also a glint of mischief in her eyes, mixed with a little bit of hope. The underlying sadness that was in her face later in life was missing from those pictures. It must have crept in bit by bit as she accepted what my grandparents thought was safe for her life. "I could have been, I should have been, I would have been, if not for . . ." is a constant refrain that has always haunted me, whether in my mother's voice or in the many forgotten voices from around the old neighborhood.

So when you ask me if I knew that "Girls Just Want to Have Fun" would be a hit, and I say I didn't want to do the song at first because I didn't think it was especially good for women, maybe you understand better why. But then my producer Rick Chertoff said to me, "Think of what this song could *mean*." And then I saw my grandmother's, my aunt's, and my mother's faces in my head. And I thought that maybe I could do something and say something so loud that every girl would hear—every girl, every color. And I said to myself, "Hell yeah, I'll make an anthem! Maybe it'll be something that will bring us all together and wake us up." It would be a movement right under all the oppressors' noses, and no one would know about it until there was nothing they could do to stop it. I was going to make it work come hell or high water. I'd make it work for every poor sucker whose dreams and joys were dashed out.

CHAPTER TWO

I HAD WANTED TO go to a performing arts high school so badly. But when my mom went to discuss this with my eighth-grade guidance counselor, he asked her if she wanted me to end up waiting tables like she did. He made her cry over the idea that I might wind up in her shoes one day. That rat—I never liked that guy. So this so-called authority told my mom that because our family had worked in the fashion industry and my uncle had made a name for himself as a pattern maker, the High School of Fashion Industries would be a better fit for me. Miraculously, I passed their entrance test.

The best thing about going to Fashion Industries was the adventure of going to a vocational school in Manhattan on the A train. I spent a ton of time on the subway watching the straphangers. I took a great pleasure in being part of that community. Manhattan wasn't remotely like Ozone Park, Queens. As a high schooler, I was living the life my mom never did. I was going to school in Manhattan! My grandparents had it so wrong. This wasn't about becoming a whore. It was about becoming cultured and educated and wanting more. I was going to the mecca of art, music, and fashion. I was traveling every day to a place where people were more glamorous. Maybe they were afraid that if my mother became cultured she wouldn't accept "safe" and "meek."

I was never good at time management, so there were many frenzied moments. Once I cut and sewed together a dress for school and then ran up the six blocks to Liberty Avenue, like I always did, in chunky high shoes, carrying my portfolio in my hand and my books under my arm and a handbag over my shoulder. The dress had the seams sewn on the outside, which I thought looked good—it was just that the idea of deconstruction hadn't really come into its own yet. I must have been a sight.

As a freshman at Fashion Industries you took different kinds of sewing classes, like the power-sewing machine class or the fine-material machine class. I got a little depressed in the shoe-making class because all we sewed was a calfskin knife case. I also imagined that the class led to a job at a shoemaker under a pile of broken shoes that needed to be mended. My fine-material machine sewing class teacher dressed in a very old-fashioned way, with a knee-length straight skirt and a short-sleeve shirt with cuffs, and she'd always stuff a pressed handkerchief up the left sleeve. She gave me a seventy and told me the knots on the end of my needle and thread for hand stitching were like torpedoes.

The art class was the kicker. I actually loved it but got on the far wrong side of the teacher. She wanted me to move my seat and I didn't understand why, so I said I wouldn't. Then she said the only way I'd pass was if I brought in twelve paintings by the end of the term. So I painted and painted. And I loved it. I would stay up all night in my room with poor ol' Elen in the other twin bed next to mine, with her head under her pillow while I painted. Looking back, I see that I was very selfish for having the light on. But my big sister was a good sport. I used watercolors and poster paint, which was very easy to maneuver without an easel. I just painted on the floor. I created pictures of the woods at night or my grandmother's garden, which was moonlit right outside my bedroom window.

Then the day came when I proudly handed them in to my teacher. But she was being threatened by one of the bigger girls in the class, who told her that she better not fail her. The school wasn't exactly in the best neighborhood and there was always some rough trade to maneuver around. Since she was busy, I said, "Here are the paintings," and put them down in front of her and left.

When I got my report card, I received a zero in art. The teacher said she never got any paintings from me. I should have remembered one of those Aesop's fables—the one with the moral that goes something like "Always get a receipt." I was crushed about losing all that work. There were other failures, too, like my English and math classes. I had mostly spent my time painting and I never got much else done.

Everybody told me to study hard, but nobody ever taught me how to study. I was just told that I'd better learn or I'd wind up like everyone else around me, which was very upsetting. But I just never knew where to start, and it was always a daunting task that I would put off, until I just fell asleep. There were times when I would open up a book and leave it open next to me, completely terrified. I was too anxious to study and felt doomed to fail. So I failed. I figured if I was going to fall, I might as well hit the bottom and get the worst of it over with. I remember bringing home a report card with every grade a failing one, and the zero in art. I guess there was a moral I should have learned from that experience, too, but it was too crushing to think about. I remember my stepfather looking at my report card and saying, "You failed gym? Isn't that like failing lunch?"

But before I flunked out, I was put in something called a non-achieving-genius class. There was this English teacher in there who actually was very inspiring. She brought in a Janis Ian song and laid it out like a poem instead of lyrics. Song lyrics at their best are poems, and that part interested me. What inspired my English teacher to think I was worth helping was my understanding of the Hemingway novel *The Old Man and the Sea*. I guess she didn't want to throw me back in the water once she saw how that book caught my interest and how I understood the metaphors that she loved so much.

But in the end I wasn't a nonachieving genius—I was just a nonachiever. And that's how I entered the Richmond Hill High School annex as a freshman again. My sister, Elen, was a senior there and I was always welcome at her lunch table, and there I didn't feel so left back. And when Elen graduated, I stayed on with younger friends and did half the freshman year again. I got very depressed, though. I just failed and failed. I started to feel like I was in a recurring bad dream and that somewhere there had to be a different reality.

For me, the little pleasantries, like the sunset or sunrise, or when the trees bloomed, or birds sang, or I saw the flowers in my grandmother's garden, were the only distractions I could find to keep myself going. I never felt inside that I fit into this world. I always had one foot where I stood and one foot somewhere else. They used to say I was just a daydreamer. I did daydream, but I used to write a lot of poetry, too, and draw whatever I could.

The few friends I had after Elen left school declared themselves gay, and when they came out, I thought, "Ooh, I'm gay because they're gay." So I tried. One of my close friends said she was in love with me. Well, I didn't want to lose my friend, so we held hands, and then we would kiss, but it wasn't how I was feeling. I even read *The Fox* by D. H. Lawrence, but no matter how I tried, I just wasn't feeling what she felt. I loved her, but not like that. I had to tell her the truth: I wasn't really a lesbian. I had to come out as a heterosexual.

As graduation kept slipping a year ahead of me, and my extra time in high school started to feel like serving a double term in misery, I quit. I was washed up. I was seventeen. After I left, I had a few friends who helped me forget my predicament. One was a girl from the neighborhood, Susan Monteleone. She lived around the corner and across the street from me. She even had an older sister the same age as my sister. And best of all, she played guitar like us. She was always a better guitar player than me. (I'm grateful to just be able to play at all. I find it soothing, even though now I usually just play dulcimer and only use guitar for writing. I even tune my guitar in fifths, like a dulcimer.)

Susan also turned me on to the women's movement. We went to a demonstration for women's rights together at the *Alice in Wonderland* statue in Central Park. First we met some women Susan knew at a hotel. They seemed a little angry and some looked like hard-core lesbians. Once I heard some older men from my neighborhood refer to the women's movement as "a bunch of angry lesbians." I guessed at the time that what they meant was that a woman just needed to get laid, and then she would go back to the old boys' system quick enough. But when I listened to these women talk, it seemed they had a lot to be angry about. They were talking about civil rights for all women, theirs and mine too. This was beyond all stereotypes—this was revolutionary. Susan was talking to a woman she knew, and then when everyone started to leave for the park, somebody said we could go with them in their limo.

There was a lot of hubbub and excitement in the car. Susan and I had been practicing what we would say and what we would burn for a couple of weeks. Susan was burning the hard plastic rollers she slept on for years to make her hair look good. That, I understood. How long can you put up with that before throwing the damn things out? That was thrilling, as thrilling as riding in the big long limo with all of those different types of women, whose mere chatter was the most inspirational information I had heard in a long time.

I understood everything they were talking about in that limo and for the most part agreed. But deep down I secretly still loved some of the fashion they looked down on, even though I agree that there are elements of fashion that are anti-women, like high heels that slow us down. Being in that car at the age of fifteen was so intense though that I could never say, in my hand-me-down Queens vernacular, "I still love them shoes, though."

As for my big moment in front of the trash can, I brought one of my mother's old bras that she gave me after I outgrew my training bra. It was pointy and old-fashioned. I walked up to the mesh trash basket, held up my mother's old bra, and said, "I burn this for me, for my mother, and for my grandmother!" It was a good moment in my life that offset a lot of not-so-victorious moments. And I also felt my mom should have thrown that bra away, anyway.

This was a new time. It was the time of protests and thinking free and being free. Although I always thought that "free love" thing seemed like a dirty deal for women. It was free, but for who? Say you felt like you wanted all the liberties a man was afforded, and you wanted to sleep with whomever, right? You still were considered a tramp. And say, like a man, you chose not to sleep with someone? Then you were frigid or a lesbian. You should be able to have control over your body and your life—just like a man. But birth control had come into play over the previous decade. And at the time, young women and girls were dying all over the United States from illegal and unsafe abortions.

Susan and I also formed a folk duo called Spring Harvest. (What the heck? I shoulda known that wouldn't work. There's no such thing as a harvest in the spring.) But it was still a great experience. We performed twice together in a small café in Queens, on a road that ran from Woodhaven Boulevard to the Alexander's store on Queens Boulevard. It was a cute place, but they didn't pay, and we had to get our friends to come see us. Later on in my professional life, I would come to know that setup as a "pay-to-play" situation. Instead of the club paying you, you're kind of paying them by bringing your friends.

At our first gig, a comic opened for us, and Elen and Wha came with their friend Dominic, who heckled the poor guy. Unfortunately Dominic was funnier than the comic, which was a big problem for us. When we went to check out everything before the place opened, the owner said to me, "Look, girlie, there's no microphones here. But there's an acoustic tile right up there on the ceiling. Aim up there, and everyone will hear ya." Now, as far as I know, acoustic tiles control sound reverberation and are used to make the room sound better. But this guy didn't have a whole ceiling of acoustic tiles like you're supposed to—he just had one tile hanging slightly on a diagonal from a dropped cork ceiling, like the kind my friend's father used to refinish their basement. I aimed for that tile from not really a stage, but more like a wooden dance floor in the center of the room. I aimed and I aimed all night, especially on the soft high singing parts I did in Eric Andersen's "Thirsty Boots." The guy had me believing that it worked. (Hey, it was my first gig.) Funny how now I can still aim my voice if I need to.

The duo was a distraction and contrast to school and home and my sister leaving. All of a sudden I could function and define myself. I felt like maybe there was something for me to be good at. But that didn't work out, because we were so young. We did have a meeting with an agent/manager once. Susan found him. Susan was one of those really informed take-action types of people. Susan was even writing Joan Baez's mother letters. I guess it started as fan mail and turned into her asking for advice. And to Joan Baez's mom's credit, Susan got responses. Anyway, we played for this agent/manager and he informed us that we needed to have some boys in the band, so that if we got married, we wouldn't split up. What the heck?

While this was happening I was still struggling in school. I will always remember that zero I got in art, because of how I felt like such a zero sitting in what felt like a remedial art class. I remember being handed small round-edged scissors, like the kind you used in kindergarten. I was told to cut paper to make paper cones, which we would glue together with a nontoxic glue (because some of the kids in the class were already in-toxic-ated).

So I went to the head of the art department and asked not to be punished anymore. Somehow I talked my way into taking his course instead. He liked my work, so I was able to go to an art program at Washington Irving High School in Manhattan for summer school, which I really liked. But after that, I was back at Richmond Hill High School, failing again.

So this time, they put me in a different program, one for kids who will never go to college. They teach you things like how to be a file clerk, so that's what I did. The building overlooked the docks, and I used to look at the boats and wonder what it was like to be Tugboat Annie. In my mind, I was living the secret life of Walter Mitty. And on that dock I used to find myself staring at, I wrote out a wish on a piece of paper that I folded into the shape of a boat and cast off to sea in the East River. I wished that someday I would meet someone like me who would be an artist and create and understand. Someone who remembered the child in themselves. I guess that's like that *Snow White* song, "Someday My Prince Will Come."

About four years after I became famous, in 1988, Richmond Hill High School asked me to go to a reunion. As a "famous person," I got a lot of stuff in the mail, and sometimes I actually got the time to open and read it. I was really on the hamster wheel at that time (when I sang "Money Changes Everything," I knew exactly what that meant). One of my closest friends, who was also my first publicist, Katie Valk, was sitting at my kitchen table in the loft I owned in the American Thread Building. She worked with me when I was in the band Blue Angel. We had become really close the night we sat together when my band broke up. She patiently listened to me cry to her about it at a bar in the West Village and then she said, "Don't be such a victim." And she was right. So I moved on.

Katie worked for a public relations firm called Solters/Roskin/ Friedman, and she was one of the best publicists at that time. When I opened the letter from Richmond Hill asking me to go to a reunion, I said to Katie, "Yeah, right—they expelled me!" Now, at the time lots of famous folks were getting honorary college degrees. So Katie started laughing and said, "You should call them and tell them that you'll only come if they nullify your expulsion and give you an honorary high school diploma." So I said, "Yeah!" But I never thought they'd go for it. Silly me—they did. So I got an outfit for graduation with the help of my stylist at the time, Laura Wills, who said, "You should have shoes with fruit on them sticking out from your gown!" And I thought, "What a hoot," so of course I did it.

My mother came to the graduation and I saw her standing with her Polaroid camera. She was snapping furiously and calling to me from the crowd. She was so proud that I was getting that diploma. She had a tear on her cheek when I walked down the aisle, and I realized how important this high school diploma really was. This wasn't just the General Equivalency Diploma I attained to attend my failed year at college. Nope—this was the genuine article.

My mother even had a graduation party for me at a Japanese restaurant in Queens. She had some of her close friends there, too. She was so proud. She said, "You've finally done it."

As a teenager, I was searching for a better me, or a better way. I lived inside my head: I'd talk to myself, hum to myself, sing to myself, and chant to myself. There were certain songs that helped me get by. Joni Mitchell had songs about freedom and ones that offered a refuge to share my loneliness with hers. There was also a Beatles song John Lennon sang called "Across the Universe," which is where I felt like I lived anyway. I also started going to Greenwich Village a lot.

I first went to the Village when my sister and brother and I were little, and my mother used to drive us through it. She'd go, "Look, kids, those are the beatniks. Look, those are the hippies." My mother always loved exotic things. She didn't want us to have her life. She was very sheltered, and she didn't want us to be afraid of the world. She wanted to be a bohemian. No one in Queens went to museums, but she did, and she read about Chinese architecture and yogis and Shakespeare. But she's Sicilian, and they have this mind-set that keeps women down.

My mom was pretty cool. When I was eleven and the Beatles were coming to New York, my mother drove my sister, her friend Diane, and me to the Belt Parkway where the Hilton Hotel is by the airport, so we could see the Beatles drive by, and she left us there for a while. She knew we weren't going to run in traffic. So we waited. And waited. All of a sudden we saw cars coming and *it was them.* So I started screaming, and I shut my eyes, and by the time I realized I should open my eyes, I'd missed it. I was all dressed nice, too. I had dark jean clam diggers with pointy shoes and a sleeveless green, blue, and black plaid shirt with a man-tailored collar. I've never actually met a Beatle, but I saw Tony Bennett once when I was a kid at the 1964–1965 World's Fair. Later, I got to sing with him, and I said to him, "You know, I met you once at the World's Fair. You were coming down the escalator and I was going up. I waved and you waved back. Remember me?" I thought that was funny, but I think it scared him. Russ Titelman, a producer who was working with me, said I sounded like a stalker.

IN 1970 I left home to stay at my sister's and Wha's basement apartment in Valley Stream at 6 Ash Street. At that time everyone was reading J. R. R. Tolkien's trilogy, so we used to call it a hobbitshire. I remember wearing green jeans and a yellow T-shirt and I thought, "Hobbits wear yellow and green and brown and live in a hole in the ground. That's me!"

My sister and I tried to get my eleven-year-old brother to come live with us, too, but my mom took him back. It killed me to leave him. But now I had to deal with my life and how I would live. And to my mother's credit, she came again to take me shopping for clothes so I could get a job. And through the kindness of Wha's mother's family, the Pepitones (yes, like the baseball player), somehow we survived. Wha's uncle Lou lied for me and gave me a recommendation for a job as a gal-Friday receptionist at a publishing house called Simon & Schuster at 251 Park Avenue South—in fact, the same one that's publishing this book.

But really, I was a gal Friday the thirteenth. I tried my best, except I didn't know what the hell I was doing. My clothes were maybe too sexy. I got a mohair dress that was a little on the tight side, because it was a sweater dress, and some pony-hair boots, and some false eyelashes, and I used to sit at the desk like that. And when I got lunch, I brought back a beer. That wasn't a good look—sitting in the front with a beer—and they came up to me afterward and said, "Uh, you need to get rid of the beer." I really did try so hard, but I sucked. One day I was in my boss's office and I picked the phone up to answer it for her, and when I put it down it was covered with sweat.

I was there a couple months. That was kind of tough for them. Also, I'd fall asleep reading the mail. I would try my hardest not to, but it was dreadfully boring to me. There wasn't a window in the file room. I could never find what the callers asked for. A lot of them yelled over the phone. Some hung up. But it wasn't until the electric typewriter came in and I could only manage nineteen words per minute that my boss brought me into her office. She was a beautiful black woman who was smart and stylish and very kind to have put up with me that long. She said she liked me a lot, but I was the worst gal Friday she had ever seen. And, regrettably, she had to let me go.

While I was struggling with my job, my sister was fired from hers. (I'm not too clear on why but the consensus was that it was because she wore the same thing every day.) Wha's dad was a guitar teacher. He played in a wedding band, too. It was hard raising a family on that. So Wha's mother was checking in on us and helping when she could. Sometimes she'd bring food. Wha knew how to make spaghetti and pea soup, which was pretty good. But the food and money situation wasn't good. So I practiced not eating and learning how not to be hungry. And the one thing I didn't know was if you fast you need to drink a lot of water, which I didn't do.

It was the winter of 1970. One day, when I was coming home from work, a little dog started following me. The little dog looked like a fox and a beagle. She walked beside me and never strayed. And in that minute I loved her, but I didn't think I could have a dog. We had no money and what looked like no prospects at the time. But the dog didn't give up. She started sleeping by our doorstep. And when Wha saw her, she took her in.

Wha named the dog Sparkle because she had a mark on her back like a star. I had been reading *The Little Prince* at the time, and Sparkle looked like that fox to me. But unlike the fox in the book, not only wasn't she a fox but she was pregnant with puppies and it was winter. She wasn't going to be put back out in the snow. I had been reading other books aside from *The Little Prince*. There was *Siddhartha*, *The Hobbit*, Paul Twichell's book on astral projection, and *Grapefruit*, which I refused to burn even though it said to in the back. I was looking to change the way I thought about the world. I was trying to become enlightened, awake. There was also a book on groupies that came out. Their sense of fashion was so fresh; it was this great mix of street and couture, which was so new to me because where I came from high fashion was Lord & Taylor and Gimbel's.

At the time, Eric Clapton's song "Layla" was huge. George Harrison's *All Things Must Pass* album came out, the one with the song "What Is Life" on it and "Wah-Wah" (which of course spoke to Wha). We would listen and dance to the albums and stare at the covers. We would discuss life, love, what our future could be. Elen and Wha would play guitar. I would play too and sing or play recorder. Wha would get frustrated listening to us though. Sometimes she would explain how to change keys by counting on your hand to find the right progressions. (For example, C, F, and G is 1, 4, 5 in the key of C but it switches to D, G, and A in the key of D and A would become 5. You got that?)

Sometimes she'd just get so frustrated that she would ask us to shut up. But that never bothered me, although it did my sister, and she'd eventually stop playing. I never cared about what other people felt about my playing and singing. I cared about how I felt. It provided a pause in life when I could feel sound vibrate through my body, and there's nothing as soothing as certain notes vibrating through your body. For example, high notes make me feel like I am soaring high above the fray, never looking down or back.

It was a different time then. There was a revolution of culture going on. The Age of Aquarius was coming. Times would radically change. The civil rights movement had come. I used to go down to the Fillmore, a club near Union Square. You could go down there, and even if you didn't go inside, you could hang out on the line with the people. It was a scene, and they were just as cool as the people going on the stage. One night Elvin Bishop and his band were opening for Johnny Winter with special guest guitarist Rick Derringer was opening for them. Somehow I decided to go. I wanted to see the stylish groupies, too. I saw some of them sitting on a wall in the alley and called out to them. There was a small blond girl who called back to me and said, "Now when I say go, you go. Got it?" I said yes. So when she told me to walk directly behind Johnny Winter and Rick Derringer as they entered the building I did. I followed them backstage. Then a guy who was very agitated started scolding me. His name was Red Dog. He was the tour manager. He saw me and said, "Where were you? You're supposed to be onstage now." He mistook me for a backup singer. I tried to talk but I was having trouble forming the words, and he just threw me out of the dressing room. It was pretty amazing that later on in my life I got to know and work with Rick Derringer.

During that time, I sang folk music and played folk guitar. There were the folkies, and there were the rockers, and you just didn't mix them, because the rockers hated the folkies. But I was starting to lose my taste for folk and had become more intrigued with rock and roll, although I never thought I could sing it. I remember hearing Bonnie Bramlett from Delaney and Bonnie and thinking, "Oh, my voice will never do that, it's way beyond what I can do."

But that day, when I watched those background singers from backstage, I realized that I could sing rock, too. They had a simple sound to their voices, and I thought, "My God, that's really easy." It was like the dust had cleared.

I wasn't thinking of singing as a career in those days. I was going to be an artist, but I had to take a bunch of different jobs to pay the bills. When I moved in with my sister and Wha in Valley Stream, we learned where we could work and eat. Like you could go to the Hare Krishna temple and if you cleaned for them, they would feed you. This was when George Harrison came out with the whole Hare Krishna action. And when I started seeing Hare Krishnas around town, they had a good vibe. I was into all kinds of spiritual stuff and I liked the chanting, and the idea that a god could be your friend instead of all the brimstone and fire I'd grown accustomed to growing up as a Catholic. It was a refreshing change from the yelling I'd heard from the pulpit as a child. I'd sit there trying to understand what the guy was going on about and think, "Wow, look what God did to his son, Jesus. Now imagine what he's going to do to me. I'm not even related."

I could deal with a kind of god like Krishna. A god who doesn't hate women and doesn't stone them to death. Funny, I had always looked at the heaven represented in different books as my idea of hell. I always felt like, "Okay, let me get this straight: While I'm alive, you're going to freakin' torture me and deny my human rights as an individual, so that when I die, hoping for a better place, I get the same raw deal in heaven too?" No thanks.

So I would clean the temple—I mean, granted, the food they served was loaded with sugar but at least I was eating. It's just that after being so hungry and then eating all that sugar, I was basically seeing stars. So I'd be cleaning the bathrooms and the pictures would kind of move, or Krishna would wink at me, and I'd laugh so hard because it was funny. But whenever I cleaned the temple, I felt like I was cleaning my heart. Then they pulled me aside and asked me if I wanted to join the Hare Krishnas. They felt I was special. They told me the head guy would choose a husband for me and I'd marry him and have children. The pièce de résistance was when they said that as a woman, I'd have to eat in the kitchen with the children, while the men ate in the main dining room after I served them. I busted out laughing and said, "Listen, I'm Italian and I already know this story about women as chattel. I don't do that shit anymore."

I watched my mother struggle her whole life, and my aunt and grandmother, and the whole Sicilian mentality of keeping the women in the house really only meant free domestic help under the guise of protection and reverence. Yeah, my ass. I always thought, "You can sell that to another mule you happen to meet on the road, but it ain't gonna be me." When I was growing up, Gloria Steinem was always a big hero of mine, and Yoko, and then I read *The Female Eunuch* by Germaine Greer and all of a sudden things started to fall into perspective.

John and Yoko always talked about helping the world. When I was living in West Hempstead, I saw an empty factory and thought it would be a great place for recycling. So I went to the town hall to make my case. Even though people argued against me, when I came back to visit years later, there was a recycling center there. I realized then that you never know how you can affect life, even if you don't see yourself as doing something big. Sometimes it can just be bringing up an idea that makes sense. (Although some folks said the recycling center brought rats. So maybe it wasn't such a great idea.)

When my sister and I and Wha moved out of Valley Stream we found a place in West Hempstead, in a new apartment complex right across from the West Hempstead stop on the Long Island Rail Road. The apartment was really sweet, except for the fact that I had some roommates that were hard to get rid of: roaches. There were so many that some of them were albino. You know how many thousands of roaches you need to get an albino? We kept spraying every week. They were in the kitchen cabinets. Once they were in the bed.

Times were not so good. The guys next door were dealing drugs and then everybody became boyfriend and girlfriend and I still had no job and had trouble paying for food. One time I was so hungry that I looked at a picture of Krishna and thought for a minute he was giving me food, and then my hunger went away. I took that as another little miracle in my life and maybe a little payback for cleaning his temple. Either way, it was a blessing.

I kept trying to get and keep a job. I finally got a job as waitress at IHOP, on Hempstead Boulevard on the other side of the railroad station two blocks away. My mother was a waitress, and she tried to train me, but I just wasn't very good. It was hard for me to work really quick. We were given little cards with tiny boxes to check when people placed their orders, I guess to speed things along. But the print was so small I kept confusing the fried chicken with the chicken pot pie. And let me tell ya, you can't believe how pissed people get when they're served fried chicken instead of chicken pot pie. I used to think, "They're both chicken, ya know! And don't think it's any healthier eating all that dough in the pie, either!" Eventually the manager pulled me aside and said, "Look, kid, maybe waitressing isn't your cup of tea. What about being a hostess?" And I told him I needed to make more money than a hostess and he said, "Yeah, but your mistakes cost more than your salary." We were sitting at a booth and he reached down and started rubbing my legs. I pushed myself right out of there.

So I tried something else. Two blocks down the other way from the apartment was a place that did mailers with samples of cosmetics and coupons. It was the kind of place that might have sent out those tampons that turned into pillows and gave people toxic shock syndrome. I'd stand at my station and take samples from the conveyor belt and put them in a box. As I was doing it, I'd start to giggle, because of course I couldn't do it quick enough. And there was a guy in a pulpit—there was actually a pulpit overlooking all these women at their stations—who kept making up little contests. He'd say things like, "And now we're going to see who can be the fastest at putting these ten items into the box!"

So I'd try to keep up with the faster and faster pace of the conveyor belt as the little items went speeding by. I felt like, "Okay, where's Ethel?" And the guy thought it was no laughing matter so he said, "Hey, Lauper, wipe that smile off your face." Well, I couldn't then, and I still can't now. I think that the only way I get through sometimes when things are so ridiculous and so bad is that I've gotta laugh.

But I was very scared all the time because bad things would happen. When I was young I would compare living in the world to being in an ocean. I didn't know how to fix what may or may not have been my fault as a child, but I knew that if you were bleeding, sharks would come. I didn't have money to get around then, so I would hitchhike to places. Hitching is really, really, really dangerous. I jumped out of cars; I was in car accidents with men driving like idiots. I don't even know how I made it out alive. But somehow I did.

For instance, I once had a job interview, and I wore pantyhose and a dress that my mother had made short to wear with matching pants. But you could still wear the top as a minidress, so that's what I did. And all I had was some old high heels that I used to wear at my first job with Simon & Schuster. At the time, I didn't have enough money to even buy underwear or a bra. And I didn't have money to get to the interview, either, but I needed a job, so I hitchhiked. A guy stopped and picked me up, but then he wouldn't let me out of his car—not until I went down on him and he on me. It was a bad experience and then I felt I deserved it because I must have looked like a whore.

When I got out of the car, I walked into the interview. I felt stunned and disgusted and sad. I tried to answer all the questions put to me as best I could, because I really needed a job. And then to get back to the apartment, which was a few towns away, I remembered how I saw the railroad tracks running alongside the highway. So I just started walking home on the side of the train tracks so that I wouldn't get lost. God, it was a long, hot walk in those heels. Obviously, I didn't get the job.

I was so depressed afterward. As kids we used to have a saying: We didn't feel like shit, we felt like the ground that shit fell on. I didn't know how to make it stop. I was so lost. I felt like I couldn't figure out why I was even born. I kept chanting in my head John Lennon songs, the ones that made it possible to stand and continue, like "Across the Universe." I sang it to myself all the time, because it had a prayer in it and it would help me to free my mind instead of agonizing over my life.

I had so many almost-jobs while living in West Hempstead, but finally I started working at Burt's Shoes at the Roosevelt Field Mall. That was steady for a while. I actually thought I did a good job at times. I met a young woman who worked there too, who was tall and pretty. I remember she told me once that the best way not to get pregnant after sex was to douche, which was actually the opposite of what you should do. She also taught me how to steal from a department store by putting the clothes underneath my own. She explained to me that it was a big department store and no one would really get hurt too badly.

At that time, I couldn't make enough money to buy a coat for the winter. I never had enough money to buy something and eat and pay rent, too. Getting through to the end of the month was a struggle. I couldn't keep asking my mom for money, either, because she didn't have much, and there wasn't anyone else I could ask. So the first thing I stole was a coat. It was around Christmas and very cold. And then I stole a dress for Wha and a skirt for Elen. I just figured, the hell with it, but I felt bad doing it. I had never stolen before (and I never have since).

Three weeks before Christmas at the mall, the Christmas crèche went up. I always loved Christmas, and a crèche to me was like a big Christmas ornament. I couldn't wait to walk around it. And when I saw the baby Jesus, I thought I'd buy him a big chrysanthemum for his birthday. So during a lunch break the next day, I went to the florist at the mall and bought a big mum and walked up to the statue of the baby and laid down the flower in front of him. I went by every day to see the baby and to see if the flower was still there.

It was there for two weeks without any water and it looked as fresh as the day I laid it down. I wasn't sure if someone else had changed it from time to time, but I decided to take it as a sign—take it as another little miracle that could happen right under people's noses. It was as if that little group in the crèche was telling me that someone was watching over me and that someday, everything would work out. As my life took on changes, I never forgot that little miracle. And every time I passed a crèche around Christmastime I would stop and sing quietly for the little group. Sometimes I would stop in front of people's houses if they had a crèche and I think my neighbors thought I was nuts. I was, a little. I think I just took the "little drummer boy" song too far. And I think it scared folks too, so I wouldn't recommend it. But sometimes, I remember it when I'm singing onstage, and I sing to the little crèche again in my head.

When I didn't have big things happening for me—especially then—I would just try to find some happiness in the little things. So if I was cleaning or straightening or whatever, I'd try to stay exactly in the moment and enjoy the little joys of doing the task. I believed, at that time, that everything was alive and had a vibration—even a cup or a table. And when I was sad and had no hope, I'd think, "Well, you can either stew in your sadness, or you could say, 'Oh, look at this, isn't this beautiful.'" And that's how I lived. I don't always remember to do that now.

I saw this black woman once in Jamaica—Jamaica, Queens, I mean—when I was still living at home. She was going to work and I was just wandering, coming from the only place girls could buy decent jeans, a men's shop, and not wanting to go home. I was just looking at the sky and thinking how pretty it was, and I looked at her because she was looking too, and she smiled and said, "That's the Lord." I thought that was beautifully put. I had started to read about different religions at that time and that's kind of what held me together, too. I tried to teach myself not to want anything.

So I continued to not eat much when I was at Elen and Wha's. We still never had enough to really go around. But like I said before, I also hadn't been drinking water, so I got a serious kidney infection and had to go to the hospital. I wound up at Hempstead General, which I thought was an awful hospital. They never came in to check on anything, so basically I was a pain in the ass because I was never a silent sufferer. There was an old lady in the bed across from me who had told me that she'd had almost everything removed from her and that there wasn't much else left to take. When she heard me wisecracking to the nurse, she looked at me and said, "Listen, kid, nobody likes a wise guy." So I tried to listen to her because I kind of liked her. At night she would talk to dead people and I thought maybe she didn't have much time. So why upset her?

Then they brought a priest in. Yeah, well, that set me off. I wasn't sure if he was there to do an exorcism or what, but I made the priest give me communion. He said, "Have you anything to confess?" I looked at him and said, "No, because I don't think I sinned." I knew I had him on a technicality; he had to give me the host, which really pissed him off. I think maybe I was still mad about when my sister and I were asked to leave Catholic grade school the first time, when I was in the third grade and Elen was in the sixth.

While living at the West Hempstead apartment, I met this fellow named Phil. I slept with him, and I liked him, but I was scared. Like I said, I was frightened of everything. I was eighteen—a kid. Phil was twenty-four, and I felt like sometimes there was nothing to talk about. I was too scared to say anything anyway. But he must have liked me because he kept asking me to move in with him.

I was always hoping to find a romantic partner. I would hook up with people thinking, "Okay, this guy?" I know it's a weird way to think. I guess I've thought that way since I was a flower girl at my godmother's wedding. I was four and thought I was marrying the ring-bearer boy. Of course that didn't work out for me because he didn't like to dance. Anyway, Phil and I wound up getting a place together. This was the era of free love, and I believed in that, because of the love part. I thought we might be married one day as freethinking people—kind of like John and Yoko. Unfortunately, like the ring boy at my godmother's wedding, it didn't work out.

I was never any good at what Phil wanted. I was reading how John and Yoko were on a macrobiotic diet. So I made adzuki beans and brown rice and sesame-seed shrimp with miso sauce, while Phil would have really liked meat and potatoes. Phil wanted me just to cook and clean, and to stop spending time drawing all day and be like a wife, but with no strings attached. I thought, "Okay, a grown-up life without the complications of marriage." And then I would play guitar and sing and he'd say, "You know, you're very good but you'll never make it. There's so many people who want to do the same thing and somebody's got to clean the fish." Well, that was kind of the big gong for Phil as far as I was concerned. And again, what he said didn't deter me. I never really cared who thought I was good or who thought I sucked. I would sit up and play anyway until people would tell me to please stop. I kind of understand that if you're singing the same song over and over and over, just to get the inflections right, after a while anyone might say, "Cyn, can you please shut up?" But I never seemed to pay attention.

And at this point, I'd come to realize that my parents' dream for me was no longer mine. Even though I couldn't figure out what that dream was, other than just to survive. Although I was grateful to them for carrying me on their shoulders, there came a point where I had to carry my own life. I was in a new phase. And I realized that if I was ever going to meet someone who would see me as an equal and who I'd be able to live with happily, I'd have to learn to live on my own and accept myself, so that someone else could accept me, too.

Whenever I sang, it always felt like the division between the outside world and the inside world teetered on a very fine line. I was aware of what it felt like to look at life from the inside out and the outside in. It's just part of my gift and I had rationalized myself out of it like most people who can do that do, and then I realized I needed to welcome it back in. I've always heard voices. I'm a singer, and I hear poems in my head—that's how I write. I always thought I was crazy until a few years later my boyfriend Richie said to me that sometimes your gift can also be your curse. Not that I think it's a curse, but if you don't come to an understanding about how your brain works and use its strengths, then what could be a great gift does become a curse.

On the one hand, feeling like I walked with one foot inside and one foot outside myself could be called crazy. But on the other hand, it could be called a much-needed perspective to create. It has been a great tool for me, whether I write or draw or sing or act or art-direct. Being in touch with your insides and understanding how to see from the outside gives you a broader view—what people now call "thinking outside the box." As a dear friend of mine, Bob Barrell, said (you'll hear more about him in a minute), I would become a student of life.

After my job at the Roosevelt Field Mall, I worked at a racetrack. I was a hot walker. It's just what it sounds like: You walk the horses down when they're hot. I had never been around horses before, but it didn't matter to me. It was a job and I love animals. I would sing to the horses, too, which would kind of calm them down. I'd sing Hare Krishna chants in their ears and walk shoulder to shoulder with them. And the sunrises over the track were really beautiful too. I thought the scenery was so stunning that I could have painted it. I thought at first that the job would be perfect for me, but the hours were hard, and the older men hated the young girls for taking their jobs away. Eventually, the older guys would spook the horses on me as I'd come into the shed row, and the last time a horse reared, I did a figure eight in the air on the end of the lead. That was enough for me. I didn't go back and was fired.

I was still living with Phil at that point, but it wasn't going too good. I thought I loved him, and I felt betrayed when I realized he didn't love me. Because the only reason I actually moved in with him was to be loved. And when we'd fight, he would always throw me down, sit on me, and say, "Can't you hear?" I started to think, "This isn't a good idea. I've got to get out of here."

At the time, I had been going to visit my friend and great teacher/ mentor Bob Barrell. I had met him when I was flunking out of high school. It was after one of those more hopeless days that I found this unlikely ally, in an unlikely place—under the El in Richmond Hill/ Ozone Park, Queens, on 106th Street. I was walking home and there, in a little storefront, were all these paintings in the window. They were beautiful and had a depth, soul, and passion to them. They didn't just speak to me, they screamed to me, "Wake up!" These were pieces of genuine art in the vast, desolate landscape of those who were too busy struggling to exist to be bothered with culture. Next to one painting was a sign that said, ART SCHOOL, UPSTAIRS. So I went upstairs and met Bob. He wasn't just a wonderful artist, he was a wonderful teacher. He taught me to paint, and he thought I had talent, and that gave me a newfound courage.

He also taught me about history and politics and life. He gave me a glimpse of who I could be. He had a whole gaggle of misfits that came to class on Tuesday and Thursday nights. Who knew? I had thought I was all alone. He was a great philosopher and talked to me about things that I never learned in school—about Gandhi and Martin Luther King and civil disobedience and Thoreau. So I'd go back and visit him, and we'd paint and talk.

Bob put a name to what was going on around me. He would say that the struggling masses were a "product of misery." He said that misery begets misery unless we break the chain. And that's where the title of the song "Product of Misery" that I wrote all those years later, on my album *Hat Full of Stars*, came from.

I told Bob about how Phil used to go camping with my other friends, but that I couldn't ever go, because I didn't have any equipment. But Phil didn't know that I took two unemployment checks that I got after I left the hot walker job and bought camping equipment, because I thought, "Fuck it, they don't ever take me camping, I'm going to go camping and I'm going to leave him." Then I got some friends to help me move out on Phil, so that he couldn't try to hold me down and shake me or whatever.

Bob helped me work out what I was going to do. He said I could go to Canada, to a provincial park, and do a tree study. Everyone was hitchhiking in those days, and I could live on an apple and a dollar a day. So that night we knelt on Bob's kitchen floor with the map opened up, and he helped me draw out where I was going in Canada and how I was going to do it.

I told my sister, Elen, about my trip, and she thought it was a good idea. She had been going through a rough time herself. I thought then, even though at the time I would never have said it, that she loved Wha. (Elen's gay, but she felt pressure to act straight then and was living with a fellow named Mitch.)

So off I went to the airport with my dog Sparkle. I was eighteen and I had never flown anywhere before. Beforehand I brought Sparkle to the vet to make sure she could make the trip. The doctor said the dog would be fine but asked if I would be okay. I thought I'd be fine, so I put Sparkle in a crate with some sleeping pills and told her I'd see her on the other side. I had never camped in my whole entire life, but I didn't care. I wasn't going to let fear stop me. I had a backpack on filled with camping equipment and canned food for both human and dog. I had some charcoal drawing sticks and drawing pads, a Bunsen burner, jeans and T-shirts, a pup tent, and a sleeping bag tied to the bottom of the backpack. I guess I just never travel light. But those were the things Bob said I'd need. I paid $125 for that ticket and an ax—because I'd have to chop wood. I had a window seat and got a tuna sandwich, too. I thought it was delicious, and the stewardess was very pleasant. I was living large!

When I landed in Toronto, I went to get Sparkle. There she was, barking her head off. The poor thing must not have cared for the ride. I would never do that to a dog anymore, now that I know how cold it is where she was in the plane. Then I went to customs, and a lady said, "Anything to declare?" I had a crumpled pack of Marlboros in my pocket and I said, "Nothing but these." I was promptly sent to a more intense customs check, because nobody likes a wise guy, as the lady in the hospital told me.

There they asked about my trip. I told them I was an art student going to the Algonquin Provincial Park to do a tree study for about two weeks. I guess I was a sight. With my dog in tow, I had on the red-brown suede jacket I had stolen from the department store in Roosevelt Field the year before, and a floppy red-brown suede hat that I flipped up so that I could see. I wore green jeans and a yellow T-shirt and some walking boots that tied at the ankle (so that I wouldn't turn it when I was up in the park, which is what the man who sold them to me said).

I was so excited and scared all at once, I could barely hear what the other customs man was saying because I could hardly wait to finally go camping. I thought about all those times that Phil said I couldn't go because I had no camping equipment, and now I was going camping big-time. And I was going without him and his friends—I was going as the artist I had always felt I was, the one trying to live and make ends meet in a nonartistic world. I had always struggled to live in a world whose language I couldn't speak and didn't want to know. In that world, everything about me was wrong.

I was going over and over in my head the plan that Bob Barrell drew out on that map that led to Algonquin Park, my destination. I was to take Thoreau's *Walden* with me and read it. It was part of my assignment. It was what he called "walking on the path as a student of life." On that path, it didn't matter if I was different or stupid or lost, because I was going to find myself on my terms. That day, at the border of Canada, I was on my way to find out who, and what, I was.

My plan was that Elen was going to wire me my unemployment check while I was in Canada, which would give me enough money to eat and to stay at youth hostels. But at the moment, all I had in my pocket was twenty-five dollars, and the customs agents said I'd need more than that to enter the country. They suggested I call my parents and ask them to front the money. So I called my dad. My poor dad didn't understand why I had to do the things I did. When I called he said, "What are you doing in Canada? And why are you there in the first place?" He couldn't afford to front the money, and I think he felt I'd stiff him anyway. I wouldn't have, but everyone in my family thought I was trouble walking.

When my father couldn't help me, I was a little heartbroken.

I tried to explain it to the customs agents but then I just started to cry a little. The funny thing about that group of customs agents was that when they heard how I had planned it and what I would do, they were rooting for me. They began to try and figure out how I could still do this tree study. My recollection of Canadians is how kind they were to me when I had nothing and I was nobody. I'll never forget it. They allowed me to come in and told me, "Listen, get some bug spray because it's June, which is blackfly season." Another told me where to go in Toronto for a youth hostel. Then they wished me luck and let me go. I was in love with Canada.

Then I hitchhiked to the park. It was so wild. When you're in the woods and you don't know anything, you do everything stupid. Like I brushed my teeth and spit in the water. I didn't know. Somebody who was canoeing past me gave me such a dirty look. Okay, the spitting in the water: not good. When I built a campfire, I remembered how my sister and I used to watch the Smokey the Bear "Careless Camper" commercial and reenact it under our kitchen table. We'd take turns being Smokey the Bear and the Careless Camper and light a fire, then recite, "Only you can prevent forest fires." Then my mother would come home and ask us about the new dark spot under the table, and I'd say, "I don't know what that is, maybe you should use Comet." I'm glad that before I left for Canada, Wha taught me how to build a proper fire pit.

I was scared, but the one thing I always felt was that I wasn't alone. I felt like I had some protective force with me. I drew, I wrote poems,

I acted out things, I made myself laugh. At one point I bent down in front of a little tree and said, "I think that I shall never see a poem as lovely as this tree." Stupid things. I could do that because I was by myself and it didn't matter.

I was there for maybe two weeks. I wanted to find myself. Like I said, I felt that I would never find anyone who would understand me if I didn't understand myself, so I needed to make this journey. It's kind of dangerous in the end, when you think about it. There wasn't a spot on me or poor ol' Sparkle that wasn't bit by blackflies. I don't know how the hell I lived (although I was carrying that ax with me and would have killed somebody if they fuckin' came at me). It was an interesting time. That was still at the end of the whole hippie thing. There still were people who were gentle souls.

I don't know how I got from the campground back to Toronto, but when I did, I met a guy there who had a bus and he was going to drive down to New York. It was a magic bus, like a hippie bus. A few people were going, so I figured I'd go, too. On our way there, he stopped at the Saint Lawrence River and we all got out. And I took off my shirt because in my whole life I had never had the wind blowing on my chest like a man. I thought, "Wow, *that's* what it feels like to be that free." Then I put my shirt back on and met a fisherman in the Saint Lawrence River. He taught me how to clean and fillet a fish. That came in handy later on. Then we got back on the magic bus with everybody and we drove to New York.

CHAPTER THREE

In New York City, I visited my sister, saw some old friends, and wound up coming back home to my mother, who had divorced her second husband. That was one of the great things about my mom. She always said, "You could come riding in on horseback—you're still my kids." I took her at her word. I didn't exactly ride a horse back home, but I'm sure my outfit made just as strong an impression.

My mom didn't just get a divorce, she was moving away from the house she and I grew up in. It was a little traumatic and freeing all at once. She found a place on Ninetieth Street. It was a little bit of a fixer-upper. My younger brother, Fred (who we called Butch), was still living at home too. I got a bedroom, and my brother was staying in what would have been the living room, as is usually the case for folks without a lot of means. So our bedrooms were right next to each other. Yikes! No privacy. It was kind of like college. We also lived with Ralph, my mom's one-day-to-be-third husband. Because Ralph was in construction, there was always a project to be finished, which is always the case for folks who like a fixer-upper opportunity (my mom loved that).

I also saw Phil, who decided he wanted to get back together. He said, "You made your point. You can come back to live with me now."

I thought, "Are you kidding me? You didn't love me, and actually, from a distance, I realized that I didn't love you, and I can't live your kind of life." I had been through so much that I just felt free of it and stronger—although I didn't really have a plan beyond that. I took the dog to the Village and panhandled for money. I always panhandled. You know: "Can you spare some change?" Sometimes people would tell me to sell my dog. I didn't care what anybody said. You've gotta understand, it didn't matter to me, because I had had horrible things happen to me before. You're going to give me money? Good. You're not going to give me money and you're going to insult me as you walk by? Fine.

I had my guitar, so I used to busk, too, but I only knew how to play two Joni Mitchell songs—"Carey" and "This Flight Tonight"—because I tuned the guitar to them, and once it was tuned, that was it. I got a couple of dollars, which is all I needed (although it would have been great if I had a bigger repertoire). Some guy came up to me one time and gave me two dollars and said, "This is for your second album—remember me then."

After Phil, I met a guy named Richie, who used to date my sister's friend. Then he hit on my sister, and then me. I said, "Hey, Richie, not for nothing, but that ain't gonna happen. We're friends." He was a terrific illustrator but a troubled soul. We decided to hitch to Massachusetts to find a place where I could live. I couldn't live in New York by myself because I was eighteen, and you have to be twenty-one to sign your own lease, and if my father wasn't going to give me money, he was not going to cosign a lease. So Richie and I headed to Massachusetts, and we would set up camp and sleep in the woods along the way. We were sitting by the fire one time and he said to me, "You know what? You shouldn't spell your name 'Cindy,' you should spell it C-Y-N-D-I." So I did.

Then we kept going, to Vermont. Sometimes I would have dreams before things happened, and a long time before we got to Vermont, I had one where I saw Jesus in a field with my dog Sparkle. Jesus was opening his arms and smiling, and the dog was jumping all around in the grass. When we got to Vermont, my dog ran down a hill and there was this field and she was jumping around in it, and the only thing that was missing was Jesus with his arms open. Vermont was so beautiful. It looked like a nature show, or like *Walt Disney Presents.* I had never seen anything like it, so I stayed.

But Richie had to leave when we arrived in Vermont, and I was on my own. I went to a youth hostel in Burlington. When the other kids in the hostel heard me approaching, they would say, "Here comes New York." They didn't like my accent. I met some people who said they would help me, and they enrolled me in this program to establish myself in an apartment. They put me on welfare and got me a job. First, I was a mother's helper. The people were very nice and had these two little boys. They bought an old farm but had this modern house, and they had two cows, but they were pets. They had a room for me in the basement, and that's where Sparkle and I lived.

I tried to be what the lady wanted, and the two little boys were all right, but one day she gave a party for one of her sons, and twelve kids came over. The father had given the kid a tractor, and the kids piled into the large shovel attached to the front, and the son was driving them around. While this was happening, my dog was running back and forth, and it was making me nervous. I kept telling the kid to watch out for my dog. I went to the mother and told her things were getting a little out of control, and she said, "That's your job, isn't it?"

Well, the five-year-old kid driving the tractor ran over the dog. I couldn't believe it. I loved that dog. We slept together. We lived to-gether. She was my family. The tractor ran right over her ribs. The father and a friend of his drove me to the vet and they talked about how they lost their dogs. I'm thinking, "Nice, can we see what the vet says first, you silly old goats?" We took her to the doctor, who said, "Listen, if she lives through the night, she'll live." I was really shaken up. They brought me back to my cellar and that night I had another dream, that I saw the Blessed Mother, only this one didn't look anything like I was taught. She had a kind face, and freckles, and sandy hair. She was smiling at me, and the dog was there, too, and there was a rainbow in the sky, just like there had really been earlier. It was as if she was superimposed over the scene from that day. It was a great comfort to see her in my dream. Growing up as a Catholic, Mary and Jesus are kind of like your secret friends who you can call in times of trouble. And the next morning when I woke up, I got the news that the dog lived, so it was a miracle.

I quit the job—big surprise—took the dog, and left. Eventually I got another job and an apartment in Burlington, but I was so lonesome. I remember when it was Christmastime, I kept hearing that Joni Mitchell song "River" bleed out of the bars on Church Street. You know the one: "It's coming on Christmas, they're cutting down trees." I was so sad, and I met this guy in a bar. He seemed to be a kindred soul, and he came back to South Burlington with me. We began seeing each other, and soon enough he was moving in. My feeling was, "Okay, whatever." (Remember, it was the seventies.) We both used to paint, but his paintings were so raw that they were almost childlike. I thought it was like van Gogh. He wasn't working, but I had recently found a job, after I went to the welfare office and said, "Can you just give me a job, please?" I really did not want to be on welfare.

They got all excited and brought me to this one man at the office, who asked me what I'd like to do. I told him I wanted to be a painter. He said that if I lived in South Burlington for a certain amount of time, I would be able to apply for a grant and go to school. In the meantime, I'd have to work. He asked me what sort of things I liked, and I said animals. So he got me a job at a kennel/pound. I used to love to work in the pound more than the kennel because those dogs were so much more loving and sweet, and appreciated everything. I loved those animals so much. The woman who owned the place used to like to put them to sleep (she had this weird thing going on). Whenever I would see that she was coming to put one to sleep, I'd take the dog for a walk. Then she kind of got wise and killed them on my day off. There was one dog that I just loved. He had a broken leg, and I nursed him back to health. I named him after an actor called Herschel Bernardi. He was very funny. He used to run around all the time and the owner would catch him. Well, the last time she caught Herschel, she put that poor dog to sleep, too.

I tried to get my boyfriend work at the kennel, because they wanted some help. Then one day the owner came to me with her husband, and they sat me down. He said, "Cyn, listen, I did some checking on your friend. You know that he got a discharge from the army because he had a mental breakdown, right? You know those childlike pictures of his? There's a reason for them."

I was like, "Ooohhh." It made sense. There were times when I would talk to him and he was very quick to get angry over nothing. And when I asked him to leave, he got a little weird with me. He was very upset and was yelling while I was helping him pack. He was still yelling when I was helping him to move his stuff into his car, and then he pushed me into the Christmas tree. I got up and continued to help him, and when he finally got out, I locked the door. Because I grew up seeing violence, I remained calm.

I went through a lot in that apartment. I had no television, no stereo, nothing. I was still a kid, and I was alone. A lot of times I couldn't take it anymore, so I just lay in bed all the time. When I really couldn't deal with anything, I used to get the shakes, just complete anxiety attacks. When they happened, I'd hold myself and try to talk myself down. I'd say to myself, "You'll be okay—take a deep breath." Then, if I was feeling like I really needed to feel protected, I would empty out the cupboard underneath the sink and crawl under there. I'd stay in there because it was enclosed, and slowly I would begin to feel better. Because I was alone, I'd allow myself to do things that had they been done in front of other people, they would have said, "Whoo, she is *crazy.*"

Sometimes I would sit in a closet if I felt really fearful, and I'd tell myself, "Okay, now you're sitting in a closet—good. Go ahead, sit anywhere you want in the whole apartment. It's your apartment. Wait until you feel better, then come out. If you want to sit in that chair over there, sit wherever you want until you feel better. If you can't handle it, and you want to get into bed, stay in bed. When you feel better, get up and try again." That's how I got better: I allowed myself to fall apart.

One of those days when I stayed in bed all day and all night, I woke up in the middle of the night and saw an angel in my head. He was sitting at a desk with a big fat book and he was showing me the scene of a courtroom. My mother was in it and she was crying. Then a mean judge told me that I judged my mother too harshly. The angel was sweet looking, with wings and curly blond hair. I looked over his desk to read the book and in the pages, I saw myself just lying on the ground with chariots running over me.

As time went on, I got really sick. Apparently, the guy with the mental breakdown had given me hepatitis. He had been throwing up a lot, but I was used to cleaning up puke because I always cleaned the vomit from the dogs. Hepatitis was going around in Burlington that year. I went to work anyway but got very, very sick one day when I was there and they had an ambulance come. They took me away in a stretcher. I was so tired but I could feel Krishna inside of my body as a young boy showing me how to rest, and I knew it would be all right. When I got to the hospital, I was told I had hepatitis. As I lay in my hospital bed with an IV in my arm, I heard the nurses talking and one of them said, "How did she get hepatitis?" And the other nurse turned around and said, "An affair." All of a sudden I felt like I was in a Bette Davis movie—I had an *affair*. I called my dad and he was going away on his honeymoon with his new wife. "Poor thing," he told me. "Please call your mom." It's not like anyone could really help me; I was fine, I was in the hospital.

When I got out, I was too weak yet to work. Sometimes if the hostel had some interesting people I might like, I'd put them up at my place for a while. There was a kid named Ann Marie who stayed with me once who was a runaway. She had an older boyfriend—who was really a pedophile, if you ask me. They were going to put her in a cor-rectional juvenile place for delinquent kids unless someone adopted her. I wanted to, but I couldn't because I was too young, I was still nineteen. I felt so bad. She never forgave me.

And while I was trying to get better, a couple came and stayed with me—a guy named Tommy and his girlfriend—and they took care of me. And then she left and he stayed, and he became my boyfriend after a while. He wouldn't leave (I know, again with that). Tommy was such a charmer and could talk you into anything. He wasn't work-ing, so he spent a lot of time hunting. One time there was nothing to eat for dinner, so Tommy went out with his gun, shot a squirrel, and brought it home.

There it was, on the kitchen counter. All I could think of was that one time when the Magic Bus had made a stop on the way to New York, and I saw a guy fishing, and he taught me how to clean a fish.

Thank goodness, I remembered how to do it, because that's how I took care of that squirrel. So I did what I had to do. I cut its head off and peeled back the skin, and I thought, "Hmm, there's not a lot of meat." But I took whatever was there and chopped it up. Then I cut up an onion, put olive oil in a pan with some basil, a little garlic, and a bay leaf, and sautéed the squirrel. Then I threw in a can of tomatoes, some wine, a little sugar, and a little salt and let it cook for a while. Tommy took a cab home and invited the cab driver to dinner. The cabbie loved it, and after dinner he said, "This is really delicious. What kind of meat is this?"

I told him it was chicken and he said, "No, it's not."

I said, "Yes, it is."

"No, it's not."

"Yes, it is."

"No, it's not, it's gamier."

I said, "All right, it's squirrel." He didn't believe me and we went back and forth a couple of more times. The squirrel's head was in the trash, and the pelt, too, so I showed him the pelt, and he got really upset.

After a while, I realized that Tommy was never going to work. It hit me that although there was something very charming about him, he was a bum, and he was really dirty. He didn't like taking baths or showers. That got old pretty fast.

In the meantime, the people in the welfare office worked it out so that I could go to Johnson State College in Johnson, Vermont. They had this thing called the PROVE Program where you could get a scholarship if you proved yourself through your work. I just wanted to take art, but they wanted me to take English and history. As I mentioned, I always had a lot of trouble with English and didn't want to take it. I couldn't write a paper or read the amount you needed to in college. I couldn't focus on a page. I had attention deficit disorder or something; I still don't read a lot. I could do things visually then and I could write creatively. But I never learned the basics of writing out a report.

Of course, at the time, I didn't know that what I might have had was ADD. And I couldn't figure out if my problem was from a traumatic childhood or if maybe I was just fuckin' stupid. I just thought that maybe my short stint in a convent school where the nuns got a little brutal might have contributed to my condition. That lovely boarding school run by what I've always called the Sisters of No Mercy or Charity at All, especially if the children wore their patience a little thin. Maybe I was just hit in the head too much. And listen, I got by as a stupid person pretty good, because I could do other things and I could verbally articulate some things well. Sometimes I would get up in class and talk to the teacher and ask questions, and then when I sat down I would hear, in my head, "You really are brilliant." I would think, "I'm not brilliant; I'm actually kind of stupid." Then I'd hear, "No, you're not." I've always felt like there was this really strong presence of a guardian angel around me. Either it was a guardian angel, or I had to completely schizoid out to survive.

While I was living in Vermont, I still made trips back to New York. I'd hitch, and take my dog and my easel. I would be on that big highway that goes from Vermont, and I would be so scared. It was cold, and I was frightened for my life all the time. I got in this one car with a guy who brought me back to his house and let me rest before he took me to the next spot. He was very kind. I was very lucky that I wasn't killed or something. (But, I mean, I had the dog too. It's kind of hard to kill you *and* the dog, right? Well, I guess if you're motivated, you could.) When I made it back to New York, I would visit Bob Barrell, and we'd paint, and he would teach me about painting. He once told me that a painter is a great liar because you're taking a flat surface and making it look like it's three-dimensional, not flat but something with depth. It's the craziest thing, but some of the techniques that he taught me I use in my makeup when I paint my face or when I'm adding color to my blond palette of a head.

So as I was taking courses for this art scholarship at Johnson State, I got a job as a nude model in one of the classes. I modeled in the watercolor class. I loved watercolor but didn't get into the class, so I worked there so I could watch the teacher. Unfortunately, artists hardly ever view the models as people who might be attending a class they couldn't get into. The great thing was that because I was also taking art history classes, I was able to pose like the models in the paintings I studied and then watch how the students translated those poses in pen, ink, and watercolor. Which I loved.

Most of the art history books I read were dreadfully written though. I had a hard time reading them but I loved the paintings so much I made myself get through the writing that made no sense. And I was making art with my body. I would twist myself to make a line that would run down the page or pose in a shape I would have liked to draw myself. And I could stay that way for a long time. Then I would watch the students draw and paint, and listen as the teacher came over and talked to them. I don't think any of them really realized how much I was watching. They probably thought I was an exhibitionist or some kind of tramp.

I never had much luck with young men. And I would hear gossip from men I dated come back to me. The first young man who was really kind to me as a boyfriend was this short African guy from Nigeria. I started hanging out with him, and sleeping with him, and everyone in the school freaked out. Apparently he was with another white girl from the school who was very sweet and he ditched her for me, the crazy-girl freak. We'd go to dorm parties and his pattern was that he'd get wasted and then somehow get in a fight with someone who he insisted had insulted him. Now, this guy never acted like a jerk to me, but at these parties he'd always curse and get angry and so drunk that I'd have to help him back to his dorm room or mine. I never felt I could help him the way he helped me. And then I bumped into that sweet girl with the biggest sad eyes that he broke up with one too many times. I just couldn't hurt her like that anymore, and maybe this girl could help him better than I could. So I ended it.

There was this one woodworking teacher who taught me a lot. One night, he was going to give me extra help and teach me how to use the machines. Since he thought I was such a space cadet, he wouldn't let me use the big chopping machine. I was making a wooden toilet with a wooden toilet-paper roll. (It was statement art.) Well. He walked into the wood shop and swept his arm across the table to clear off everything—very dramatic, like, "All right, are we gonna do this thing or not?" I was thinking to myself, "That's really fuckin' nice."

Listen, if you're one of those girls who slept around, it was supposed to be free love, but like I said, it wasn't. Not for the women. I used to hear the things they said about me. If you went on a date and had sex with someone they would tell everyone if you gave good blow jobs or whatever it was. I used to think, "Should I talk about how *you* were? Unattentive and jiminy-quick-like in bed?"

But I was glad to have a real college experience. At first I was in a dorm and that was pretty cool, but I kept trying to sneak my dog in and they weren't happy with me, so I left. I ended up staying at a bunch of different places. I had this one awful roommate who rode his motorcycle in the house. To get some air, I'd walk my dog at night but there were graveyards everywhere. She'd run in one to take a leak on a gravestone, and I'd run in after her trying to get her out. I was freaked out; I would think, "Oh my God, that person would be so pissed. And, actually, they were." I also lived in a place called the PROVE Program house, since I was part of the PROVE Program. There were other folks in the house who were doing the same thing, including people from prisons who were trying to rehabilitate—ex-drug addicts, ex-felons. They also housed people who had nervous breakdowns. Some of those kids had a very tough time in moments of stress. One kid was freaking out and wouldn't get out of his chair, so his family just carried the chair out and put him in the back of a truck. But the people in the PROVE house were good kids. People would always pass judgment on them, and I know very well what that's like.

At that point, I was still determined to be a painter, so I painted on every surface I could find. One time I took the shoes that I had worn in Algonquin Provincial Park and put gesso, which is like a white surface primer, on the bottom of one of the shoes, and painted on that. I took one of the sketches I made on the trip, of a place by the river where the water washed over the rocks, and painted it in acrylic. Then afterward I took real rocks and glued them on, so the rocks would come out of the painting. It was pretty neat. I also took a small tree branch I saved and put it through the toe of the shoe. I showed that piece in an art show at school, and it was stolen. But I was told that only the really good pieces were stolen, so that's good.

I was also deejaying at the radio station at school. I got the gig after I called the station and complained that they weren't playing enough women. The early seventies was a time when people were still in that hippie mentality of wanting to change things and make them better. The guy at the station told me, "If you don't like it, come down here and be a deejay for us, and you can play all the women you want." I went in as a belligerent kid, but then I saw how fun it was. I loved it there. I played all kinds of music, and in between I'd put in bits of comedy things, and then segue into aeolian harps or something. I always made sure there was some kind of story going on with the music. It was very trippy. In fact, a lot of people used to trip to my shows.

I brought more women to the airwaves, and I was the first female streaker on campus, too. It needed to be done—there were a lot of guys doing it, and it was time for a female. I had my boots on and a hat, and I ran naked through the cafeteria. One of my art-student friends said, "Cyn, I couldn't help but recognize you, because I draw you all the time."

And of course I played music too. I had some friends who lived in a different dorm that was an old converted farmhouse. Sparkle and I would run across a cow patch (sidestepping the cow pies) between my dorm and theirs. I'd bring my guitar and we'd all sing and jam together all night. I had a guitar that I'd play called Athena—the one people gave me money for playing when I was sixteen. She had a thin neck and a nice sound. We'd sit around playing and any sound was welcome. You could play glasses if you wanted; it didn't matter what you picked up, and I kind of loved that. One time, a teacher told me that I could join his band but that I'd have to pull my weight by writing songs. I was so excited. After dinner, in Johnson, everyone sat around and played.

During that time, B. B. King came to the college for a show. I shook his hand, but I remember I was so scared that I couldn't look in his eyes. I went from that frightened handshake to making a record that he played on two years ago. The arc and the miracle of a lifetime is what really stuns me. It reminds me, "Don't count yourself out." A lot of stuff happens in life for a reason, and for all I know, that handshake, on some spiritual level, might have been carrying the message, "Hi, in twenty or thirty years you'll be a musician, and I'll be playing on your record."

I was at college for a year and two months. I tried really hard, but once again I was failing, and I just couldn't bear it. My art grades were fine, but I flunked Greek history, I was failing English, and in addition to that, I was in debt. When I made up my mind to leave and hitch back to New York, I cried my eyes out. I stopped at a church, like any good Italian, and prayed to Jesus, my secret friend, and all of a sudden I felt him standing on the side of me with no sadness. In a way, he was telling me without words that this failure was okay, that I should just go home. I'll never know if it's just my imagination that makes me hear and see things, but I'm glad I do. It helps me get through life.

When I came home from college in 1972, I walked down from Jamaica Avenue and people threw rocks at me because of my clothes. I remember I was wearing a long green coat, which was really kind of cute; my "hat full of stars" that I had created after reading Yoko Ono's *Grapefruit* book; socks that were like candy canes, white and red; and big red clogs that were size 8. I was a 7 but I liked them, so I wore thick socks, but that's how I got my bunions. So never do that, okay? Get shoes that fit.

Soon enough I was back in Bob Barrell's studio. One night he was having a party, and I was playing guitar for everyone, and another art student named Fran Kissinger sat her butt down next to me and said, "You know, you have a professional voice—you should really sing professionally." Well, why not? I started looking at ads for singers in the newspapers, but what they usually wanted were black girls to sing background for these white guys. (Which, when you stop and think about it, is like, "An all-white band and black background singers? What the fuck is that?") Then I heard about a company that was looking for singers. I met with a guy who told me that I should learn all these different songs that were on the radio. I performed for him, and it seemed to go well, but then I got in trouble.

He invited me to his house for dinner and I thought it was a date. So I went, and it was really nice—candlelit and everything. I was probably twenty at the time and thinking, "What a nice guy, he's actually making dinner for me. Who does that?" And then, of course, he came on to me. I was flattered and went for it, then all of a sudden he got a phone call. He hung up, said his wife was coming home, and ushered me out and put me in a cab. That was the end of that. I was such a stupid kid.

But then I went to another audition, for a cover band. This time Fran came with me because I decided that I wasn't going to go on auditions alone anymore. I sang the Gladys Knight and the Pips song "I've Got to Use My Imagination," and I made a mistake and sang higher than I should have. I just pushed a little, and I couldn't believe the big voice that came out of me. It was so loud and so strong that I was thinking, "Holy shit, where did this come from?" You should have seen everyone's faces, too. They were looking at me, surprised, and I'm thinking, "You think *you're* surprised?" I once had a dream where an angel told me I was a sleeping lion, and at that moment I thought, "This must be my roar." I kept going, though, because I was in an audition situation. I joined the band. (I'm leaving out the band's name, for reasons that you'll see later.)

There was a gay singer who looked a little like John Travolta and a bass player who dressed like Bootsy Collins, although he was a white guy. I was a background singer, but every once in a while the background girls would sing lead, so whenever the band was sort of losing the crowd, they'd have me step up and do something like "Lady Marmalade," "I've Got the Music in Me," or "Tell Me Something Good." I sang background with this other girl, Dale, who was awesome. I sang the high harmonies, so they started calling us Chip and Dale.

Along with my new band, I got a new place to live: Fran's apartment. She made a deal that I would be a live-in nanny for her two kids. So I did the gigs at night with the band, but then I had to get up early in the morning and take care of the kids. And soon it started to get really weird. Fran was going through a very traumatic time because there was a lot of turmoil with her ex, and the kids were a little out of control. And one time I slapped her son. The kid did something to me, and it was a snap reaction. He went into the wall, and I never forgave myself. I was a kid myself, but I should never have ever, ever hit him. It's just wrong, because if you teach violence, violence begets more violence. I could never get it right because I didn't know how. I couldn't be the nanny that she needed and I couldn't bring stability to the place, so finally I just left.

So I moved back to my mom's place in Queens, and Fran started working in a bar as a barmaid to support her kids. Through her bar, I met a couple of guys I thought I was going to be with, because I just wanted to go out on a date. They never worked out. One guy was a Vietnam vet, but I was not sensitive to his plight and I told him I had marched against the war. He freaked out. That date ended abruptly. It should have because no one treated those guys fairly when they came back and I was a stupid kid who didn't understand that. Then later, when I was the lead singer in the band, I started seeing this other guy who was friends with the drummer. But that ended when he became a nervous boyfriend who had to make sure everything ran smoothly at the clubs, even though he wasn't our manager.

The band got some good opening gigs. We opened for Wayne County—once when he was Wayne, and later when he was Jayne. Remember that musical *Hedwig and the Angry Inch*? It reminded me very much of Wayne/Jayne, although actor John Cameron Mitchell said that the character Hedwig was based on a combination of a couple of people. Wayne was wild and funny. I was always afraid of him. He did say some nasty things to me, but I didn't care. We played at the Coventry Club on Queens Boulevard, where Kiss played their first gig. We opened for Isis, whose lead singer was a beautiful lesbian. She had white-blonde hair that she sprinkled with glitter. She also wore a white glittery shirt and shiny pants. She looked like an ice queen, but her guitar playing was on fire. In those days it was cool to see people living alternative lifestyles in those glitter bands—but even though a gay man could break through then, a declared lesbian never could.

All of the club owners always had a problem with me, because I couldn't stay on my feet when I danced. They would ask, "Why can't she just stand there and sing?" I used to fall a lot because I'd be wearing high heels, or big platforms, and the lead singer would bend down and help me up, and then he'd fall and Dale would try and help us up and then we'd all be on the ground. That's how I learned to talk onstage—because you gotta say something.

We would drive to gigs in an old van and once we got in an accident. I think we were on the Southern State Parkway, way out east on Long Island, by exit 60, and we were all piled in with the equipment. There were no seat belts then and the guy driving the van had a blowout, and it turned over, but the skillful way the guy was driving, the way he could maneuver, actually saved our lives. I remember I was pulling at people flying out the window, and then finally I was flying, too, but I wasn't alone. I was flying with an angel above me, and I passed these dead musicians who were on the side of the road just watching—Duane Allman, Berry Oakley. Then the angel said, "That's a good place for you to land," and it was a bush. That's where I landed. I just ended up with a scar on my leg.

Singing in Long Island clubs and dives wasn't easy on my voice. These were places like the Glendale Lounge, where Fat Jack used to walk through our setup with a pizza, because the kitchen was right behind us. A lot of times, the guitar players would have two-hundred-watt Marshall amplifiers, which were very popular then, with Gibson Les Paul Goldtop guitars—those are loud, sustained guitars. So in order to be heard, I had to get a fifty-watt amplifier for my voice and I only had a little fart box to hear what I sounded like. But after a while, I would still be hoarse. I'd start out singing with a full range and end up with nothing when I finished, and then I'd go to sleep and try and regain my voice.

While we were doing shows, a manager came to see us a couple of times. He said to us, "I'm not going to manage you unless you make the girl in the back who sings good, and falls all the time, sing lead. Let the guy in the front who dances good but sings a little off be a background singer with the other girl—let's see how that works." So we did it, but of course the band kind of hated me for that. And the club owners always had a problem with me because they said I looked like a boy and danced like a boy.

This manager, Phil, was a little screwy. In my opinion, he was a sexist, manipulative asshole. He came in one time at a place we were playing called the Three Ships, which had a huge bar with a stage and served five-cent drinks (so kids would get really plastered and have car accidents on the highway on the way home). I was singing Janis Joplin covers, and after one set, he pulled me aside. I had makeup on, like I usually did, and he made me take it all off and go onstage without a drop of it, because he said Joplin never wore makeup. Which is not fucking true—sometimes she didn't, sometimes she did. You know how embarrassing it was to go in front of all those people with the bright lights and not a stitch of makeup?

And there was tension in the band because they were a little mad at me. One night, some of us were at one of the band member's house. He was a little nutty and very provocative—the sort of guy who talked about sex and what he did with his girlfriend all the time and thought it was funny to pee into his beer. For some reason he and his girlfriend had a whole box of dildos at his house. And they said to me, "Go ahead—pick one up." I thought it was funny, we were all laughing about it, so I picked one of them up, looked at it, and then put it back down. His girlfriend's sister was also there and it was all fun and games until all of a sudden it was like the atmosphere in the room changed. He grabbed it, and then two other people grabbed me. I ran away from them, but they caught me and pulled my pants off. And that guy took the dildo, and he used it on me.

The gay guy in the band was there and he started freaking out. He was yelling, "Oh my God, oh my God, don't hurt her!" I couldn't believe it was happening. I tried so hard to break loose and I couldn't, because I was being held down by his girlfriend and her sister—and she was a big girl. I was stunned, in shock.

I finally broke away and grabbed the dildo, and I was going to shove it up his ass, and they were like, "Yeah, yeah, go, go!" But I dropped it. I was nauseated and in disbelief that it wasn't just men—it was a guy and two women. I just could not understand why. While it was all happening, I saw somebody sitting on the bed looking at me and crying and I thought, "It's either me, or an angel crying." The girlfriend went into the bathroom, and I went in, too. I still wasn't dressed. And I said to her, "Why? Why did you do this to me?" And she told me it was because she loved the guy and wanted to make him happy.

I just got dressed and left. I was kind of stunned for a long time. I thought that when you're in a band, you're family. Because you're the same. I always felt a kinship with musicians. I was always so glad to know that there were people in the world who felt just like I did before I found them. Like, "What the fuck am I here for? I'm a nothing. What can I do? I can't do anything. I can't keep a job." I thought there was an honor among thieves.

And then afterward, I realized that maybe it was because this guy had started the band, and then the power slipped away from him, and it had come to me. So this act was like a very animal instinct to dominate. I told him that I would tell the others what happened and he said, "Go ahead, tell them—they won't believe it." Sure enough, I told the other guys in the band and they didn't believe me. And after that, if you can believe it, I still stayed with the band because I refused to let them break me.

The only reason I never talked about this publicly before now was that I didn't want to give that guy any power. But here's what God did. In 1989, after my first two albums had come out, I was shopping for Christmas presents in New York. I had this wonderful car service—really great guys who would take me around shopping. It was snowing, and I was standing in front of Bloomingdale's. This guy came over and said, "Cyn, how are you? Look at you: You really made it. I'm so proud of you." It was him. I asked how he was, and he said he was working in a deli or something. I asked him, "How's your girlfriend?" and he said, "Oh, that ended years ago."

At the end of our conversation, I didn't say anything to him about the whole incident. I didn't have to. You know when you get the grander picture? I just went back in my car and continued on. I thought, "You know what, pal? As you treat others, at one point in your life, whether it's now or later, you're going to get it back."

Everything in my life has been a lesson like that. Every freakin' thing.

CHAPTER FOUR

I DIDN'T LEAVE THAT band, but they fired me, anyway. I don't know why and I don't care—I was not happy; I wasn't listening to them anymore. But ultimately it was good, because I started another band called Flyer. At that time, a lot of bands had come to see me and I became friendly with other musicians, so with Flyer, we had a really good group. There was a guitar player named Jimmy, Richie on rhythm guitar, Eddie on bass (who still emails me), and Charlie on drums. We were going to be rockers. In my last band I was doing Janis Joplin covers, but in this one, our sound was more like Rod Stewart.

I ended up falling in love with Richie. He was my first real love. He was funny and bright, had a BA in English, and could play a wicked lead. He had a lot of promise, but he was haunted. I've found that most musicians are haunted by something or some idea that they are always at odds with. He had nightmares about his late father, who passed away when he was maybe around twelve. In his dream, his dad, who was an alcoholic most of his life, would be sitting in his kitchen, laughing at him.

Richie lived with his mom not too far away from me in Richmond Hill, Queens. She hadn't had it easy with his dad and was a little bitter about the turn of her life (who wouldn't be, I guess). But she also was never too supportive of Richie's choice to play in a band. He could have been a teacher. He used to talk about Shakespeare, and I told him I had been seeing Shakespeare since I was small and went to Central Park's outdoor Delacorte Theater with my mother. Once when I was watching a performance on channel 13, Richie said, "Cyn, you don't even know what they're saying." I said, "Yeah, I do. Basically, he said that guy's a fuckin' asshole." He didn't understand that you could understand Shakespeare without translating it the way you are taught in school. There are many ways to see it.

He taught me a lot about what made performances great—how if you always sing a high note in every verse, it takes away from its being special (which I guess I was doing at the time). On our long trips back and forth to Long Island clubs in his little Volkswagen Karmann Ghia car, we'd listen to David Bowie's *Heroes* album. We listened to a lot of Clapton, too. Richie adored him. Clapton was a god to any guitar player coming up then, but especially to Richie. He also loved the Kinks and Elvis Costello, which I did too, as well as Joni Mitchell's *Miles of Aisles*. She was a successful woman who wrote, produced, art-directed, and did her own clothes. What was not to love?

Richie's Karmann Ghia had a two-inch hole in the floor on my side, where he told me once he put a hibachi in just to keep the car warm. In the winter, he'd use a blanket to block the wind. The wind off of the Long Island Expressway really blew hard, especially when trucks went by. I tried to put my foot there once to block the wind but I could see the road so clearly that I just kept my feet away because I was so afraid they would somehow fall through. (One time a guy yelled as he passed, "Why don't you get a bike?") And in this little warrior chariot we'd talk about sex, life, or the last gig. Or we'd talk about how we could learn from the rock gods whose altars we knelt at every time we'd hit a stage singing one of their songs again.

We also talked a lot about what it was that made David Bowie and Elvis Costello such great poets. Especially Elvis Costello. Richie would play his music and explain, with his English BA, the literary references that Elvis used. And although in my heart I knew I would never write like Elvis Costello or even be as great as David Bowie, it didn't stop me from trying every night to find something, some escape note or move that would help me step off the platform into my own fantastic elastic interior world where I could be Bowie or Elvis for an instant. And that was enough for me to keep going, because in my heart I felt that maybe all those little great moments would add up one day. There was never a doubt in my mind I would sing for a living. I would keep trying to learn as best I could, as much as I could, about my craft. I didn't care what anyone thought of me because onstage, in that state of mind, I could be anyone I wanted to be and because I was on a stage, it would be accepted.

One time when Flyer did a show, my mother came to see us. The gig was at the church where I went to school until the third grade— where I was baptized, and had the Holy Communion, and all that nonsense. In those days the church would host dances, so we played a high school dance. Afterward my mother said, "You know, Cyn, I think you're really good. You've really got something." I always knew I could sing. No one had to tell me. No one had to teach me. When I was little, the nuns at my convent school were out of their minds and wanted me to be an opera singer. They used to tell my mother I should be trained for it. Then my mother had this idea that she would put me up for adoption to rich people so that they could train my voice. (I guess that's why I never really liked rich people.) I was like, "Ma, I don't care about this. Hello, let's not get crazy." My mother always dragged me to everything she could—ballet lessons, tap lessons where I was gangly and danced like a scarecrow.

There were people who would come up to me and say I sang like a rat. I didn't care, because there were other moments where it was really great, and I could see how I had the power to get a reaction out of people. I would go out into the crowd and make them nuts. I would climb on somebody's back and sing at the same time.

We had to do covers, covers, and more covers, like "Born to Run" (in that case I really did sound like a rat because it was never in my key). I often got in trouble because I drew too many people away from the bars in the club. They were supposed to be drinking and instead of doing that, they would come in the front and just watch—and that was a big no-no. You're supposed to say things like, "Hey, drinks for twenty-five cents at the bar!" But I wouldn't promote the alcohol, because when Richie and I drove home at night after a gig, I would see the car accidents.

Obviously, that wasn't the right gig for me. I really felt like a failure, although Deborah Harry told me once that if I had stayed, I would have been up to doing cruise ships in my career by now. (Which is really horrific for me, because I can't swim. I mean, I saw *The Poseidon Adventure* with Shelley Winters and she just didn't look good in the water.)

We couldn't win. We played at a beach club in the Hamptons, but it was the middle of the winter and fourteen people showed up. We had our first NYC gig at the famous music club Trude Heller's. I don't know whether they paid us or not and I didn't care, because it was the first time that people sat and listened to us because they wanted to. A lot of places in New York City didn't pay, like the Bottom Line. (Later when they asked me to help them, I was like, "How about when you could have helped some young artists but instead you just fuckin' wouldn't pay them?") Even at CBGB, the owner, Hilly Kristal, wasn't like a sweet pussycat type of guy. He didn't pay anybody either. Cheap bastard. They were all cheap—they squeaked when they walked. They weren't very nice.

Along with trying to preserve my voice, I started feeling ill, just out-of-my-mind sick with stomach pains. I was throwing up all the time and finally I went to a doctor. I couldn't afford medical help at the time so I was always going to a clinic, where they'd have a student examine me with the doctor behind him. I couldn't have been more surprised when the doctor said, "Listen. You're pregnant." Richie was the father. I had always been told that I couldn't get pregnant because my cervix was tilted.

The doctor told me that if he gave me medicine to make my illness better, then I couldn't have the baby. He said, "Think about what you want to do." And I remember saying, "Just give me the medicine." You have to understand: at the time, I was so fucking sick. But then afterward, when I started to get better, I wanted this kid. All of a sudden, I wanted this kid a lot.

When I told Richie that I was pregnant, I didn't tell him about the medicine, just to see his reaction. He said, "You know, we can get an abortion. I'll be there with you." And even though I had already taken the medicine, it just broke my heart that there wasn't even a thought to keep the baby. But I still loved Richie. Poor guy. He drank too much, smoked too many cigarettes, and in the end he worked at the part of the airport that was very toxic, near the fuel tanks, but they paid you a lot of money to work there. He got sick and later died of some kind of cancer.

So I got the abortion. Afterward I bled a lot, and cried a lot, because I couldn't believe what happened. The kid was almost twelve weeks—that's a lot. And I wanted it, even though with the medicine

I had taken, the baby might have been deformed. I just wish I was smarter then, but I wasn't. My mother wanted me not to have the kid too. She thought it would mess up my chances in my career, because I was twenty-three. But other people have had kids and still managed to have a chance. I don't know. I used to cry for a long, long time, onto a pillow that became tear-stained—like that Little Anthony and the Imperials song from the 1950s, remember it? "Tears on my pillow, pain in my heart." Even when I was famous, I felt the need to hold on to that pillow, so I had it stuffed into another pillow.

When I was bleeding so much after the abortion, I decided to go to another clinic. In those clinics, there was so much sexism and bullshit and arrogance. While the student was examining me, I told them that it hurt, and the doctor said, "Well, why didn't you just keep your legs closed in the first place?" I realized that if you didn't come from a rich family with a parent there to protect you, you were at the mercy of the clinic and a bunch of powerful men who put themselves in charge. In college, though, I used to go to Planned Parenthood, and they were always kind and generous to me even though I didn't have a pot to piss in, so when I did have money later, I gave to them.

Later, I was so happy when my son, Declyn, was born in 1997. I wanted another baby after him, but it just wasn't in the cards, and I cried all over again when I saw all my friends who had been pregnant alongside of me knocked up again while I was going back to work. For a long time, I dreamed that there was another kid, a little girl in a car seat behind Declyn saying, "Yay, Declyn." Listen, you can't have regrets, because everything is supposed to happen the way it's supposed to happen.

After the abortion, I had to get back to work. As usual, I had bills to pay, and I needed to get a PA, which is a speaker that the band goes through and a monitor system that you can hear yourself through when you sing. It would make things easier on my voice, which I couldn't lose again. One of the guys in the band said to me, "Not everyone has a rich uncle, so a lot of people get a job as a go-go dancer. They make a lot of money, and then you can pay for your PA."

It sounded like a good idea. Why not? I'd worked at every other kind of job. So I became a topless dancer. There were lots of topless places in midtown Manhattan, but new girls were usually sent out of town, so I started at a place upstate in Nyack, New York. Then I worked in a place called Gracie's Lounge, in the industrial part of Queens. It was kind of like we were pole dancers, only without the pole. My stage name was Carrot, because I had red hair, and my performances were free-form dance and pretty creative. Instead of just shaking my tail feather, I would make believe I was with someone, or I would make shapes. I used to put myself in a world and tell a story through my dance. (And as long as it had sex in it, the people watching didn't care.)

Some of the girls would go up to the guys in the audience and take money from them with their knees during their performance, so I had to do the same thing. It was weird because the men would sometimes insult you. I remember one guy, who clearly hated women, would say horrible things like "I can smell you from here." And then of course I'd think, "I smell? Oh my God." You'd try to clean yourself like there was no tomorrow.

But when I was onstage, the policy was that nobody could bother the performers. Then, after you danced, you had to put on a night-gown and sit at the bar and drink. Dancers weren't supposed to really drink—instead we were told to ask for white wine spritzers, and they would make it mostly with soda. Then you had to sit and talk with the customers. Some of the guys were real characters. They were truck drivers and factory workers, and their philosophy of things was very interesting to me, and very funny.

The whole scene was really like a play: the customers, who had a specific way of talking and acting; the people who danced (who were nice enough but all kind of strange); the security people; the club owner; the bartender, who had to work in the middle of girls dancing around him—all of them were characters, really. I love talking to people, because they're all walking books. Sometimes you only meet them once, but they're a chapter. So you try to enjoy them. (That's why, even if you're in the ladies' room, you should always talk to the woman next to you. When you're in the stall, you can say, "Hey! No toilet paper! I guess it's drip-dry tonight!")

It was intriguing at first, so I stayed. And of course I was trying to earn money for my PA. I made two hundred dollars a day sometimes, and that was a big pile of dough. I even had a signature move. I did this acrobatic, stupid thing where I would be lying down on my back, and then I'd take my legs and put them up over my shoulders so that you could see my butt with the G-string on, and then I'd shake my butt back and forth so it was just a butt with no head. It was very funny to me but sexy to the customers. It was so silly, so nutty, but any acrobatic thing that you could do was a big plus to your gig, because as I said, we didn't have poles. Think about it: If you have a pole, you can do so many more things. The poor things who dance now have to do lap dances—we didn't have that. Sometimes if one guy wanted extra, I would say, "I don't really do that, but I know somebody who does."

But after a while, I got really depressed. Even though I was ultimately doing it for the PA, for the music, it was hurting me. Part of it felt like it was a safe place to be sexy, where no one was going to hurt me, and that was freeing. But the things that people would say and do, like throw coins down and tell you to pick them up (what fuckin' circus world are you living in, guys?), made me feel bad. I remember when I was dancing at the club in Nyack, they liked me there, and the owner called me into his office one day and said, "Listen, I know you sing at a club, but let me tell you something, you were made for this. You can't try and be something you're not. You're great at dancing, you've got a lot of talent, you should just focus on what you do well." Everything he said made me realize the exact opposite—that I was a singer.

So I danced until I got the PA, but I just couldn't keep going long enough to get the monitor system. It started to get to me. Because my job from the stage was to seduce people, I started to look at men in my everyday life in a weird way, just to see if I was able to do it offstage, too. And I thought, "Oh, no. It's still going. This ain't for me." One night I went to CBGB with Richie, the boy I was in love with, and one of my dancer friends. We were going just to go—it wasn't like a big act was there or anything. We always tried to see whatever we could because this was in 1975 or '76, and a music scene was starting to happen in New York. And I noticed that my friend started rubbing his leg. She was doing the seduction thing to Richie, too.

Since I still had the same crappy-ass monitors, I couldn't hear my voice, but I was so bored with the way I sang, anyway. I thought, "Okay, you're still doing Joplin covers, and now you're singing Grace Slick. If you sing 'White Rabbit' one more time, just shoot yourself," because that's what the crowd wanted on the Long Island bar circuit.

And even though I tried to take special care of my voice, I ended up losing it. I was devastated, and so scared, because I had to stop singing for two months. I couldn't talk—I had to write everything down. Three doctors told me that I would never sing again. In the meantime, the guys in Flyer had hired a girl named Ellen to take my place. When I was watching her once, I noticed she could really keep her vocal range when she was singing. When I did shows, I would always start out with a range and end up with nothing at the end, because I used it all. I asked her how she was able to sing so well in her range, and she said that she studied with a vocal coach named Katie Agresta. I decided to go see Katie, and I brought her a tape of the Joplin covers that I did. I played her the tape and I'll never forget what she said to me: "This is fine, but where is *your* singing?" What she meant and what I understood her to be asking were two different things. Katie thought that I had brought her a tape of Janis Joplin, instead of me imitating Janis. But what I thought she was asking was what I was aching for—to sing my own songs, in my own voice, in my own style, that I made up myself. I wasn't using my voice to my advantage at all, but before I could work on that, I had to get my voice back.

She sent me to a doctor who looked in my throat and said that one of my vocal cords had collapsed. It just couldn't take it anymore. He told me that I shouldn't be singing rock and roll music, and because of the way I'm built, I should try country and western. He said that people have different vocal cords. I have a small frame and I'm white, so I have completely different vocal cords than, say, a man who is on the large side, or a black woman. Really, I'm a lyrical soprano, which is different from what I normally sing, but I have a big, three-and-a-half-octave range, or on an extraordinary day, a four. So despite what he said, I wanted to use my voice that way, anyway. Because when I sang, there was something in me that was bigger than me and I somehow had to learn how to use what was inside without wrecking the outside. I just had to find a way to fix and maintain it, and I thought Katie might be able to help.

So I started studying with Katie, who changed my life, and I'm still with her today. In fact, I saw her last Tuesday. She taught me vocal therapy. A man named Dr. Dwyer was her teacher, and he developed this technique based on operatic and therapeutic stuff that he used to help Broadway and opera singers. Katie taught me about vocal exercises and warm-ups, and how your diet affects your voice, and the damage that alcohol and drugs can do to it.

I mostly stayed away from drugs anyway, but one time at a show, somebody said to me, "You sing great—you want some coke? This will make you sing even better." Of course, I would do anything to sing better. So I tried it and sang great for about two seconds, before all of a sudden I couldn't sing at all. Coke numbs your throat so you don't feel what you're doing, and you blow your vocal cords out and: the end. I freaked. I couldn't sing and all I kept thinking was, "I thought that person *liked* the way I sang."

I was always leery about the coke thing. When I was around fourteen, my friends and I used to hang out at a park on 106th Street and Atlantic Avenue, and dealers used to drive by and hand out coke, like free samples, and tell us it wasn't addictive. People didn't know then that it was.

After I rested my voice and, with Katie's help, got it back, I got a gig singing at Trude Heller's. What I loved about it was that it was a nightclub (now it's gone) where people didn't pick up each other but really sat and listened to music. All of a sudden, they really *heard* the things I was doing. Like we did "Magic Man," the Heart song, and you know the two guitar parts that they play in "Magic Man"? I sang one of the guitar parts. I wanted to sing like an instrument. And people noticed it and actually liked me. So when I got a taste of that, I told myself I wanted to keep playing in Manhattan and stop doing cover material.

I tried to write with the guys in Flyer but they were just goofballs—every time I'd get a melody they'd change the chord, over and over, and we never got anywhere. Then, when I sang at Trude's one night, my friend Rose brought down a songwriter named John Turi, who also played saxophone and keyboards. We hit it off and started writing together, and eventually I just quit Flyer, and John and I formed the band Blue Angel, named after the Marlene Dietrich movie. We went through a bunch of different versions of the band, with many different guitar players, and we went through many kinds of sounds before we settled on rockabilly. John and I wrote a song called "Flyer"—which Flyer kept. At the time I was influenced by Queen and Freddie Mercury. Later I changed so radically and totally away from that influence that when I had an opportunity to meet them at the height of my career, I didn't. But I was an idiot kid. You know how you get when you think something is cool and then something isn't? Actually, by then I was thirty—I wasn't a kid. Everything was late for me. It's a shame when you don't know the value of what's in front of you.

In Blue Angel, we recorded expensive, bad demos to send around to record labels and played clubs like Great Gildersleeves, which was (physically and sort of symbolically) right down the block from CBGB. Gildersleeves was never *the* place, never the "scene." Instead it was always the corny rock place that had the straighter bands. And things didn't go so well with our manager after a while. He had put out money for these terrible demos, and after a while he wanted his money back—which I don't blame him for, but there was no way we were going to make the money back because we just could not get a leg up.

So one night at a gig, he got really upset, and took the money we earned and just left. So we needed a new manager. One night when we were playing Trax, a club on the Upper West Side, a guy named Steve came to see the show. He was the Allman Brothers' manager and had heard our demos. Not that he was impressed—he thought they were bad—but somehow he had been persuaded to see us. Then John arranged for me to meet a new manager in his office in midtown. (I don't know why John didn't go, too, but he didn't.) It was one of the weirder meetings I've been to. I was supposed to go in at five, and when I did, everyone was leaving. That was a little creepy. I went in there, sat down, and while I'm talking to him, he started scratching the corner of his forehead, like by his scalp. Then, when it bled, he would reach up and blot the blood with his finger, and then put it on the blotter on his desk. Pick, pick. Dab, dab. Blot, blot. He was totally comfortable, talking away. After he made a pattern, he picked up a pen and started *drawing around the blood on the blotter.*

I didn't know who was nuttier: him, or me for being there. I was thinking, "Okay, this ain't right, and I'm gonna be killed." We talked awhile, and then I got the hell out of there really quick. I told John about it and said, "Listen, we can't do this." He said, "Oh, Cyn, come on. You're not marrying the guy. He's gonna manage you, that's all, and we're gonna get to the next spot. We need that help." I told him I thought he was wrong, but I'd do it. So he became our manager and set up a showcase for Blue Angel for all of his industry guys to come see.

We ended up getting a record deal with Polydor, a major label, in 1980, which was so exciting. There was a lot of enthusiasm around the whole New Wave rockabilly thing, and it was really happening. We had our picture in *Billboard* magazine, and the world seemed open to us.

Even though Blue Angel was signed, we had already been through so many versions of the band. And even then, we were convinced that this latest version would really happen for us. At that point, I had been writing with John Turi for four years and trying to come up with a formula that would be the sound and the style of the new band. We were kind of expanding the rockabilly pop thing to a more New Wave rockabilly pop sound, and we'd sit for hours just listening to Wanda Jackson, Elvis Presley, Elvis Costello, the Police, and the Specials. John would play me these great fifties and sixties singers who I didn't even know existed but kind of sounded like me.

When we first started Blue Angel I was living in Woodhaven, Queens, with my kid brother Butch, not too far from my mom's apartment on Ninetieth Street. Every night that I wasn't working in a club or practicing with the band, I'd go back to the apartment. I finally had him living with me like I wanted to do when I first left home. But by that time, he was no longer eleven, and it was hard to be living together when we were both in our twenties. I did my share of knuckleheaded things, and so did he. Except this was his first shot at being an adult—this was my third. I had already tried to live in Long Island, Vermont, City Line, in between Queens and Brooklyn, and wound up coming back home to my mother.

But then I moved out of the apartment with Butch in Woodhaven and into a little studio apartment in Manhattan on East Seventy-seventh Street. I fixed up the place with all of my family's old furniture and curtains and whatever I could buy cheaply (but looked cute) from McCrory's, where I worked. It was one of the day jobs I took. Usually they didn't last because I worked so much with the band, but I had gotten this job through a friend of mine. He told me he was my first fan and had been coming down to see me for years. He was the assistant manager of McCrory's, a Woolworth's type of five-and-ten store across the street from Alexander's in Rego Park, Queens. He introduced me to a woman named Doris, who ran a jewelry concession in the front of the store. At Christmas she personalized Christmas stockings with glue and glitter. She sold T-shirts, too, and you could purchase the picture you wanted her to iron on. My favorite iron-on was a cartoon of a grimy-looking soldier type who had a bubble coming out of his mouth that read, "Though I walk through the Valley of Death I fear no evil, 'cause I'm the meanest son of a bitch in the valley." That made me laugh. Doris made me laugh, and everyone around her too. I liked her so much right away. She was small and had bright red hair, the exact shade I used to search the drugstore shelves for in the early seventies (and she didn't mind that mine was purple and blond, either). She had a big smile and reminded me of the Italian women I used to see on 101st Avenue in Queens coming out of the beauty parlor. She and her mom (also a bottled redhead, but not as deep and rich as Doris's) used to know Barbra Streisand when she lived in Brooklyn. Her mother would visit and tell me her friend Barbra lived upstairs from her—Barbra, who was just like everybody else.

Doris was a woman who knew how to do a lot of different things. And sometimes if I had a gig, she would let me miss work. I was usually a little late for the job—my friends always called me "the late Cyndi Lauper"—so I'd always be running in at the last minute. But Doris liked entertainers. At McCrory's, my job was to engrave cheap jewelry. I used to practice my handwriting on a pie plate with an engraving pen. Little kids would be excited about their Christmas present for their grandma and would bring in a little, inch-long silver- or gold-plated heart with rhinestones. They'd ask me to write, "Dear Grandma, Merry Christmas and Happy New Year, Love, Tommy, Judy, Larry, and Susan." Then they'd say, "Oh, and can you put the date on it, too?"

But I was doing well, and Doris, who was so funny, liked me. She moved me up to the front of the store one Christmas Eve and had me doing Christmas stockings. She told me to start barking. I had to say as loud as I could (which was pretty loud), "Get ya Christmas stockings! Personalized Christmas stockings!" And the price would go down the later in the day it got. But I remember getting into the spirit with that glue and glitter.

She asked me to pierce people's ears, too. I figured I could do it because when I was a kid, I helped my mother reupholster the kitchen set. My mother really knew how to sew and could remake anything (remember, we all came from the garment industry). So we kids helped her with the vinyl and Naugahyde; we'd stretch it over the chair and staple it.

So piercing ears was just another staple to me, right? But when I went to staple the earrings in and it passed through the flesh, it felt totally different from a chair. I forgot that I'm really squeamish— I couldn't even cut the frog in biology—and I kind of freaked out.

Doris was somewhere else in the store, and it's not like there was a panic button. I was trying to talk to the lady, but I couldn't speak Polish like she did, and I was feeling a little sick, and trying to call for Doris out of the side of my mouth, like, "Doris. *Doris.*" I couldn't leave the lady with the staple gun in her ear and she was a large woman, and then she started to laugh. Which made her sway back and forth, and the staple gun started to sway, too. Which made me feel *really* queasy, so I kept calling for Doris.

The store did not have an intercom. Instead, it had Big Mary. Big Mary sat in the back of the store in the office behind a sliding door, and she would open it and holler down in the store for whoever. So Mary caught wind of what was going on and opened the door and hollered, "Doris, I think Cyndi needs you!" And Doris came running up the aisle and made it all fine for the lady and finished the other ear, and I never pierced another ear in my life.

Doris worked in two locations: Queens and Greenpoint, Brooklyn. I started in Queens, but later they needed me to fill in occasionally at the store in Brooklyn, too. But it was in Queens where I met two older gals: Minnie and Margaret, the sweetest-looking older woman with the filthiest mouth. They were what were known as returnees. New York was having a fiscal crisis at the time, and people had their pensions cut, so a lot of people over sixty-five suddenly had to return to the workforce. My boss Steve, who had hired me, got such a kick out of these women. So did we all, because they were hysterical.

They would say things just to shock you. Margaret worked at the food counter. She looked like a sweet auntie, but then she'd hit ya with "Cocksucker." As for Minnie, if I went over and talked to her, she'd start out perfectly normal—until I kept questioning her about something she didn't feel like talking about. Then she'd say something like, "Look, you seem like a nice kid, but go fuck yourself." That one Christmas Eve when I was selling Christmas stockings, I asked her what she was doing that evening. She said she'd be waiting for Santa on a bearskin rug, naked with nothing on but a bow, and some milk and cookies by her side too. She said she'd be waiting for Santa to come up her chute.

Now, Minnie was an older woman—around seventy. Not that Santa's a young guy or anything but Minnie was heavyset with (very) wide hips. She wore black every day. Now that I think about it, she was actually kind of punk and she didn't even know it. Her hair was dyed dark brown and she wore stockings that went above her knee. She always had on the best platform orthopedic shoes that looked just like the ones that Pearl Harbor (of Pearl Harbor and the Explosions) wore. Later on, when I wrote my Christmas album, I had a song called "Minnie and Santa." That was Minnie.

There was this one woman who looked like a vision every time she entered the store. The first day I met her, it was nasty out. I was watching the rain pour down and bounce off the bus shelter by the corner and up off the sidewalk. Doris's counter was right up in the front of the store, and if there weren't any customers, I could stare out the big front windows. Well—in walks this tall woman, with her platinum hair tied up in a tall French knot in the back and curled in the front. And a kerchief with a pink and red floral print, framing those high curls in the front and her face. She wore a bright, cobalt-blue raincoat and had on the prettiest bright pink lipstick too. It was very sixties. And I said to her, "Wow, you look great." And she said back to me, "I always wear my brightest colors on the darkest days." It made my eyes happy to see her against that gray day. For a long time, what she said stuck with me. And years later, I kept it in mind when I stood in front of the old wax museum in Coney Island and took the album-cover photograph for *She's So Unusual*. I thought of that woman when I was dancing barefoot, in a piss-stained alley, dressed in red, against a bright yellow door and bright blue brick walls that I knew would strobe against the red. I thought, "In the darkest place, shed the brightest light."

The best part of working with those women was how much fun they made it. These were woman who would be nice to you all day, and at the end of the day they would get really lewd and rude. And they knew Steve and I loved them for all their nastiness. We always felt they were kindred spirits and I just thought I was extraordinarily lucky to have the job and to know those people, and for the people who ran that little department store to have enough kindness and room in their hearts to hire such characters. There was so much personality and humor in that store. It's not the same anymore. Everything has gotten so corporate that the humanity is kind of gone from those shops.

So I spent my days working at the department store and my nights doing gigs or recording. Then I'd go back to my apartment in Queens. I'd take the Woodhaven Boulevard bus, where you'd transfer at London Lennie's, a restaurant that my mother loved. She thought that the shrimp was incredible. I just loved the name "London Lennie's."

Going to any of my apartments was a challenge because I always had tons of bags with all this shit in them for my gigs. I'd bring this heavy stainless steel pot with a hot plate so I could steam my throat because I was so worried about losing my voice, and some Vicks, and a vibrator for my neck to make sure it wasn't tight, and vitamins, and God knows what else.

When I moved to the city, my sister, Elen, came with me. On the mailboxes she saw the name of a friend who used to be a neighbor of hers. She had lost contact with him, and incredibly, there he was, right downstairs from my apartment. So she knocked on his door and said, "My sister's moving in upstairs—can you keep an eye on her for me?" His name was Carl Eagleston, and that's how I met him and his boyfriend, Gregory, who became a really close friend and later inspired my song "Boy Blue." He was called Blue because his eyes were so blue. I never called him that, but his cousin Diana, who was a transgender woman, did, and another woman who took him in off the streets when she saw him sleeping in the park.

It was 1980 and Elen had just moved away from NYC to Newport News, Virginia. She was working as a pipe fitter at the shipyard there. El always wanted to learn how to do things and went about her life like an explorer trying different jobs and lifestyles. I guess I did too. El and I wanted to change the world for the better, wanted to be all we could be (who knew the army would take that line?).

El is older than me by a year and a bit. When we were small, folks would ask my mother if we were twins (mainly because she dressed us alike) and my mom would reply, "Almost." I can't even get into what the heck that means, because either ya are, or ya aren't. Some people called us Irish twins, which is really confusing since we were Italian and German/Swiss. But whatever the case, my mom always said I was born to be Elen's friend and told my sister to always watch out for me. When we were small children I took everything very literally, and because she was supposed to watch out for me, I became Elen's shadow. And as much as she tried to push away her tantrum-y, demanding little sister who felt the need to be with her every second, she still watched out for me. Basically, I thought I had to have special consideration because I was born to be her friend. It's a long story. Maybe that's what my mom meant when she said we were "almost twins." I probably would have squeezed into this world *with* her if I could have. So here she was, once again watching out for her little sis, who was moving into the big city for the first time. And if El couldn't be there for me all the time, she felt Carl would watch out for me.

Before I met Carl and Gregory, I had a dream about two little old ladies who lived in a shiny pink castle. Then when I met them, I saw that they had painted their apartment pink—like cotton candy, Pepto-Bismol pink, and they put crushed mirrors into the paint. It was just about the most amazing thing I ever saw, and I realized that these guys were the two little old ladies. Carl would cook, and I would go downstairs and eat with them. I had no money, but I'd bring something, and they'd say, "Oh, don't bring anything."

I used to wear muumuus all the time with flip-flops, and then I'd tie my hair up in a turban. Carl would look at me and go, "Mrs. Feeney!" He just thought I looked like a Mrs. Feeney, so he made up the name, and that's who I became.

They used to play all these old records and show me how to dance the fox-trot. They had a studio apartment and built a loft bed and moved most of the furniture out so there was more room to dance. They put pillows on the floor and we sat cross-legged to eat dinner. Every day it was a picnic. They'd always change the paint in the loft. Like one year it was a garden terrace so everything was bright yellow and green. Once Carl came up to my apartment, looked around at the white walls, and said, "Cyn. Mrs. Feeney. Look at this place. You're not a white-wall gal. We're going to the paint store, and we'll find out what you like, what you are." So we went to the store and I painted one wall of my apartment rust and the other walls light tan, and I covered them with, like, twenty antique mirrors, and he built a loft bed for me. My apartment also had a floor that was slanted, so whenever you dropped anything, it would roll to one side. Then they would say, "Mrs. Feeney is bowling again."

After I moved into the city, I went to the store Trash and Vaudeville and bought clothes that I liked. We were playing Manhattan clubs, and I didn't want to dress like somebody from Queens anymore. I bought this really cute black and white sheer vintage blouse with a black vest, and drape-y pants with stars on them that kind of had an Ali Baba look, but not as severe. And I would go to Screaming Mimi's, a vintage clothing store where I later worked, and try on vintage clothes, turning and swirling to see how I could perform in them and what they would look like onstage. I used to go out and find the clothes, but now I'm so busy that I have a stylist who shops for me. I look through what she brings to see what speaks to me. She and I have worked together since 2004. She's a kick-ass stylist. I always tell her, "Elegant, but not conservative—ever." And she gets it. We do have different mind-sets. For her, it's about style, but for me, it's about the performance and how the clothes will move when I'm dancing onstage.

And of course I always liked to try new things with my hair. Like, when I was in Blue Angel, my hair was blond in the front and brown, and I would twist it and do different ponytails and things. I made it up myself. The only reason the front of my hair was blond was because of Ed from Flyer. He used to tease me and say I had a mustache, so I tweezed it. Well, it came in darker, so I bought this Jolene bleach stuff. I put it on my mustache, and while it was working I was looking at myself in the mirror. There was some Jolene left over, so I put it on my bangs, so the front was blond and the back was brown. Which was a good look, I thought.

It was such an exciting time for all of us. A radio station ran a contest, "Win a date with Cyndi from Blue Angel," for Valentine's Day. So Carl and I and another friend, John, who has since passed away, and all my colorful friends from downstairs in my apartment building, helped me draw a big heart that said "Happy Valentine's Day," and put ruffles around it and cut two armholes in it so when I came out, I had a "heart on" . . . get it? That was a thrill because it was the beginning of all the performance art that we used to do.

And we did some shows in Puerto Rico, because not too many famous people from the United States would play in Puerto Rico—at the time, there were no direct flights, so it wasn't convenient. Plus, it wasn't seen as this big market. But since I didn't *have* a market, it didn't matter. As we were planning the trip, I thought that since no famous people would go to Puerto Rico, why don't we just dress like we're famous, and act like we're famous, and wave grandly to everybody? So that's what we did.

I remember for my "arrival," I wore pedal pushers like the ones on the Blue Angel album cover, and little bobby socks with hearts on them. I used to like to mix patterns, like a print and checks and plaids, and for some reason that used to upset a lot of people. I always thought plaid and leopard were really good together, but it wasn't until later on in the nineties that it became acceptable when Vivienne Westwood did it. Not that I'm saying I did it first—I just did whatever I liked. Blue Angel once got a review and the person wrote, "I can't even hear her sing because of her clothes." I didn't care. I dressed however I wanted onstage, because there were also other people who would say, "Oh my God, what a voice." Sometimes when I was onstage I would throw my shoes off and dance barefoot because I could dance better. (I don't know if that was a good idea, because now my feet are killing me.)

When Blue Angel opened for Peter Frampton, I bought this little pink fifties bathing suit and a button-down green dress for the
stage. I couldn't run offstage and do costume changes—I had to do it
right there. So I took the dress off during the show, and then I danced
around in the bathing suit. Hey, Debbie Harry did it in Blondie, and
talk about style: She wore a bathing suit with a suit jacket, which
was so sexy and great. She wore a trash bag onstage and made it look
good! So I improvised too. I'd come out with sunglasses and take
them off, or a cap, and then I'd pull my cap off and there would be my
brightly colored hair spilling out. So I basically peeled off things as I
performed, which made me feel freer emotionally, too. I was young
and skinny, and, you know, when you're twenty-seven, you can put
anything on and look good.

Then we had a meeting over dinner with the head guy from Germany (the label was a German company) and they liked our cover of
"I'm Gonna Be Strong" and told us there was going to be a big push
for that. Which was fine, but then they also told me they were going
to make me into the next Streisand. I said, "Oh no. You can't do that.
I'm a rocker. Why don't you make somebody else into the next Streisand?" Of course, because I said this to the head of Polydor, everybody
choked on their food. They kept wanting to make me into a balladeer,
because I could sing a ballad. I told them, "I can't take enough medica-
tions to stand still that long, okay? I can rock out better than most,
and I'm not going to let you put a brace on my brain and spirit."

But what really put a nail in our coffin was the way our manager
arranged to record the album. Say that we had a hundred thousand
dollars to do it—well, he made a deal to keep whatever money wasn't
used, so that if it cost, say, seventy-five thousand bucks, he got twenty-
five. Not a good idea, because in the end, there were no background
vocals, there were no extra musicians, nothing. Just us. The album

could have been better than it was if we had had some help. But that was my first album. I didn't know. And the band was happy.

The plan was to break us in Europe first, which the labels often did at the time. So we went to Germany, and there was a really wonderful woman who was assigned to us, who constantly walked behind me and said, "*Schnell*" (which meant "quick"), with a kind word attached to it, because I always had too many things to carry, like my steam pot. She helped me as best she could.

Things were good in Europe, but when we came back to America, *Billboard* had decided that bands like ours were retro and they weren't going to cover them. This resulted in another round of meetings with Polydor, who kept telling me, "You've gotta lose the band." I told them no. Producers were offering to put a choir behind me, but I just kept saying no, no, no. I felt I should stick with the band. In another meeting I had a guy draw up a pie chart and tell me how I was going to make money if I would sell all of my publishing to him. You always heard from older songwriters about how they got one little piece of the profits in the beginning and that was it. I had been raped in my first band, I had been abused every which way, and then here's this guy telling me how I'm going to make money if he buys everything I create. I knew this guy was a crook, and if he took me for a ride and took all my publishing, then I still wouldn't be making any money to this day if they ever used one of my songs in a movie or anything. That's your old-age pension, John Turi used to tell me, when you become an outsider—which, for most people, is sort of inevitable.

But I said some really nasty things. I used the N-word in a meeting because I grew up listening to that John Lennon song "Woman Is the Nigger of the World," and in this band, I was always being told, "You gotta listen to what the producer is saying," and "Sing what you're told," or that the label had "filled their quota" of women. So in this one meeting, I said, "Listen, I hear what you're saying, but you see this nigger over here? I ain't doing it, go find some other ones." Because I have always felt that women really are the N-word (especially in the music business) and honestly, if you look at the whole world today, not much has changed. But the N-word comes with a long history of abuse and slavery and horror, and I wasn't sensitive to that. I was still on the John Lennon jag, and as I mentioned, I was always on another planet. And I didn't have the wherewithal, I didn't know how to fight anybody. They thought I was racist, but what I was saying is that women were lower than low. You can spit to the bottom of the barrel, and on the bottom are women and children. But that's me—I'm always saying the wrong things to the right people.

Another time I had a taste of it with Roy, our record producer. There was one song that didn't come out so good, so we wanted to have a talk with him about it. And he turned around to me and said, "I have an idea. Why don't you mix your version, I'll mix mine, and let's see what the record company thinks—what do you think about that?" I looked at him and said, "I think that's baby shit, if you want to know." Then the people who signed us at Polydor left, and they brought in a new president. I remember one meeting in his office. His assistant came in and announced she had the new single from the Jam, and put it on the turntable for everyone to hear. Except it sounded like it was in slow motion. And everyone was bobbing their heads and listening like they were really enjoying it. I looked at the label head and looked at the assistant, who wouldn't dare open her mouth. So I got up and walked over to the turntable, and I saw that the speed was on 33, and the record was a 45. I was thinking, "Okay, now I'm in Cuckoo Land." So I moved it to 45, and all of a sudden, there's the Jam. The president's eyes lit up and he said, "Ohhh." Of course, maybe the right thing to do was not to touch it, but I was curious to see what the hell the real Jam single was.

Meetings were not my strong suit, because I was never good at doing what the record company wanted. But it didn't take a genius to see that Blue Angel was on its way out, anyway.

CHAPTER FIVE

T HE REASON I kept resisting the record company guys who told me to sing ballads was that the more I worked in the music industry, the more I realized that your first hit was what identified you for the rest of your career, and I wanted to make sure mine was uptempo so that I wouldn't be pigeonholed. I also fought because I noticed that everybody who rolled over failed. All the cool performers, all the great ones—the Clash, Elvis Costello, the Pretenders—those people did not have the record company invent them. The artists that the record company invented had a fuckin' shallow life. Because if the record company really knew how to make music, they'd be making music, not selling it, right? What I saw was, "Hey, come listen to the new 45 single from the Jam on 33." I'm going to let those guys tell me what to do?

But Blue Angel was going downhill. Our single "I'm Gonna Be Strong" reached number 37—in the Netherlands. No one would accept our demos anymore. It was getting worse and worse, and once again the money was not coming in, and we all started to starve. I remember my friend Jutta—she's German—used to tell me that there were two kinds of people in the world. There are the kind of people who sit around and think about their problems, and then there are the kind of people who sit around thinking about how to solve them.

I try to be the second type of person but at that time I was pretty down. I went to Katie Agresta's studio and told her that I couldn't figure out how I was going to make it work. She started giving me food, because she thought I couldn't sing properly if I was hungry all the time. That's why I love her. She believed in me. One time we were working together I was feeling really dejected about the whole business—this was before Blue Angel—and I told her that one of these days, they were going to see my name, and they were going to remember me. We both stopped dead. We felt a chill, and it wasn't the flu.

But unfortunately, I got really sick—again. And lost my voice—again. I was so depressed. I had an inverted cyst on my vocal cord, which the doctor said was from incorrect singing but it really wasn't. I finally found a doctor, a saint named Dr. Eberly, who operated on my throat. And Katie helped me back. It was hard and took a long time, but when I could sing again, I was really careful when we were playing live.

I also knew I wanted to get out of our record contract and get away from our manager who, for a lot of reasons, was not working out for us. I went to him and said, "Listen, we would like to break from you completely, or we would like to continue, get another record deal, and then pay you off." He said, "No. You're not going anywhere without me." And then it became a fight.

And I always needed money. I was talking about it with Blue Angel's accountant and he said, "Why don't you get a job at a clothing store that you like? You go to Screaming Mimi's all the time—ask them if they would want to hire you." So I did, and I was hired as a salesgirl. I ended up staying for a couple of years because I loved it so much. It was like a giant toy store for me, as you can imagine. I was constantly buying clothes, and they made me stop because what I was buying cost more than I would sell. They couldn't put stuff out because it was on layaway for me. People would come in and I'd help style them, which was so much fun. One time Lene Lovich came in, who I adored, and was looking at shoes. I just circled her, though—I didn't even say anything to her because I didn't want to bother her while she was browsing.

So at least I could pay the bills, but we were still trying to get out of the contract. My lawyer said, "Cyndi, now the whole industry is saying that when you get tired of dragging that little red wagon around with you, they'll talk to you." He meant the band. So then, of course, the band hated me.

This was the end of 1981, and I remember around Christmastime, my bass player, Jim Gregory, had a little party. There were other singers and bands around, and I was sitting with my friend Debbie. She was a studio singer who had worked with John Turi and Jim Gregory, and who also sang background with Billy Hocker, a guy with a kind of bruised voice who sang white soul. He really influenced me—he told me I should listen to Otis Redding and open my ear and voice. Anyway, I was sitting with Debbie, and I saw this guy with yellow corduroy bell-bottoms. You have to remember, at that time, everybody wore tight black jeans—it was just a uniform. It was how you knew the cool people from the not-so-cool people. He was dressed like . . . *ay yi yi.* Along with those yellow pants, he had on white sneakers, a beat-up sweater, a peacoat, a beard, and long hair like Jesus Christ. I'm looking at him going, "Oh my God, what a mess." It was kind of a seventies thing he was doing, and at that point I didn't see any merit in that.

It was Dave Wolff.

So we were all drinking, and Dave Wolff hit on one of the girls from the punk band the Sic F*cks. She ditched him to go to the bathroom, and then all of a sudden, he looked at *me* and I'm like, "Oh, come *on*." But he sat down next to me, and I said, "You gotta be kidding me. Now you're hitting on me? You didn't get anywhere with her, and I look like the number that's gonna put out for ya?" But everything he said was so funny and wacko, and I just started laughing because he was a character.

So we started talking and I found out he was from Connecticut. So that's two drawbacks right there—flares and Connecticut. But he wasn't WASP-y, like I thought at first—he was Jewish—and when we got to talking about rock pygmies that live underground and come up for wampanini juice, I thought, "This guy's pretty entertaining." And he had all these different jobs like I had. He had been an exterminator and a messenger. And like a lot of people at that party, he was in a band.

I found out later that he was a road manager for Vicki Sue Robinson, but he had a record deal, too. He'd done a rap record as Captain Chameleon and did rock music as the Human Fly. See, he happened to make a deal with this French-Canadian acrobat called the Human Fly who stood on airplanes while they took off, and stayed on while they flew and landed. So somehow Dave, who could talk anybody into anything and loved to mix rock and roll with other kinds of performance, made a deal with him. Dave would dress up as him and represent him as the Human Fly, and make believe that the Fly had a side gig in a rock band—even though the real Fly didn't have a band. Are you following me so far?

So Dave would be in a rock band dressed as the Human Fly, with a red skintight outfit and a cape, with a mask and boots, and he'd have a French-Canadian accent. But then he also was Dave Wolff, the Human Fly's manager, so if there were press guys, he'd be Dave and say, "I'm going to send the Human Fly out for you." Then he'd quickly get dressed as the Human Fly and come out and talk with a French-Canadian accent in the whole getup, which was one of the most hilarious things I had ever seen.

That night he just kept making me laugh, telling me all these stories, and despite the flares, he was cute and sexy. And I was very single at that point. A while back I was dating this bisexual guy, and my friend Gregory sat me down and said, "Listen, Cyn, you can't win with a bisexual guy, because you can never fulfill what they want. You'll always be on the wrong side of it. What do you want that kind of relationship for? Plus, you buy his coffee, too, don't you?" Which I did. He was a starving artist like me and was the kind of guy that—like most guys I knew, especially if they were artists—would find a girl and mooch off of her. There was something different about Dave. He was trying to help me.

So Dave and I kept talking, and the end of the night came, and I realized I didn't have any bus fare to get home. I said to him, "Listen, you've got a car. Can you just drive me back to my apartment?" Big mistake.

Remember how guys used to come to my apartment, and it was always like they wouldn't leave? I'd tell myself that I might as well have sex with them so that they'd leave me alone and I could lock the door? So that's kind of what started happening with Dave: I felt like he was never going to leave. I was thinking, "Here we go again. I want you out of here, and this has happened to me all my life so let me just sleep with you, and you'll leave."

But the funny thing was, he stayed. He kept saying, "You know, I really like you."

He was very sweet, and we became boyfriend and girlfriend. He'd walk with me and I'd talk to him about things that I'd see. I've always had this imagination that is so overboard, it could kill you. Like, if

I saw gum on the street when I was out walking, it would gross me out because I would imagine what it was like to lick it up off of the ground. Maybe I was a dog in a past life. I have no idea. But he always understood that my imagination was maybe a little different from everybody else's. He was also a little bit of a lost soul. We both nurtured each other.

As we got closer, I was still looking for a manager, and Dave would tell me the things to ask. I'd meet with all these people, but the weirdest thing is that when I came home I kept having dreams about the scenarios with my new manager, and none of them were right. In the interim, with money being tight, as usual, I had to become a maid again. (I had been a maid already in Vermont.) I made twenty dollars a job, which was a lot for a day. I started with my friend Dan and I remember being somewhere with him and a girl said, "Look—there's Cinderella." I was so embarrassed.

I remember when I was in Vermont, I answered ads in the paper for cleaning ladies and I called up one guy who told me, "Well, part of your job will be you'll have to give my wife a bath and then dress her." I said, "Is she an invalid?" He said, "No. And I will watch." I told him I didn't think I was interested and hung up.

I worked as a maid for this other woman in Vermont that I'll never forget as long as I live: Mrs. Butterfly. She was almost ninety and lived in a big Victorian house, and she would rent out the rooms. She needed a cleaning lady, and then I had to sit and eat lunch with her. She said that cleaning people had to eat lunch, too. It was the sweetest thing, and I think she knew that I was always hungry. She would talk a lot, and had all these pictures of dead people she had outlived, and she would tell me stories about this one and that one. She had pictures of Jesus all over, too, and I remember talking to him and saying, "Jesus, you've gotta help her. She can't just sit around and talk to dead people." It was not good, her just waiting to die. Even though you're old, there have got to be other things. That's why when I later married my husband, and my grandmother was ninety-one and started to get depressed, I was like, "Why don't you be my maid of honor?" Nothing like a new dress and a party! She had a nice wool dress with rhinestones and looked so pretty.

Back in New York, I told my friend Lisa about the whole Cinderella incident. And she said, "Why are you cleaning houses? You don't have to do that. I can get you a job as a hostess at a Japanese piano bar and you can make a ton of money with tips. And nobody knows these places exist!" There was a whole bunch of these piano bars in the eighties in the midtown area of the city, near all of the office buildings. They were kind of like discos, and your job was to dance with the Japanese businessmen and pour drinks and light cigarettes and just be a party girl. Lisa told me about this great family-run place called Mama's, but unfortunately they didn't have any openings. They recommended another club to me, which was more of a nightclub. I started working there and I used to come home with the most terrible head and neck aches. I remember I was dancing with this one girl to the Olivia Newton-John song, "Physical," and one of the customers gave me the old fish eye. I'm like, "Hey, I don't do that." I kind of felt like I was falling down, like with the go-go dancing gig I had. It was so against who I was. I just couldn't do it and I left.

But then Lisa was able to get Mama's to hire me. The girls working there didn't have to put out, ever. You didn't have to "get physical" with anyone. A woman called Mama-San, who was a great patron of the arts, ran the place, and she loved having someone with notoriety there, because as it happened I had just gotten into an issue of *Life* magazine that had Elizabeth Taylor on the cover. The magazine featured me in a "Girl Rockers" piece that also had bands like the

Go-Go's and the Pretenders. I wore my red pedal pushers, red stilettos with bobby socks, and a little sleeveless shirt that said JOHNNY ANGEL on it. I was in a beauty parlor, and I had orange and pink foam rollers in my hair and I was reading Carl Jung's *The Undiscovered Self.* Mama-San loved that.

She loved the singing, and it was a great place for me to learn how to deal with businessmen on a more personal level. They were nice; they had their bottles, and they just wanted to have a drink. I really loved it there. Afterward the sushi chefs would come sit at the bar. Usually those chefs gave me twenty-dollar tips, too, which was a really big deal. And Peter, the guitar player, would teach me Japanese phonetically.

My big number was "Wasureaniwa," which was translated as "I Will Never Forget You." I was accompanied by Peter and a woman piano player, and after every phrase she'd end with a little "da da da" flourish on the piano. The guitarist told me I sounded just like Brenda Lee. I became fascinated with these people, and I loved them, and I have very comforting memories of the place, of people who were very kind. I tried really hard to be a good hostess and to make people laugh.

At that point, I was going to a therapist too because I was trying to not come off as angry. When people said something to me, I would tell them what I thought, and they saw that as anger, as opposed to the fact that I didn't have a filter. Since then, I've grown a little bit of a filter—not a big one, but a little one. So I started going to therapy because it was a place where I could just be angry and complain and not have anybody tell me, "Oh, God, you're always complaining." And it helped teach me to have boundaries. We grew up kind of rough as kids, feeling that what we had to say was very important because my mother always let us say what we wanted.

But sometimes you have to think before you speak and that wasn't a big thing of mine.

So after I met Dave Wolff at the Christmas party, he came to see me at this New Year's Eve gig Blue Angel was doing. It was 1981 going into 1982, and it wasn't one of the most prestigious New Year's gigs. We were playing a small dive in Passaic, New Jersey. It was called Hitsville, but I called it Shitsville, because that's what it felt like. Our bass player at the time was Slim Jim Gregory, who drove our rent-a-wreck out of Manhattan from Seventy-sixth Street over the George Washington Bridge, and it was raining, and we couldn't find the fuckin' thing. I remember that night so clearly because it was so definitive of the time, because we were in a struggle with our old management and it seemed like we were going nowhere—literally and figuratively.

We played in a back room that they told us was a dressing room. It was typically dumpy and dirty and had graffiti all over the walls. There was this one grafitti tag that, after everything we had been through, was so profound to me, and no matter how many times I tried not to look it screamed at me from off the wall. The words were in black Magic Marker against a dirty white wall: "Are we not signed? We are demo." Like the Devo line "Are we not men? We are Devo." Which was my life: doing demos that didn't go anywhere.

So we kept trying, but it just didn't seem to be happening. Dave hadn't seen me perform before, and I was very worried about that, because every boyfriend I ever had was fine until they saw me perform, and then they freaked out.

When men see women singing so powerfully like that, it can scare the shit out of them. If a man is singing, girls swoon, but if a woman is singing, it's like, *"Ay yi yi."* Maybe they're wondering, "How will I be manly enough?" Who knows. So I was very worried, because I really liked him, and I was thinking, "Well, here goes another one to the shit heap." I had already realized that although male singers always had these cute people waiting for them, I always had the sad sacks, the ones who needed help. Which I didn't mind, but it was never going to be like how it was for the men. So I just figured, "Here we go—good-bye, Dave Wolff."

I had sprayed my hair blue with some spray paint, and I was on-stage singing "Blue Christmas." And because I was upset, I drank. And drank. And I ain't a big drinker, having one good kidney and one kidney that doesn't work so good. I gotta be careful—I'm a lightweight. And I remember a girl in the audience going, "She's drunk." I thought, "Yeah, I'm drunk, all right! I'm heading toward thirty, I felt like I could have been a contender, but instead I'm here in Shitsville with you on New Year's Eve and reading in the back room how I'm still demo, d-e-m-o." Which of course I wouldn't say, because she'd be terribly hurt after she wanted to spend New Year's Eve with me. But believe me, I thought it.

I did the gig and came offstage and was standing by the bar, and Dave had a funny look on his face so I figured, "Okay, here goes. He's going to say how great I was, but it's going to get weird from now on." But he didn't say anything. Instead, after the van dropped us off at my place, he helped me carry all my shit up the five flights of stairs to my apartment. So as he was helping me carry all this shit up, I was wait-ing for him to complain about that. But instead he said, "How do I love thee? Let me count the steps." I started laughing and thought, "Oh my God—this guy is a riot."

Here's the thing with guys: After seeing you onstage, a lot of them have to take you back home to bed and kind of own you, you know what I mean? But I always had to go back and take the makeup off, steam my throat, do vocal exercises, and by the time that's over, they were usually like, "What the heck?" Devotion to a craft is not what people equate with rock and roll music, but for me, because I lost my voice so early on, I was obsessed with not losing my voice again. Because when I lost my voice, I didn't think, "How will I make a living?" I thought, "How will I live? How can I breathe anymore?" It was not an option. There's a movie called *The Red Shoes* and in it, Vicky, the ballerina, wanted to dance. And when she met Boris, the head of the Lermontov ballet, he asked her, "Why do you want to dance?" And she said, "Why do you want to live?" He says something like, "Well, I don't know exactly why, but . . . I must." I was thinking, "Yeah, that's why I do it." Why do you eat? Why do you breathe? That's why I sing.

So after the gig, I was unpacking, I had to do my hair, and I was tired and cleaning the tub. And while I was cleaning the tub, Dave started combing my hair out. It was such a sweet gesture, and I thought, "Oh my God, this guy, he understands." Soon after that, he started moving in. He broke my alarm clock, a Betty Boop clock that I loved, so he brought a clock from his mother's house that was so loud I had to put it in the bathroom and close the door and you could still hear it. And one day he went out and bought a television set for us (I didn't have one) and carried it up the five flights of stairs. He got a hernia from it. But I liked him—I really did.

In the meantime I still needed a manager. I met with a bunch of people, including Tommy Mottola. The thing with Tommy is, he made you feel like he was going to take care of you, and it's a very seductive feeling because you feel like it's all going to be okay, he'll make it work out. I had known Tommy for a while just from being in the business. In his office there were all these hunting trophies. There was even a scorpion frozen in plastic. After I met him, I had a dream that night that he also had a singer's soul in the drawer. He collected things and I didn't want to be part of his collection.

I had a couple of similar dreams after I met with other people, and they were always very dark. I kept telling Dave about my dreams, and finally he said to me, "Well, I'm a manager. I'm just starting out, but I'll manage you if you want." I looked at the whole scenario and thought to myself, "Well, he's a rascal, and he's funny, and even when you don't want to do something, you'll laugh so hard, you'll wind up doing it, and if he could talk me into doing stuff, he could talk anybody into doing stuff." He was like that. He had this kind of boyish funny charm about him. So I told him, "I'll throw my hat into the ring. I'll sing, and you'll collect the money. But you can't ever let the business become more important than us." That was our deal. He would manage me as a solo act.

What I had going for me at the time was that my reputation as a singer was kind of great, and my reviews were pretty awesome, too. The first thing Dave said to me was, "I have someone I want you to meet." I told him I couldn't go because I had a job—I was still working at Mama's. He said, "Quit your job, you're going to get a record deal." It was Lennie Petze, who was the head of Portrait Records over at Epic. He had signed the band Boston. Dave had met with him before about other things and Lennie had told him, "When you have something real, come to me."

So we went to Connecticut to meet Lennie and his family for dinner. It was around the holidays, and it was snowing. I liked Lennie and his wife right off the bat. Lennie was so nice that I couldn't figure out if he was really like that, but he was. Then they played cards, and I did a reading with them. I was turning the cards over, and I asked about Lennie, and he came up as the King of Hearts, and I did it again, and he came up as the King of Hearts.

Then I did a show in Yonkers, New York, in a club that had been an old bank, and Lennie came to see me. I wore a fifties kind of white sweater with a cocktail skirt, fishnets, and stiletto sling-backs, and I was wild: It was nighttime, I didn't care, so I grabbed my crotch, kicked my legs up, and rolled around. (When I became famous and started seeing little kids coming to the show, I stopped that.)

Lennie wasn't sure about the rockabilly I was doing, but he liked my performance. And all of a sudden, Dave was just doing things. He introduced me to another friend of his named Gibby Silverman, a rich fellow and a really nice man who agreed to support us for a while until we could pay him back. This made me nervous, because when you like somebody the last thing you want to do is take their money, but we agreed to it.

I remember Dave and I still weren't eating too good, because we didn't have any money. Both of us lived on two hundred dollars a week in Manhattan, which was kind of tight. Sometimes the plan was that we wouldn't eat one day or wouldn't eat until the night. In the meantime, I was going through legal troubles with Blue Angel's ex-manager, who wouldn't let us go. He took us to court and sued us to prevent us from going any further without him. He wanted everything—all the music, all the demos—and wanted to make sure I remained a waitress, not a singer. I was trying to get him paid off and he wouldn't have it. One of the bright spots during that time though was one of my lawyers, Elliot Hoffman. He was very New York. He wore a suit and had a handlebar mustache, and he would pick me up and take me to court on the back of his little motorcycle.

What I came to understand about the law is that what was right had nothing to do with it—what was the law is what had to do with it. Which were two different things. I said to the manager in court, "Why do you want all the songs? They're not even good. What do you want them for—blackmail?" Everybody started laughing, and the judge said, "Order!" But I just had to say to him, "Why are you doing this? Why don't you take a settlement? You could make some money, and I could move forward." I mean, what a pain in the ass.

And here's the thing: He met my family. He saw where I came from. In what remote land could you be from, how far up your ass could you be, to think that you are going to have a standoff and think I'm not going to fight to the bitter end, like the bitter-end-rest-of-your-fuckin'-life, motherfucker? He knew the different jobs I had. He understood that I had lost my voice, was told I was never going to sing again, and came back. He understood the ferocity with which I sang. I'm always going to sing. That's the end of it. I'm going to sing until I die.

Dave Wolff just said to me, "Hold your course. We're fighting it." I did what they said and just tried to zip it, and then finally in the end, the judge looked at me and looked at everybody. He took the gavel, hit the desk, and said, "Let the canary sing." That is exactly what he said. We won the case.

Finally I was able to move forward, although I did have to declare bankruptcy after the suit. But then I had more meetings with Lennie Petze and eventually signed with him. It was November of 1982. The reason I thought Epic Records was a good idea was that I looked at what Epic offered and saw what was missing. They didn't have a big female star.

Afterward Lennie said, "I know this guy that you should meet with," and introduced me to Rick Chertoff, a producer from Columbia Records who had worked with groups like the Kinks and the Band. He was looking for a singer who could sing these songs that he had been collecting. I said I wanted to write, but Dave said, "Sing first, and then you can write."

So I sat down with Rick, who was working with this other band called the Hooters. He played me some of their music, and I thought that even though the Hooters had two guys who sang, to me, they didn't have a voice. So then when I heard this reggae stuff they were doing, I had an idea of what I could put together with them.

And in the spring of 1983, I went into the studio to record *She's So Unusual.*

CHAPTER SIX

WE STARTED WORK on the album *She's So Unusual* at a studio in Manayunk, which is a neighborhood in northwestern Philadelphia. Rob Hyman and Eric Bazilian, the guys from the Hooters who were working on my album, were from Philadelphia, so that's where we went. It was freezing fuckin' cold, even in March. Manayunk is at the foot of the Pocono Mountains, but once it was a very poor industrial place made up of a lot of European immigrants. So we called it the Polish Poconos. Then we recorded at the Record Plant in New York City, which was pretty famous. John Lennon had recorded in that studio and his stuff was all over the place. I saw his face everywhere too—as I did when I was a kid studying his voice so intently.

Kiss was using the studio at that time, and they'd come by a lot and ask what we were doing. Paul Stanley would arrive with all these women and I was always thinking to myself, "I love you guys, but can you take the whole rock-god thing outta here?"

I had this very strong vision of how I wanted to put the music together. I heard it when I sat in Rick's office and he played me the Hooters record. I wanted to combine their reggae sound with this trashy street sound—this punky, Clash, Police sound—and a gated snare drum, which was new at the time. It had come out of the street and was being put on dance records (later it became really popular). I didn't know what it was called, so Bill Wittman, another producer, made me go out and buy some albums to play him the sound I was describing. I played the Red Rockers (remember their song "China"?) and that song "The Safety Dance" by Men Without Hats. Bill looked at me and said, "That's a gated snare."

So I wanted to fuse a dance electronic sound with the reggae, which was being done by people like Grace Jones, but with that gated snare, which is *not* what they did. We had a little band—which started out bigger, but Rick and I kept weeding out people. Rick is a very smart guy, and he knew exactly who was good and who wasn't. When I said, "Listen, that drummer, he's running me down and he's always on the phone. We need him because . . . ?" we'd get rid of him. We also didn't need a bass player. We needed five people: Rob; Eric; Rick; the other producer, Bill; and me. That's it, and a drum machine—thank you, the end. I could then focus on getting these songs in shape and making arrangements. And that's what I did.

It was kind of a magical time. We'd eat Philly cheesesteaks at a place called Rosie's. We'd get really delirious from working all day and we'd entertain everyone at Rosie's. I'd do Ethel Merman singing Beatles songs. I used to do a really good impersonation of Ethel. Rob would go, "Cyn, do Ethel. Come on! Do 'She Came in Through the Bathroom Window.'" I just always thought things like that were funny—like, Johnny Mathis singing "Stairway to Heaven." I always figured, "Why not mix it up?"

But it was a tough time, too, because Rick had never really worked with somebody like me. He kept bringing in songs and suggesting songwriters, and I had to figure out how I was going to make the songs sound cohesive. There had to be a connection, instead of just a bunch of random songs. A lot of times when producers are put together with singers, the albums sound like this grab bag that doesn't make any sense.

The first song Rick really got me on was "All Through the Night," which Jules Shear wrote. It sounded like a Beatles song, except the lyrics were different. It was so awesome. So we put it on the album. When we recorded "All Through the Night" we couldn't get the first line right. Something happened with the tape and it caused a magnetic thump, and then Dave Wolff liked a line from another part of the song and kept trying to put it in the beginning. So I kept singing the first line of "All Through the Night" literally all through the fuckin' night. I just kept doing it, trying to get it right, stepping away from it, coming back, trying, trying, trying. It went on and on until I thought I'd lose my mind, and then at dawn I sang the first line and that was it. You can spend days on one tiny part of a song.

Rick then played me this Prince song, "When You Were Mine," which I also liked, so we added that to the album too. I heard that he liked my version of it. Later, I saw him when we were both at the American Music Awards, but I didn't speak to him. You're gonna think this is nutty, but I felt he was so famous that I didn't want to go up to him. But I have gotten to know him in the last ten years or so. He is still a great artist. And he's always very sweet to me. I think he's God's child. And here's why: In 2007, while I was writing the CD *Bring Ya to the Brink*, I happened to see Prince's extraordinary Super Bowl performance live on TV. He was singing "Purple Rain" and it was raining—real hard too. All of a sudden, he needed to fight the elements. It was slippery and he slipped. The large white backdrop behind him that was supposed to gently move with the wind was turning into a sail and still, it continued to rain hard. And all of a sudden, I saw how he accepted and worked with the rain and the wind. I thought, "This is God's child, right in front of us, live." It was one of the most inspirational performances I'd ever seen. So in "Same Ol' Story," the lines "People slipping in the rain, I watch them get up again / It makes me feel like I can too" are about him.

Rick also played me this Desmond Child song called "Do Me Right," and at the time I was like, "'Do Me Right'? What neighborhood did you come from? Coming from where I come from, I could never possibly sing a song called 'Do Me Right.' In my early bands, the guys used to make fun of Catholic girls, saying that they'd lie back and say, 'Do me.' And I said, 'Well, I ain't gonna be one of them.'" Poor Rick, it must have been like talking to an alien. He seemed a little taken aback by that.

I think the guys had a really rough time in the beginning with me. I can't believe that after they heard me sing they thought I was a delicate flower. But Dave Wolff kept having to come and put out fires because I'd tell them what I thought. First we'd be making these great arrangements together, and they would let me direct, because it was working, I guess. But then they'd get in the studio and keep me out and record some guitar styles that were more dated than I wanted to use. And I was very up-front about it. I asked Eric to play with more of a Clash feel against the track in "Money Changes Everything," and that worked. So little by little, I took over my album.

Dave would say, "You're so angry; you've got to work on your anger." I would tell him all the time, "Yeah, but my name is pretty big on the front of the record and the producers' names are pretty small on the back. Once this thing is done, they go on to something else, but I have to sell it. If this is going to be my thing, and if this is the only time I ever get to open my mouth and sing, I want it to be great and my fuckin' vision." I had worked so hard to get to where I was at that time. I had to go bankrupt. I lost my voice twice and came back. And when I fought for something it was because I knew I was right, and nine times out of ten, I was.

That said, it still was very much a style that all of us contributed to. I just would direct them a bit here and there, and sing with it all the time to make sure it was right. Although I couldn't articulate it then, it was all about connection. And they would genuinely try and help me get the sound that I wanted. So, bless them for that.

Rick had this one song that to him was like the Holy Grail, and maybe it was. There was a guy named Robert Hazard, who sang "Escalator of Life" and had this whole kind of cool, David Bowie–esque sound. He had written "Girls Just Want to Have Fun" a few years earlier, but it was much faster, and it was also from a guy's point of view, which made it mean something totally different. He had a verse where a woman comes into his room at night because she wants to have fun and he's telling his dad, "We are the fortunate ones." I said to Rick, "So now that I'm singing it, I'm supposed to get a lobotomy and just kick my legs up in the air and basically say girls just want to have sex?" He kept saying, "Think about what it could mean." And so I thought about what a woman's version might say. And that maybe I should try to find a new heart in the song. I started to think, "Okay, I'm not a guy. How do I feel?" If I could find the twist in it so that I could use my voice in a unique way, and in a woman's key, that could change everything. And the word "anthem" kept coming up. So I went about the arrangement in a more radical way. I took what Rob loved to listen to, which was reggae music, and asked him to play that feel but with the chords of "Girls." And I asked Eric to play a little guitar riff from an old Motown song (the masters of musical hooks with rhythm), and I remembered an old Shirley and Lee song that John Turi had played me a long time ago, "Feel So Good," that was in a girl's key. And one last time I gave it a shot. I had the drum machine on its simplest modern beat. I said, "Just play your part and ignore me and let's hear it that way." And all of a sudden, we heard the song in a completely different way that worked and kept the commercial parts and had that anthem feel.

Then Rick brought in Ellie Greenwich, who was one of the Brill Building songwriters/producers, to write with me and sing backup on "Girls." She wrote and produced all these wonderful, classic songs like "Be My Baby" and "Leader of the Pack," and I loved her. She wrote with her husband Jeff Barry, in the sixties, and even though she was right there in the studio doing those songs with her husband, only his name was on the records as producer. This was common in the old days. Which is how I started learning that you have to get credit for your work.

So when Rick brought Ellie in, she listened to "Girls" and knew just what to do. She started chanting, "Girls / They want / Want to have fun." Then she said, "Cyn, come on—sing with me with your accent! Come on, make your Queens accent prominent!" I was like, "Yeah right—ha, ha, ha." But I sang in the hallway of the studio with her, and I gotta say, she was right.

And Rick said to me, "What if you did that little hiccup sound on the word 'fun'?" I used that sound, which was a little like Buddy Holly, in Blue Angel a lot. So I said okay. That whole record was a combination of a Bob Marley blues approach to reggae, some Elvis Costello, a little Elvis Presley, Buddy Holly, Frankie Lymon, some Ronnie Spector, and of course Shirley and Lee. And I put it in the key of F, just like a trumpet. And John Lennon's picture was in the studio too. And like all good pictures, eventually the eyes move, so he was kind of there in spirit.

It's funny because later on, I became friends with Yoko. The first night I played Madison Square Garden as a headliner, in 1986, Yoko Ono walked backstage with an eleven-year-old Sean Lennon. Did ya ever? Could have knocked me down. After that, I'd go to see her at her apartment and I'd be talking to her at her table, where there was a big portrait of John and a beautiful portrait of their son, Sean. And after a while, like any good portrait, I'd be talking to the picture too, and I'd think, "Okay, what's the matter with you?" And I'd get up to go in the other room to sort of clear my head, and there was a mummy—it was a real mummy, not like the one in the *SkyMall* catalog. When I asked about the mummy, Yoko explained that she was in a warehouse buying antiques, and she heard someone calling her from the basement. She went downstairs and in this dusty room, there was a mummy case with a mummified . . . whoever. And Yoko told me that she felt such sadness that this person, this mummy, was in this dusty old basement, so she bought her and put her in this nice room. I remember thinking, "Wow, that makes sense and it's kind of her too." Later I was at a get-together at Yoko's with my friend and trainer for years, Marion, and we were both nursing babies at the time, so we went to the room with the mummy to nurse away from the fray. A guy who was a friend of hers walked by and said, "Oh, how nice—the mommies and the mummy." And I thought, "That's surreal."

My life is so funny sometimes. Everyone has these moments, but if you're not aware, you miss them. And we were so tired then nursing the babies and trying to go back to work. I always tell my son to pay attention or he'll miss something that's spectacular. Sometimes you can just sit in your backyard and a little dragonfly comes by and lands right on you and just sits there. Or it sits on a flower right next to you. Who is that? Is that a fairy? I never know, but it always feels magical.

Okay, where was I? Right—"Girls Just Want to Have Fun." I kept thinking about how the music in the song represented different parts of my life. Like the organ sound that you hear was actually from an old commercial for a drag-racing place called Raceway Park that I used to hear as a kid. (Most people who grew up in the New York area when I did will remember those commercials.) And I loved to dance to Motown while making the beds when my mom worked.

That's how I work. A little slice of life here, a little piece of a different song there, and bada bing, bada boom, mix it all together and there it is. My musical style has always been a collage of everything. Like Rick would play me "Money Changes Everything" in the style of a Bob Dylan song, and I'd say, "Can we just start it off differently? Make believe you're playing 'London Calling.'" Then I'd start singing. The producers' approach was more traditional, because that's how it was always done. Except that I didn't want to do what was always done. So they didn't want me in the studio when they were doing guitars. So I went straight to Lennie Petze and he stuck by me. And if you listen to "Money," you can hear the influences of the Clash.

But everyone was watching me sing, which I think is the worst thing to do, because they all would *watch* the performance, rather than *hear* it. I sang it over and over. As I said, I was singing in the key of a trumpet, so after several times when I was pretty sure they had it, I said, "Okay, I think you have it," and stopped. In that key, it would have been easy to lose my voice. And sometimes Rick would say to use my "head voice." But women don't have a "head voice"—only men do. Now that's biology for ya: For a woman, you either sing high and thin, or you sing low, or you sing in the middle and soft or strong. I found myself trying to close my eyes and forget who I was and try to find the spirit of the story—but there they were, watching me.

So I tried to create another world for myself where I could be less self-conscious, because the first thing I do whenever I do anything really creative is lose that freakin' third eye. Because you gotta just lose it all and throw it all down right there. You gotta open up a vein, and you can't open up a vein if you got all these scientists out there watching you and telling you, "Do this," or "Do that." So I started to look for ways that I would have freedom of expression without anyone hovering over me. When I work with new guys now it's still like that.

I also had to fight to write a song with Rob, too. They didn't think I was a good writer, but they did like the way I arranged. They had a Hooters song called "Fighting on the Same Side," which was a good song, but I thought we should take this new style and write with it. I just kept asking and asking. I started to think, "If we're fighting on the same side, why don't you want to write with me?" Eventually Dave Wolff got me together with Steve Lunt, a writer he knew from an English band called City Boy. The first time I came over to see him, he had had some drinks and was a little toasty. He was busy writing and said, "Cyn, I have this idea—it's going to be great. We're going to write a song about female masturbation. No other girl has done this before." I said, "Okay, I'm in." For a little inspiration, I said, "Let's find one of those boy magazines for girls," not realizing that the boy magazines are for boys.

My thinking for writing "She Bop" was this: I remember when I was a little kid, there was a lot of talk about the Stones song "Get Off of My Cloud." The rumor was that "cloud" really meant "my girl" or "my prostitute." I remember thinking, "Oooh! Really?" You spend time thinking about the most ridiculous things as a kid. I mean, how many times did I sit up all night in the park with my friends, discussing if Paul was dead? "Let's play the record backward! Isn't that John saying, 'I buried Paul'?" So I thought, "Hey, why not pass this legacy on? The kids hear 'She bop, he bop-a-we-bop' and think it's about dancing. Then when the kids grow up, they hear, 'They say I'd better stop, or I'll go blind,' and realize what the song's about and have a giggle." And that adds a different dimension to a song and deepens their relationship to it. I wanted the song not to be blatant. Steve was on board so we made sure that that song did not refer to hands or touching anything, because if it did, then we wouldn't be writing a song that was multilevel. And covert is always the tradition in rhythm and blues anyway. We had a lot of laughs writing it. We sat next to each other with these lyrics all over the page, which is how I write sometimes, with a basic melody. But we didn't know how the song was going to begin. So I said, "Wouldn't it be funny if the sound was kind of like the Big Bopper, which is what John Lennon did when he did *Rock 'n' Roll*, his rockabilly record?" The thing about the beginning riff of "She Bop" was that it was rockabilly but still held true to that electronic, pop modern sound we were doing, with the gated snare. And come on, the Big Bopper? That was funny, too.

A lot of times, I didn't know a song was going to happen a certain way until I tried it. Because everything is always like a puzzle, and you start out this way and then all of a sudden the puzzle starts to come together, and sometimes it's good and sometimes it's bad. Sometimes you and your writing partners are smacking each other on the back going, "We're geniuses! It worked!" It's like when the oil gushes through the derrick, and you're like, *"It's alive!"* Then the next day, or the next week, after you get shot down a little by the powers that be, you're sitting there looking at each other going, "What the hell were we thinking?" But that's how it always is.

I recorded "She Bop" in a room in the back of the studio. It was the big rectangle warehouse room where Kiss rehearsed. I started singing there because it unnerved me to have Rick watching my performances so intently. I was able to convince Bill to run the wires for the microphone and stuff back to the room so I had total privacy.

So that's where I sang "She Bop." I could even take my clothes off and sing and no one would know. So of course that's what I did, and I tickled myself too. That's why you hear me laughing, because it was

116

so ridiculous. I was singing half-naked. I heard Yoko took her clothes off for "Walking on Thin Ice," which I think is cool.

But most people didn't get what "She Bop" was about until much later, when I went on Dr. Ruth's radio show. I was playing along with her, making believe I was in a psychiatrist's office, but then everything I said was blown up later by the press. Suddenly "She Bop" was on the Parents' Music Resource Center's "Filthy Fifteen" list of songs that they said should be banned, like "Let Me Put My Love into You" by AC/DC. I was so mad, because I had made sure that I never mentioned touching myself so that little kids would never know. And then I was found out because of my big mouth. Now every kid knew what it was about, and it wasn't supposed to be that way. Oh, *c'est la vie.* That's French for "whatever."

I always tried so hard to make music that would not become dated. And then I had this conversation with Dick Clark and he told me that I was making disposable music. That's what pop music was—disposable. I said, "No, I did not work my whole life to make disposable music." After "She Bop," I wanted to write another song, and Dave Wolff kept saying, "Wait, wait—it'll come." But it didn't, and I had to fight tooth and nail, and finally when the record was almost done I started writing with Eric. It was hard, though, because at the time he seemed a little scattered. Once we'd finally get a sound after working on it for hours—or days—he'd change it. His process would make me forget the melodies I was singing after a while.

With Rob, his temperament was different and he was easier to remember melodies with. There was a sweetness about him. I felt I could show him poetry. And we were both going through similar things with our relationships: He was just coming out of one that was long and hard, and Dave and I were having a lot of bumps. So Rob and I started writing together. Sometimes in our conversations he'd say something that struck me, and I'd write it down. Like he referred to a "suitcase of memories." I thought that was a wonderful line so I used it in "Time After Time." Other lines came from my life. "Lying in my bed I hear the clock tick"—that came from the really loud clock that I mentioned Dave and I had in our apartment. And the part about "the second hand unwinds" was from Rick's watch. For some reason, it was going backward instead of forward. He kept saying, "Look at this, the second hand is unwinding." I just looked at him and I'm like, "Oh my God, the second hand unwinding?" and wrote it down. I try all the time to take stuff from conversations. I always look for words that chew well and sing well.

When we started writing the song, I needed a fake title as a place-holder for the time being. So I was looking in the *TV Guide* and saw a couple of movie titles. There was this movie starring Malcolm Mc-Dowell and Mary Steenburgen called *Time After Time*, and I said, "Okay, that sounds like a good fake title for right now; it'll change." And did I mention I am a huge fan of Mary Steenburgen? She is so funny and a terrific actress. Anyway, when we started writing it, it was like the song title lodged itself into the song. I kept thinking it would be thrown away, but no matter how I tried to remove the freakin' title, I couldn't take it out without the song falling apart.

When Rick heard the song, he became very protective of it. If he thought people could kind of hear the song outside the door, he'd shut all the music off because he worried that somebody would copy us. Pretty early on, he felt it was really something extraordinary. The record company loved that song, too, and I kept saying, "Why did you make me do all this other stuff? I could have been writing more songs all along."

We recorded the album in a couple of months, and we became like a little family. Lennie Petze likes to live, he likes to eat, he's just a joyful person, so he'd come by and take us to that Japanese steak house Benihana, which we called Beni Ha Ha. One time during the Fourth of July he brought firecrackers, and we shot them off at the studio. Lennie was always so real and a good guy, very nurturing. We were like kids. And I thought that Rick was pretty fantastic, and I had a great time with him, but he wasn't used to the singer being so damn vocal, I think. He is a great producer and I did learn a lot from him. And we made an album that has lasted a long time.

We didn't know what to call the album. There was a song we were doing, just kind of playing around with, called "He's So Unusual," recorded by Helen Kane, a singer from the twenties who was the inspiration for Betty Boop. And we used to laugh because my friend Rose would come over and talk about her boyfriend Joe. It was Joe, Joe, Joe, all the time (her husband now for some time). My downstairs neighbor Carl and I used to laugh that the lyrics to "He's So Unusual" sounded just like Rose going on about Joe ("He's handsome as can b-e-e-e").

I would always find wacko songs like that and just stick them in the middle of other music we were doing to make Rick laugh. And of course we kept *She's So Unusual* for the title.

Everything for that album came from my life—even the record cover. I was inspired by a picture that I had seen in a book of photos of South America that my friend Ken Walls had. He worked on Blue Angel's three videos, and I dated him for a while, and we stayed friends. He always showed me books of art and photography, and one time I found this photograph of a girl standing in the midday sun. She had a colorful skirt and a bouquet of flowers and the sun cast a shadow that was just right. I said that there should be a beach umbrella on the cover photo with me, and it was the art director's idea to go to Coney Island. We went there (after getting lost) and started walking around, and I found this one street that had really great color, like in South America, and it was in front of an old wax museum. There was midday sun and that was it: We found the location.

Then I went to Screaming Mimi's, where I had worked, to pick out my wardrobe. In the shop I had seen this wonderful picture of Jane Russell, a beautiful actress from *Gentlemen Prefer Blondes*. In the photo, she had a blouse that was off the shoulders; espadrilles, which were popular then; and a full green skirt that looked like this red skirt that had come into the store. Her outfit had a whole South American feel. And I had already worn a bathing suit under a big dress when I opened for Peter Frampton in Puerto Rico, so I knew that could work for the top. Laura Wills, who owned the shop and was a genius, helped put together the look. I used to see how stylists would come in and ask Laura to put something together for them, and they'd take the credit. I'd say to her, "When I get my album, you're going to be named as the stylist." (Of course, what did I do? I misspelled her name in the first round of credits. I'm such a fuckin' idiot.)

For the cover shoot, I didn't have anybody doing my makeup—I did my own. Laura did the styling, but we got Annie Leibovitz to do the shoot. I found the Polaroids recently, which are wild to look at now, especially the one Annie gave me after we figured out the back cover together. I had gessoed my shoes for the shoot. I had been dreaming of my feet in the air with the parachute jump in the background ever since we first went to Coney Island. If you're from Coney Island, or New York, you recognize that scene immediately. To me, it's the Eiffel Tower of Brooklyn. I didn't have time to paint so I found a book with prints of van Gogh, my favorite painter. I studied him in school too. I gravitated to the color and broad strokes of his work. I'm also fascinated with the soles of shoes, because when you look at them, you see how a person walks through their life.

Celebrating Christmas. Left to right: Elen, my father, my mother, Butch, and me (age 4½).

With my cousins Vinny and Susan in Queens. I'm on the right (age 8).

Playing with my dolls in the alley next to my house (age 6).

In my grandmother's garden on the day of my middle school graduation.

Me and Elen in front of our house in Queens on 104th Street. This is proof that girls don't always have fun in dresses. I'm on the right (age 13).

On my uncle's boat in Jamaica Bay. Left to right: Me (age 13), Elen and my cousin Linda.

At Bob Barrell's studio.

With Elen (age 13) and Butch (age 7) on the day of Butch's First Holy Communion. I'm on the left (age 12).

The day of my confirmation with my godmother, Tina.

Wha's high school graduation photo.

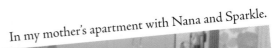

In my mother's apartment with Nana and Sparkle.

This is what I looked like when I first left home. I'm on the left with my dog Sparkle and a counselor from a home for runaways.

Hair modeling at Vidal Sassoon for Justin Ware.

From left to right: Elen, Nana, Butch, and me.

Elen, age 24.

Photo taken by Elen's photographer friend in his studio. I'm in my early 20s.

On Coney Island with Richie, 1976.

Elen graduating as an acupuncturist, 1980.

With Gregory and Miss Piggy in his and Carl's apartment, 1980.

At Limelight, NYC, 1984. Left to right: Aunt Gracie, Aunt May, me, my mother, Aunt Helen.

In my living room in the Thread Building, 1990.

In Puerto Rico with Blue Angel, pretending to be famous, 1981.

Me with Cheryl and my assistant Paul, who introduced me to David Thornton, 1989.

Shooting "She Bop" video. Left to right: Gregory, Diana, Johnny, my mother, 1984.

Performing in the second phase of Doc West in a small club on Long Island on a small, crummy stage, 1975.

Another incarnation of Blue Angel.

In a Long Island club with Flyer, 1976.

With Blue Angel when we thought we were really going places. I bought those clothes at Screaming Mimi's, 1980.

Jamming with Rick Derringer, 1981.

RON AKIYAMA

With Patrick Lucas, 1985.

With Justin Ware.

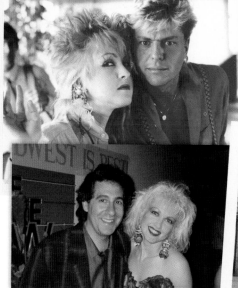

With Rick Chertoff.

Laura Wills, me, and makeup artist Jody Morlock, left and below.

Rob Hyman (on the left) and Eric Bazilian.

BRUCE ANDO

In Houston singing "Money Changes Everything" for video, 1985.

BRUCE ANDO

On tour in Montreal, checking the sound, 1985.

Performing in Toronto.

BRUCE ANDO

Old Quebec City, Canada, 1985.

BRUCE ANDO

At the Richard Avedon shoot for *Rolling Stone* magazine, 1984.

On tour
for the
greatest hits
album, 1994.

Taping the video
for "You Don't
Know." I was
directing. I built
a camera that
went all the way
around to create
movement.

ROZ LEVIN

With Lennie Petze at Epic Christmas party. I was dressed as Santa, 1984.

At a motel outside Houston, preparing for "Money Changes Everything" video. They gave me the best room in the house, with a heart-shaped tub, 1985.

With Al Arashita in Japan, 1986.

On the set of *Vibes* in Ecaudor, 1987, practicing finger waves on Peter Falk's hair.

Nashville, 1987, Katie Valk with a 3½ lb striped bass.

My birthday on the set of *Vibes*. They got a cake for me.

Russia, 1989. The blonde on the left is Laura Wills.

David Thornton and David Wolfe at the Berlin Wall, 1990.

With Biff Chandler and Queen Latifah at my first DIFFA Ball, 1991. I went in drag.

At DIFFA Ball with Howard Kaplan.

Also Berlin, 1990, with David Thornton. We went for a walk in the park.

Going to a television show in Europe, 1989.

Being honored as Princess of Good Fortune in Kobe Japan, 1996.

With Russ Titelman when we did *At Last* at PIE Studios, 2003.

With (clockwise, from top left) Muhammad Ali, Hulk Hogan, wrestler Wendy Richter, and Liberace backstage at WrestleMania, 1985.

JIM MARCHESE

TIMF & LIFE PICTURES/GETTY IMAGES

With Mr. T and Hulk Hogan during the buildup to the first WrestleMania, 1985.

RON GALELLA, LTD.

Me and Lou Albano at Studio 54, 1984.

Filming and directing "Hey Now," 1994.

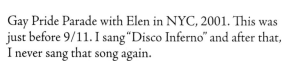

In Washington for NOW convention, 1992.

Gay Pride Parade with Elen in NYC, 2001. This was just before 9/11. I sang "Disco Inferno" and after that, I never sang that song again.

Poster for Stay Close campaign with Elen, 2002.

Inspired by a Man Ray photo, I did this shoot with
Caroline Greyshock in 1986 in New York City.

The photo on the left was shot by
Kim Stringfellow in Los Angeles, 1994.
I styled the clothing, and Cheryl and
I glued the feathers on that hat.

Walking down the aisle with my father to "A Whiter Shade of Pale," played by Rob Hyman, 1991.

In the red double-decker bus we rented to take us from our wedding ceremony to the reception.

KEVIN DORNAN

At the reception with Patti LaBelle.

In Hawaii on our delayed honeymoon, 1995.

KEVIN DORNAN

Outtake from photo shoot we did for the Christmas album, 1998. David is dressed as Santa and Declyn is the elf.

KEVIN DORNAN

With David and Declyn, 1999.

KEVIN DORNAN

Declyn, age 3, on drums. I was his roadie, 2000.

So I cut the painting *Starry Night* along the outline of my shoes, so that I had pieces of van Gogh, I had art, on my soles. When I went to art school, I read Vinnie's letters to his brother, Theo. I kind of wished I could have written Vincent and told him I used his work to make living art of *Starry Night* in a photograph nearly a hundred years after his death and hoped it was okay with him.

For the front cover, I wanted flowers like the girl in the South American picture, and I wanted a chain on my ankle and on my hip, to stress that woman is the slave of the world. Slavery is not just black and white. As I said, for Sicilian women, slavery was a mind fuck, a way to keep them in the house, as domestic slaves and bearing a man's children. So that chain was very symbolic to me.

I placed the flowers, the shoes, and the umbrella on the ground. And I brought the unfinished tapes from the studio so that I could play the music and dance to it while Annie was shooting. I wanted the sound of the music and the visual to marry, and that was the only way Annie could understand what it was she was taking a picture of.

Annie kept going, "Cyndi, pull your dress up." I just felt like, "No, I don't want to do that. I want to do the strong dance art thing." So I did both, and when it came time to choose the image, the record company was really vying for the one of me holding my dress up with the slip showing. I went around and asked people, "Which one do you like?" The people under thirty liked the strong one, and the people over thirty liked the more passive one. So when I presented it to Lennie, I told him that people under thirty liked the strong one, and I said we should go with that. He did. Lennie allowed me to have some freedom of speech and mind, and I'll always be grateful to him for that.

I'll tell you something else: I also did nude pictures with Annie. I was always an artist's model. I thought we were going to make great art, and some of it was, but I was a pop star and you couldn't have those kinds of pictures around. (I had them in a drawer; when my kid was born one of my assistants cleared all my pictures away, but I just found them.)

When the album was completed, the label wanted the first single to be "Time After Time." But I kept saying to them, "Listen to me— releasing a ballad first defines you in a certain way. You become known as a balladeer, and it can kill your career." Dave Wolff fought for me and kept saying that "Girls Just Want to Have Fun" could be an anthem, and finally everyone got excited and agreed it would be the first single.

The album was released in October of 1983. I was about to become famous, and it wasn't at all what I pictured.

CHAPTER SEVEN

WHEN IT CAME time to choose a director for the video of "Girls Just Want to Have Fun," I had Edd Griles in mind. I liked how he directed the Blue Angel video "I Had a Love," which won an International Film & Television of New York Award. And I liked him because he was personable and had a sense of humor (that was so important) and he was visual. For instance, when we shot the "I Had a Love" video, I had this idea of my boyfriend in the video and me watching TV; I'd then go turn the TV set off and my skirt would wipe the screen, wiping you into another scene. Visuals like that always went through my head, and sometimes it was kind of hard to get other people on board, but Edd and I were in sync.

He was open to doing the video, and once he was in, we started having meetings. He had this concept of having all these girls in it, like a Busby Berkeley musical, which I thought would be great. (I didn't really have time to write a treatment because at the time I was doing so much promotion for the album.)

What Edd did that was so special was that he was open-minded enough to see that the whole video was a creative collective. People in the public eye often see things as "It's either all me or all them." That's

123

not true. It wasn't all me or all them: it was us. The video was made with a combination of input from all the creative people on the set— the set designer, the stylists, Edd, my friends, me, and Captain Lou Albano, the wrestler who played my dad. Everyone felt free to contribute. I met Captain Lou when I was in Blue Angel. We were on a plane ride coming back from Puerto Rico. Originally they wanted the wrestler Gorgeous George to be in the video, but I said, "No, Captain Lou's the one." I had kept in touch with him and had his number, so Dave called him and he signed up immediately. When I was in Blue Angel I had an idea for a funny radio commercial with the voice of Tom Carvel, the founder of a chain of ice cream stores called Carvel's. But we couldn't get him, so we used Arnold Stang for the radio commercial and Captain Lou for the video. The rest became rock and roll history. Lou was sweet, and kind of a rock and roll character, too. The band NRBQ loved him as well. He was so funny. He made all the promotion fun. He was like this wacky big kahuna with his Hawaiian shirts and bushy eyebrows. He was so ahead of the curve.

Edd was not only a really wonderful director but a great teacher as well. He taught me so much. I had very strong ideas about what I thought the video should look like and mainly I was trying to make sure that it moved along with the music. And you don't shoot a dance scene without showing the feet! I saw that all the time. I asked Edd so many questions during our meetings. "What's the apartment going to look like? What's she going to look like? What's her room going to look like? Because it's gotta have a certain look."

The aesthetic I was going for was again Screaming Mimi's. And of course Laura Wills, the owner, was styling my clothes for the shoot. That store totally inspired me. I shopped all around the city and always went back to Screaming Mimi's because it had this fun approach to fashion. It had humor, it had wildness, it had sexiness, it had the old-movie vibe. And I had always felt like I was born in an old movie. To me, the whole Screaming Mimi's look wasn't just a style—it was a movement. And it wasn't just them. There were a whole bunch of people in the city who saw fashion, and home living, like that—reminiscent of the fifties, yet a Jackson Pollock thing, and that modern, cutting-edge thing where you mix elements together that would never have been mixed together in that time. When we did this video, the style that we presented was current but still underground. That look was really hot in New York and in England, but it was not big in middle America.

I started working with the art director—the guy who was doing the furniture and stuff. I wanted the kitchen to be very fifties. We couldn't really afford wallpaper—it was really a low-budget shoot— so I brought in a tablecloth from Screaming Mimi's that had a pattern I liked, and the art director kind of painted the walls like that. I also found furniture for the bedroom and painted it with bright paint. I wish I could find that furniture now. I think it's in storage.

I really saw my work as a kind of social movement, and not just when it came to the visuals. When I asked my mom to be in the video, I said, "Mom, think of what this could mean if you're involved—then you and I will make it popular to be friends with your mom." I told her we couldn't afford to pay a bunch of extras, and she said, "Of course I'll help you, Cyndi. What do you want me to do? I'm not really an actress." I said, "Ma, we're gonna play together, that's all." So Laura dressed her up, and they fixed her hair up, put a little makeup on her. On the set, she sat at the kitchen table and she didn't know what to do. Edd said, "Maybe when you're at the table cracking eggs, you should take the egg and slap it on your chest, like you're doing a mea culpa." So after I come in and sing, "We're not the fortunate ones," she takes the egg and breaks it on her chest like Edd said and then realizes it's there. That's all she needed to do.

My mother was frightened to death of Captain Lou. When he was talking to her during the shoot, he was really getting in her face, and you could see her sort of backed up against the wall, but it was so funny. My mom is such a good sport. She even came to work at the age of eighty on *The Celebrity Apprentice*. There was something about her on film that was so vulnerable. She wasn't an actress, but she had this charming presence that was so endearing. I know this is my mother, but she looked like she was from an Italian film, or the woman from the 1950s French film *Mon Oncle*.

We shot it in the summer at a place called Mother's, a studio in the East Village. Again, we didn't have a big budget so we all opened up our closets and shared all our clothes, and we got a whole bunch of my friends and family to be in the video. They're all in it except my sister, Elen, who was in LA, and my cousin Vinny. Everyone's generosity is what got the video made. We were all in this together. My videos became almost like home movies of my friends and family. I remember we got all the beauticians from Vidal Sassoon to be in it, too. Not Vidal himself, but everybody else joined in, including this really talented guy named Justin Ware, who did my hair for the shoot. I knew everybody at Vidal Sassoon because I was a hair model there for the longest time. In 1975 or '76, it was the cutting-edge place, and they would do demonstrations on my hair. Everyone was doing all kinds of wild and creative things at that time and had absolutely amazing hair. You'd come in and somebody had hair dyed like a tabby cat, and you'd say, "Man, that's fuckin' awesome—how did they do that?" The hairstyles were art pieces. As you could imagine, there was a lot of experimentation done on my hair. In the seventies I had a Suzi Quatro kind of haircut, and it was brown, and then they went with red in the back and blond in the front. I loved it.

They looked forward to rock and rollers like me who wanted experimental haircuts. They'd discuss it with you and say, "How about we dye it black just on the last few inches?" and you'd go, "Yeah, yeah, that's good." I once told Justin to cut my hair short on one side and gradually long on the other, because there was a picture of Mamie Van Doren on the wall at Screaming Mimi's, with her hair pinned to one side. I thought, "Why pin it when you can just cut it?"

So we had the beauticians from Vidal Sassoon, some secretaries from Epic, the girls from Laura's shop, Myra from the Japanese place where I had worked, and this black girl we cast who looked awesome with her dreads. It was very important to me that every girl was represented—Hispanic girls, African-American girls. I told Edd that we had to have multiracial people too. At that time, everybody who was in videos was either all white or all black. I figured, "You know what? Here's what I see missing. Let's go for it." There still wasn't as much integration as there should have been, but I feel like a lot of little girls who saw the video saw themselves, and that was the most important thing. As long as I got to them, I didn't care anymore.

So many people showed up for that shoot! It was extraordinary. My brother, Butch, played the pizza-delivery guy. Joe Zynsczak, who was my manager along with Dave, was the waiter in the bedroom. I had a friend named Bonnie Ross who was a nurse, and she was there dressed up in her uniform. (Bonnie was a direct descendant of Betsy Ross and used to tell me there was this horrible feeling in her family that Betsy might have slept with George Washington to get the gig.) You know the man with the handlebar mustache? That was my lawyer, Elliot Hoffman. Edd said, "How about getting Steve Forbert to be your boyfriend?" I said, "I love Steve Forbert." So there's Steve Forbert holding flowers. They're all in that fuckin' room.

The shoot took place over one long day that turned into a party. We got up really early for our first shot at the Metropolitan Museum. We stood in front of the fountain because it was supposed to look like a Busby Berkeley production. So all of us were lined up, Francis the cameraman used a Steadicam that he owned, and I took all my sunglasses that I had gotten at Screaming Mimi's over the years and handed them out, so everybody put on a pair. So that's the shot. And I was happy because everyone looked young and kind of hip. I brought all my makeup to the shoot, too, and ended up getting pinkeye because all of us shared everything.

Even my dog is in the beginning of the video—Rick Chertoff is walking him as I'm dancing down the street. For that part, I was inspired by a scene in this Sophia Loren movie where she comes dancing down the street in Naples in the fuckin' early morning light with her shoes slung over her shoulder. Then I had to go find the right street. I went down to the West Village, where there would be cobblestone streets, like in the movie, and I found this one street that had a great depth of field because it curved around. It's called Gay Street, oddly enough.

And then, for a scene later in the video, Edd told me to lead everyone down the street. I said, "What am I supposed to do, the cancan?" (Funny, I kind of did do a can-can.) It was me and this kind of motley crew. I mean, the girls were pretty, but it was still motley even though we took a glamorous approach to the whole thing. You had all these radical girls behaving like they're America's sweethearts in the Ziegfeld Follies. Edd said, "Keep leading everyone through the city until you get home, and then your poor mother has to deal with all these people traipsing through to get to your room." It would be like the Marx Brothers film *A Night at the Opera*, where everybody keeps coming into the room, until Captain Lou opens the door and they all fall out—which I think was Dave Wolff's idea. Or was it Edd's? Or it might have been Dave's friend Johann, who was also in the video. Dave had his own language and he called his friend Johann Von Bep Bep. His first name was really Johann, but I have no idea what his real last name was.

After we finished shooting, Edd was kind enough to allow me to be a part of the editing, which I really wanted to do. So he showed me the first edit and I said, "Wait a minute—where's all the other shots? They're not in here." He told me that the editor, Pam, had cut some scenes, but if I wanted to add or change things, I should go in with her and get them. I have a good visual memory (especially with clothes) and I busted my ass to do certain things. So I was literally sitting with Pam and pulling out strips of film from a bin. I changed a few shots around with her, and all of a sudden it was moving better and Edd said, "I think you should stay in here with her." So all of a sudden, I was learning editing. I only did it because I wanted my video to move the way it should move, because it was about music—and I know music.

Edd was looking to get in some kind of special effect, so at the special effects studio at Broadway Video they showed me a technique where you take a photograph and kind of wrap it in a ball. I was under the impression that each girl would be in her own ball—again, kind of a Busby Berkeley effect. But that was not the effect—we only had a certain amount of money, so they were going to do dots of random shots. So I said, "What the hell can this ball do? Can it bounce? How much does that cost?" He said it would cost the same, so then he bounced it and I said, "Bounce it to the time of the music."

We didn't have the budget to really do the kind of thing that Busby Berkeley would do—we would have had to have a crane over us to film from above while we all lay down on the floor and moved the way they did in those musicals. Which is what Macy Gray did in her video for "Beauty in the World"—they were all in a circle holding up pink circles and she's in the middle. That's a very strong visual. But you also have to figure out that kind of thing in advance, and we were kind of in a rush.

I did love the part in the video when the silent-movie version of *The Hunchback of Notre Dame* is playing and I'm singing, "Some boys take a beautiful girl and hide her away . . . ," and of course it's Quasimodo, taking Esmeralda away to the tower at the exact same time, which is very funny. And the way it was edited, it looked like Quasimodo was waving his arm to the beat and singing the song, too, which was even funnier.

There were so many bits and pieces in there of different things that influenced me. When I pick up the phone backward and then turn it around, it's because I had seen a David Bowie piece somewhere, where he had a phone receiver upside down and then put it right-side up. I thought, "Yeah, that's a good idea." And I love the French film-maker Jacques Tati (if you don't know about him you should rent *Mon Oncle* or *Mr. Hulot's Holiday*), so there are elements of his style in there as well. I used to watch channel 13 a lot, the public TV station in New York, because I loved old films and they showed a lot of them, like *Mon Oncle*. And because I was an art student, I knew about studying the masters. You need to know what was, before you know what can be.

People think "Girls Just Want to Have Fun" was a big hit right away, but it wasn't. MTV played it a little at first, but not much. When it went to radio, it only got seven adds in two weeks, meaning only seven radio stations played it in the whole country. I got a letter from a powerful national radio programmer who said that the record would never be big because I sang too high. He offered to have me and Dave come see him so we could discuss my career options. But Dave looked at the letter and decided to cook up a different idea. He said, "This is what we're going to do: We're going to start to go to wrestling shows. I'm going to call this guy Vince McMahon and propose a cross-promotion, and we'll start by doing stuff with Captain Lou." And that's how my record really broke.

It was Dave's dream to do something like this. I mean, this was the guy who set up press meetings in that ridiculous way when he did the whole Human Fly thing, using a horrible French-Canadian accent. Dave really was a pioneer of cross-promotion. Here's how he explained it to me: There were three wrestling shows every weekend, Friday night, Saturday morning, and Saturday night. If you had your music videos on all three of those shows, which had big numbers, lots of people would see them. So I said okay.

So then publicity photos started coming out of me and Dave at wrestling matches cheering on the wrestlers and booing the bad guys. And they showed parts of my video before commercial breaks. But he also thought up these on-air scenarios with Captain Lou and me that were played during the show.

You know how those sixties beach movies had all these ridiculous comical characters—like in the Frankie Avalon and Annette Funicello teen movies where there was a biker named Eric Von Zipper? And the straight people in the movie would be in there going, "Who the heck are these people?" Well, those comical characters were very influential in everything I did. So along with Captain Lou and the wrestlers, I had my mother become a character and dressed her up like this eccentric, sexy, kooky woman with pointy sunglasses and a Chinese robe, and a long cigarette holder and foo-foo shoes with cha-cha heels and pedal pushers.

I thought we should start doing stuff like that because it was funny, and because every time you saw artists, they would try and tell you about their work and their music and basically it can be boring as shit. Just like when I sit there and try and explain my work—it's probably so fucking boring. What's important is the end result: Is it entertaining? So I thought, how hilarious would it be if my "spiritual adviser" Captain Lou, as this big fuckin' nut, just talks you senseless?

So when I did promotion I'd have my "spiritual adviser" standing there, with two giant Samoan guys standing behind him. And he'd launch into the P-E-G principle: Politeness, Etiquette, and Good Grooming, which is something that he, as a manager, had taught these two men. It mimicked a scene that was very familiar in old-school wresting promotion—there's some screaming nut-job manager type with a big stupid guy nodding his head in the background. We used to think, "This is brilliant and very on spot." It was improv, too, baby!

And then things started to pick up with the album. I remember I got on David Letterman's show right away. At the time, he was new, and he was on at 12:30 A.M. And I was new, too, and I was funny—that's all the people booking the show knew. At that point, Dave would play a little clip from your video and then he'd let you talk. So when I came on, I decided to pick my foot up and put it on the chair in a certain way that was irreverent and comfortable.

I really wasn't nervous. I was ready. Dave was so funny when he started talking to me, so I had fun with him. He asked about my mom, and I told him that we used to have some pet fish, and one of them got fungus and had a tumor, so my mother decided to operate on it. She got out a cuticle scissor and sterilized it and everything. Then she laid the fish out, kept it wet, and cut away the tumor, then painted mercurochrome on it and put it back in the tank.

And the fish lived. Dave said, "So your mom is a fish doctor." Yes, I said. Unfortunately what happened was our fish were Siamese fighter fish, so when my mother put the female fish back in the tank with the others, a male fish killed her. My mother was so upset, she took the male fish out with the net and put him down and said, "Bad fish, bad fish!" and smacked him a little with the net. Unfortunately, that chopped his tail off. Then she tried to put him back in the water because she didn't want him to die. It was all a terrible thing, but you can't take a fish out of the tank and spank him. The story got so crazy and then Paul Shaffer started chiming in . . . it was pretty funny.

So Letterman was the first adventure, and then the record company realized that they had something. Until I came along, they never understood how to put together fashion (well, my version of it) and humor with music. Music had become a visual medium, so Dave Wolff and I created this whole world that we brought with us when we did appearances or press, which is much more intriguing and interesting, if you ask me. My mother became a regular character in my entourage, and she made up a stage name for herself: Catrine Dominique. Like I said, she liked everything French.

And then there was always Captain Lou, who would go ranting about something, and then I'd chime in, and it would get silly. Captain Lou became famous all over the world because he was in videos like "Girls Just Want to Have Fun," "She Bop," and "The Goonies 'R' Good Enough." We were walking a little bit of a fine line between earning respect and not being taken seriously, but it was still really fun. I'd think, "Who cares if they think I'm a good singer or not? I *am* a good singer." When I sang "Girls Just Want to Have Fun" and came back with "Time After Time," that's when I proved that you can rock out, be a good singer and writer, but also use humor.

Then Dave Wolff made a deal with Vince McMahon that if he continued to play my videos on his shows, I would go on Johnny Carson and promote wrestling. So that's what we did. And you know what? It worked. Johnny Carson was huge for me. Although he always called me Sydney and never Cyndi. But hey, it was Johnny Carson, and that was his pet name for me, which was kind of cool. When I first went on his show, I wore the sparkly, full skirt I wore in the "Time After Time" video and this wonderful rust-and-yellow Hawaiian-print shirt that I loved (I still have it), and I tied tulle around my head in a bow. I saw that tulle on a mannequin named Esther at Screaming Mimi's first. My friend Biff Chandler, who was Laura's partner at Screaming Mimi's, came up with that idea. (Sadly, he died of AIDS in the nineties. At that time, we were losing a lot of visionaries to AIDS.) All the mannequins had names. And I thought, "Wow, that tulle is good." (My hair never seemed big enough for me; I always felt like I was this small person.) And I brought Johnny a pair of sunglasses. He said to me, "You dress so unusual." I said, "Really? Because it doesn't seem that way to me. I think *you* dress very unusual."

The wrestling connection kept growing to the point where the executives from the label were in on it. I was warned that I might have a fight with Lou on "Rowdy" Roddy Piper's segment because he was saying a lot of stuff that I might not like, but I said that even though we were going to fight, I still wanted to promote women's lib somehow. Dave Wolff said, "Just have him say women belong barefoot and pregnant in the kitchen, and then we'll do a whole fight thing with female wrestlers." So the Fabulous Moolah was brought in. (I've always been unhappy that I never really got to know Moolah, who died a few years ago, like I would have liked to, because she was awesome.)

So when Captain Lou said that thing about being barefoot and pregnant, I had a freakout on the show. I turned over a table and I pulled Lou's beard and hit him over the head with a bag. But they showed a clip of it on *Entertainment Tonight* as if it were real! I was watching it with Dave Wolfe, and we were laughing, and saying, "How could you not see the humor? It's so ridiculous." It was funny. But my friend Rose called me up and said, "Cyn, when you freaked out like that, people saw you angry." She was worried.

Working with Vince McMahon was very different for us. It became challenging at times because it was taking a lot of time away from making music. But we did a lot of really fun stuff that left its mark on wrestling and on Dave Wolff and me. When we were in it, Dave was like a little kid. And if you talk to anybody working in professional wrestling you'll see that same little kid look in their eyes. It was something that I was able to share that with Dave Wolff.

While all this was going on, we were getting ready to do the video for "Time After Time," the second single. Edd was directing again, and he got a scriptwriter to come in and write it. I changed some things I didn't like, which everybody does, and I said, "I want my mother in it, and I want the vision of her mother to haunt her." Dave was also going to be in the video (he wanted to be in the video—Dave liked being in the limelight), and I wanted to do something that was really going to surprise him. So I had my hair cut and shaved in a checkerboard pattern, and I didn't let him see it. So when I pull off my hat in that scene in the diner, that was really him freaking out.

It was important to me that we were natural and human in that video. I wanted to convey somebody who walked her own path and did not always get along with everyone and did not always marry the guy. At the end of the video, when I get on the train and wave goodbye to Dave, Edd said, "Okay, you'll look out the window, waving goodbye, and you'll have this one tear running down your cheek." I said, "Are you crazy? What do I look like, Bette Davis?" But much to my surprise, I was able to cry. While shooting the scene leading up to that, when I'm carrying the duffel bag, I thought about when I was hitchhiking in Vermont. All I had was that small duffel bag. It contained everything I owned. I wondered then if I'd be okay—if I would be able to make something of myself. I then came back to the present moment of shooting this video for a song I wrote after having "made it"—more importantly, I'd survived. That was the thought that moved me to tears.

To convey the sadness of this person leaving her old life to start a new one—with no one, striking out on her complete own—I thought we could show an old movie that conveyed a mood of loss, and I said to Edd, "I know a movie that's really fun—*The Garden of Allah* with Marlene Dietrich and Charles Boyer." And again we used Biff and Laura from Screaming Mimi's to help out with the decor in the house and trailer scenes, which was just as important as the clothing fashion. Because again, you don't just wear it, you live it. And a video is my record, visually. It can't just be from outer space. I wanted a sound and a look that worked together. Which quickly became a pain in the ass to the corporate people and managers, because they just wanted me to do all the promotion and have somebody else do the rest of it. But that's not what it was for me. I'm sure they thought I was some kind of control freak, but to me, it was performance art. It was creating a world—and a life and people in it.

The Airstream trailer in the scene at the beginning was in the middle of nowhere in New Jersey and unbeknownst to us there was dog shit all over because the guy who owned it had dogs. When Dave had to run out after me, he was stepping in that dog shit.

Another thing about that video is that even though the town looks desolate, a couple thousand people filled the streets, just standing around watching us. That was a big shock. If you had panned the camera around, you wouldn't have believed it. We didn't even have any security—it never crossed our minds that we'd need it.

Then I sat in the edit again, but this time with a brilliant editor that Edd was able to get. His name was Norman Smith and he used to edit for Robert Altman. From that man I learned a great, great deal. In those days, you had two reels of film and you used razor blades to cut and splice—it wasn't done on a computer. Sometimes it took a really long time, and everybody would go, "You have so much happening, so why do you gotta do that?" But I loved visuals and I loved the whole music-film thing, and I saw the possibility of film moving like music.

"Time After Time" went to number one on the singles chart in June of 1984. And here's the thing: I never had a filter before I was famous, and I didn't have one after, either. I really should have shut up sometimes. But of course I never did. I mean, listen: I'm not Saint Cyndi. I used to say I was Saint Cyndi of a Feces, because wherever shit fell, there I was.

CHAPTER EIGHT

There were a lot of highs and lows during that time. Like I was on the cover of *Rolling Stone* in May of 1984. A very famous photographer took the photo, Richard Avedon, and all I wanted was to look as pretty as Annie Lennox did in her *Rolling Stone* cover. But instead they used a photo that I thought made me look ugly. I cried when I saw it and thought, "If I look that ugly, who's going to buy it?" You should have seen the photos they didn't use, which were so much nicer.

And *Ms.* magazine voted me one of the women of the year, which, let me tell ya, was such an honor for a bra-burner like me. But it was hard to take it all in, because I had basically been working since 1983 promoting the album or touring. When you're doing that stuff, you're away from home like three-quarters of the time. I'd go to Los Angeles, then to Japan, and then to Australia. That's how it was—I just kept going around the world. I'd come back, maybe get a day or two off, but it wasn't really a break because I'd be dealing with jet lag. Then I had to get back to work.

Fame was happening on a level that Epic had hoped for but didn't expect. I mean, I had four top five hits in a row from *She's So Unusual.*

They had success with other female artists, but people were screaming over me.

No one ever really prepares you for success. I think every kid, to some degree, wants to be famous. I know I did, but it was because I wanted to make a record, and the only way you could make a record and have a recording career was if you were famous. So I spent a good deal of time preparing for fame—like, I would do interviews in my head when I was in the shower. I don't know why. (I was also a little nutty.) And if I felt wronged by someone, I would also, in the shower, give my acceptance speech for the big award that I was going to get—like the Grammys or whatever.

But fame is nothing like I could have imagined. It seemed to turn everything backward from what I remembered my life to be. I always lived on the outside, and it was so bizarre when I became famous because all of a sudden I was on the inside. Funny thing was, I started to see a strange irony going on: The same mental idiots who threw rocks at me for what I used to wear went out and bought the same kinds of clothes.

I'd see versions of myself everywhere. And my funny little dirty trick was that I was always teasing very normal-looking people that I was perfectly normal—that I was the girl next door. Then the normal sucked up the abnormal and made it normal. All of a sudden, there was a movement of people dressing in things they wouldn't have dared to wear before they saw me.

Maybe I made it a little easier for kids who were different from the norm. Because for one minute, everything was reversed, and the different people became the norm and the more conservative people became different. And it really wasn't just young people. My music bled through generations.

My hairdo, my clothes—everything—became fashion. I wore corsets like you would wear a blouse, and then Madonna did it after me, and after a while, everybody wore corsets. It was weird to be totally sucked up and taken. And what's also ironic is that a lot of my looks came from the fact that I couldn't afford to get what I really wanted, so I had to be innovative. Like when everyone was wearing long chains, all I could afford was a chain or two, so I would get strands of rhinestones that you could buy for a quarter from the flea markets and hook them together to make a kind of belt. And then somebody actually started selling chains with rhinestones.

People would write about my "grab-bag fashion." Then I did a show in Detroit, and while I was performing—really getting everybody going—people in the audience started pulling things off of me. At that time, I was still shopping for every little thing, saving for this and that, and was finally able to buy stuff like the chain-and-rhinestone belt. So when people just reached out and took my stuff, I was kind of like, "What are you doing? You're ripping this skirt that I got on layaway!" It was really upsetting at first. That, and the screaming.

But I knew I was doing something good when I saw three generations of women come to my concerts: grandmothers with rhinestones, mothers with spray-dyed hair, and their little kids dressed as some weird-ass version of me. I realized then that I had their attention. I was speaking to three generations, and that's what I wanted. By bringing my mom into the mix, and people like Captain Lou, I was able to speak to a very wide and diverse audience. And my feeling is: When you climb to the top of the mountain, you better have something to say. I never had a problem opening up my big mouth, and it didn't change when I was famous. Like I said, I was always saying the wrong things to the right people.

I especially spoke up for women's rights. In the beginning no one really came out and said they were a feminist. I did. I never said "humanist" like a lot of other women artists did. And when the "Papa Don't Preach" video came out, with Madonna dancing around in her sexy outfit, I had something to say about that. If you're a teen mother who wants to keep her baby—number one, you're not going to look like Madonna, dancing around. Number two, it ain't gonna be that easy. Fathers don't always come around at the end to give you their blessing. The guy who knocked you up doesn't always stay around. Number three, every woman should still have a choice. I was proud to have spoken out for what I knew was right, but the record company and my manager freaked out.

Another time, I went to Japan and the reporters brought up "Girls Just Want to Have Fun," and asked, "Do you think it's right for a young woman to stay out all night long?" I said, "It seems so to me. Men do it." There were still women in kimonos walking behind their husbands in Japan at that time and when I saw that, I was like, "That's gotta change." So everything I talked about when I was in Japan was about equality—everything. I turned every conversation back to, "Well, look at it this way—if you want a strong society, if you want to compete in the world, you can't just use half your people—you need to use all your power." They would look at me like I was presenting a new idea—and of course I wasn't. But it was coming from this little fuckin' woman who looked like an alien to them. But they like aliens. When I went to Japan, I realized why I had caught on: My hair was bright orange, I wore funny clothes, and I had war paint on my face. Just like some of their cartoons.

I did the same thing when I went to Italy. I took a page from Gertrude Stein and told the press that the three biggest oppressors of women are the church, the family, and the government. It's true.

God, I did a ton of press that year. And after a while when I was repeating the same thing over and over and over, I just felt like saying,

"Listen—forget the questions, don't be silly, stop everything, run right out, get yourself a ticket, purchase the album. It's the best thing you'll ever buy." But of course you can't do that.

So I was working nonstop, but Dave and I had some fun. We were riding around in limos all the time. I was jumping on beds in hotel rooms (but then, I've always jumped on the beds, in hotels and at home). It was like, "Look at us! We're livin' large!" But it was also surreal. I'd walk into an event and people would be screaming at me the way I used to scream over the Beatles, ripping at my clothes. And it was usually girls, which was strange for me. I understood why young girls would scream for guys—they'd think they were cute. But girls screaming over girls, I didn't understand. After a while I realized that it was admiration—that I was kind of their hero for opening my knee-jerk big fat mouth. I said things that other people wouldn't say. I guess it made me endearing—but of course it also made people hate me.

I couldn't believe what was happening—that I couldn't go anywhere, that there was hysteria when I did go somewhere. I'd go out to eat and somebody would always come up to me, always. I couldn't have one single minute to myself, and the sad thing was that the people I was with that I hadn't seen for a long time—the ones I could finally afford to take out to eat—started to get upset. It's strange to be constantly interrupted and they weren't used to it.

Going to dinner was mostly what I did socially. I had a boyfriend, so it's not like there were any wild parties. For my thirty-first birthday, I celebrated at a Chinese restaurant and invited all my friends—that's about as wild as it got. After shows, I'd go back to the hotel with Dave, take a hot bath, stretch, and go to bed while he went and played cards with his friends. Or if we were home together he would go to the other side of the loft we had gotten downtown in the Thread Building, and play video games like Super Mario or Pinball. After watching him play awhile I'd head over to the other side of the apartment and watch old movies because I couldn't take it.

Since I was with Dave, there was never any going out on the town or going dancing. He didn't dance. Our life together was business stuff and homebody stuff. I loved Dave, but I wished that I could have known other artists and done more things. Sometimes when he wasn't around, I'd go to clubs and sing at open-mic nights. I tried to find other musicians because that's the one thing I missed—other musicians, other artists, not just people that the manager finds for you to write with. There was only one musician who came by my apartment to see me and I really liked: Boy George. He came with Marilyn, the transgender singer. I loved Boy George and I was so excited to see another artist. We sat around talking, and then when it got late, we were like, "Let's go eat." And at that time, which is hard to believe now, there weren't any places to eat near us that were open late except for one place, called the Green Kitchen.

Usually with other famous people I was a little goofy. I'd trip over my own feet a little. Because I was still me. You know? Even at Epic I was more comfortable going out to lunch with the secretaries than with the record people. Although I was the one who was supposed to be the spoiled brat, I didn't really feel like that, because all I did was work (and fight for getting what I wanted).

For my first major tour, I played a lot of colleges. And I always wanted women on the tour because my band was filled with men, but every time I asked for a woman, Dave Wolff would say, "They don't play as good as men." Which isn't true.

Concrete Blonde opened for me once. They were a trio, and on the first night, they did not do so good. So I told my tour manager to call up my agent, Barbara Skydel, and say, "Hey, I don't know what's up with this band." So the tour manager took them off the tour. But they were committed to open for me the next night. Well, that night, they were awesome. So I called Barbara back and said, "Wait a minute—these guys aren't really bad at all." They did not want to come back, though. They were mad. That's all right, because maybe that criticism was a catalyst for Johnette to try even harder. I think sometimes anger helps you move forward.

Basically, I didn't have background singers or any of that stuff on my tours in the beginning. The guy who played guitar kind of sang background and I would sing lead and then switch to background and join him so the sound was a little fuller, and then go back to singing lead. He was a terrific guitar player and he had red hair too. So that looked really good onstage. It was a lot for my voice to handle. My band was wonderful, but I always felt like I could have really used some background singers. I would have loved to have some women with me on tour, either as singers or musicians, but again every time I brought up hiring a female musician Dave would say there weren't any good ones.

The audiences kept getting bigger. Usually, before I went onstage, I was a wreck. It was always a rush backstage. Sometimes while my makeup artist was doing my makeup—I did my own hair—I'd start doing my vocal exercises. Like I said, I always had a pot and a hot plate so I could steam my voice (for around ten minutes because I never had the time to do it longer). I'd blow up a balloon to work my lungs. Then I'd get dressed and walk around, being nervous. I was always worried that I was not going to be good enough. I was always peeking outside and counting filled seats to see if I did okay, and then wondering if they were going to get their money's worth. If the place was not sold out, I'd tell myself, "Well, that's okay—then you show everyone what the people who didn't buy tickets missed." Ya know, I kind of still do the same thing.

I'd try and meet up with the band beforehand, to say, "Have a nice show," but I was always kept apart. And no, I didn't do a prayer circle before the show. I hate the whole prayer-circle action. Because my Lord is probably not your Lord. I mean, look at me: What do you think? A woman, or a drag queen, or someone who is really interested in fashion and music and the arts—maybe that's the leader of my house of worship. Or maybe my house of worship is the House of Chanel? The only time I liked the whole prayer-circle thing was when I did it with Cassandra Wilson. I adore her. She called me up one time when I was having a big fight with my husband, David, and I said, "Cassandra, I can't talk right now, I'm having a big fight with my husband, I'll call you later." I thought that she was very insulted and thought I was rude. That was the last I spoke to her for a while. But as life would have it, we orbited back toward each other again in December of 2011, when she performed at the True Colors Fund show "Cyndi Lauper & Friends: Home for the Holidays." I got to sing and play dulcimer while she played guitar. She's still awesome.

Where was I? Right: performing. When it was time to go onstage, I'd go out there very unassumingly and quietly, and say, "Hey, how ya doin'?" Sometimes when the audience was very appreciative it almost choked me up and made me cry. Then I talked because I was nervous. After I was done talking, I felt less nervous, and when I started singing, I really calmed down.

But I always felt like I had to prove myself. If I messed up the lyrics, I'd say, "Oh my God, let's pretend that didn't happen," and count the band back in. I always tried to include the audience, like "We're all in this together." I always think, "How will the people in the crowd get their money's worth? They bought the ticket. Maybe they got a babysitter. Now, how do I make it worth their while?"

As I did in the Blue Angel days, I really thought about how I would begin the show. I always thought it's all about how you open. I'd come out covered up, and then kind of take my clothes off as I performed. I would have my hair dyed the brightest orange and yellow and red, like fire, and shove it under a hat. I'd also wear glasses and an overcoat when I came out onstage. Then I'd pull the hat off and shake my hair to reveal this burst of color, which was exciting to them, or I'd take my eyeglasses off, and that was like a moment. But I would do that for myself too. Because, like I said, it helped me peel off layers emotionally.

And then I started to sing. I knew the first and second song had to be strong. I learned that from watching the Allman Brothers when I saw them in the seventies. They always came out with up-tempo songs first, to get the audience's attention, and then slowed it down. I would move and sing, move and sing, stop, talk, do a little ballad, and then just when they'd relax, I'd move and sing again until the crowd was in such a frenzy that by the end they were crazy. I'd hit them really hard. I wouldn't give them a chance. I've never given up on an audience, ever. I keep hitting them until I got them, even if I have to go out in the audience and sit on their chairs. I always wished that I could be like the Rolling Stones and sail over the audience in a cherry picker like Mick Jagger. Instead, my act was climbing into a fuckin' garbage can onstage because I couldn't afford the cherry picker when I did "Money Changes Everything." And I thought the garbage can was on an automatic pulley system, but instead it was actually ten men holding me up. They had me sign my will before they hoisted me. I only went up a short distance and as soon as I started shaking and getting off balance, they pulled me right back in. They musta been like, "The golden goose, she's going down—pull it in, boys, bring her in!"

There were a lot of times that I felt totally isolated backstage, so I always tried to connect with people when I was onstage. With the college audiences, we had no barriers, so they could touch me and I could touch them. We would hold each other, or they'd put their hands out and hold my feet and legs and I'd put my arm out and sing. They never did anything weird—if they did, I would have smacked them. Listen, I was never a sex symbol. Because I didn't dress like one. I had fishnet stockings with one black sneaker and one white sneaker that I painted in Magic Marker. And I didn't act like a sex symbol, either. I was selling freedom of expression and the freedom to be different—not sex. I'm telling ya, there were no men who chased after me. Instead I got the sad people, because that's who I was trying to heal when I sang.

But I couldn't believe how sexist some of the guys on the tour were. I'd hear about guys sleeping with a mother and daughter, and things like that. I was like, "What the fuck is that? These people are all coming here because of me, and I'm preaching women's lib onstage, and look what you guys are doing." It was my moment, but they wanted to have their moment, too. In the end it was really Dave Wolff's band— he hired them, they listened to him, if they had a problem with me they'd talk to him. (Believe me, that changed a few years later.) But at the time I was kept very busy and I was just trying to keep up with everything. And when people did deal with me, they'd freak out, because I was so direct with them.

Sexism in the music business wasn't just limited to the record companies and the guys on tour. I saw it with other artists, too. I met Ron Wood from the Stones once at some awards ceremony. His girls were all dressed up and I said, "Yeah, girls just want to have fun." He looked at me and moved the girls away. You gotta understand, in his generation, women were totally different. Guys like him were not comfortable with what I represented. Did you ever see that video from Art of Noise called "Close (to the Edit)"? There's a little girl in there with punky hair who is slamming things around and is dressed just like me. That's how that generation of men viewed me: I was frightening because when I saw women being pushed down or objectified I said, "Fuck no! That's chauvinism, I'm not allowing that."

Another time, when I was at some other event, I told my stylist I wanted to look shockingly different. So I was dressed up very womanly—still rock and roll, but sexy, which, for me, was radical. I was waiting to go onstage to present with an older rocker. I turned my back to him for a second to say hello to a friend, and all of a sudden this very famous guy grabbed my hips and kind of humped my butt. I'm thinking, "What? He thinks this is some kind of handshake?" So I turned around and said, as lighthearted as I could (I even put a little laugh in the middle of the sentence), "Hey, pal—not for nothin', but if you do that again, I'm gonna have to punch your fuckin' heart out." Then he acted like he was frightened of me. I thought, "Oh, ya mean under that mane there's not a lion, just a whimper? What the hell?" He was taller, he was stronger, and he took me by surprise.

The idea that a woman would actually take offense to having her butt humped by someone she didn't know that well was probably a shock to him. And why—because he was used to women throwing themselves at him? I just think I was in the middle of a strange generation where the idea of equality eluded these guys (at least until they had children who were girls).

I also had Bob Dylan come up to me one time, not long after I appeared on a special for John Lennon. Now, I adore him. Who doesn't? But he said to me, "You know, I saw what you did on the Lennon special, and I thought it was really great. I would have you in my band—and that's saying something, because I don't like chicks in bands."

Ai yi yi. I looked at him and said, "Yeah, well—not for nothing, but was that an insult or a compliment?"

He said, "Oh, what are you, one of those bra-burning women's libbers?" I took a deep breath and said, "Well, you know, Bob, if I'm not concerned about my civil liberties, who will be?" He just kind of nodded and said, "Oh." At that point I wanted to say, "Blowin' in the wind, Bob?" But I didn't, because it was Bob Dylan and he did write that song, and many, many other wonderful songs. And honestly, I think he is also from a generation where women put out because the men were rock gods. To me that whole fuckin' generation and their free love, with male musicians being the big peacocks and the women walking quietly behind or next to them, was a bunch of crap. As a woman who maneuvered through so much of that shit, I just want to say sometimes, "Excuse me—but ain't there light enough for two people?"

When I became famous—I mean right away—the press always asked me about one person: Madonna. They tried to create this big rivalry, but my feeling was, you don't fuckin' knock another sister, ever. But even her record company got in on it. They ran an ad in *Billboard* where she was dressed in a white corset. And it said something like, "This girl's gonna give Cyndi Lauper a run for her money." I felt really bad about it. Everybody else was fueled up by this supposed rivalry, but I was backing up, going, "I don't want to do this. I don't want to be part of this."

The thing was, our music wasn't even similar. (Although if you ask me, her voice was sped up in "Like a Virgin" to make it sound high like mine.) She was so smart about business and marketing (I never was) and she always was, and still is, beautiful. I kind of went the other way because I had on the war paint and I purposely wore clothes that were rebellious, and antifashion sometimes, especially toward the end of 1985. I remember I saw Madonna for the first time at the American Music Awards at the beginning of 1985. I was up for a few awards and was also going to perform "When You Were Mine." I should have done "Girls Just Want to Have Fun," because the whole place would have erupted, but instead I did the Prince song, which probably went right over everybody's head. But I wanted my record to move on.

Anyway, I made everything on the set black and white. I talked the producers into letting me work with the carpenters' union to build this big sculpture made of shoes. I was barefoot and wore black pants, a white shirt, black eye makeup, and a zebra-print vest. Nothing had color except some orange paint that was in a bucket onstage and my hair, which was yellow and orange. So while I sang, I swished color onto the set. To TV viewers, it looked like I was turning a black and white image into color. I wanted to bring art into people's homes. I was hell-bent on mixing art and music, the visual and the sound and the story, and I basically cut open a vein onstage. I wanted to be larger than life, to be better than who I was, to look completely different. I became a painting. That's why I relate to Lady Gaga and Nicki Minaj, because they make themselves paintings sometimes.

That year I was nominated for two awards, Favorite Pop/Rock Female Artist (against Madonna) and Favorite Pop/Rock Female Video Artist (against Tina Turner). When I got up to make my acceptance speech for Favorite Pop/Rock Female Artist, I looked at Madonna sitting in the audience, and I felt so crummy, because she had "Like a Virgin" out and it was number one for six weeks in a row. I never had that kind of success in my life, ever. Neither had she, so I thought it was awesome for her.

So I thanked everybody and then I said, "I accept this award for the people that came before me and paved the way, and for the people that will come after me." And I looked at her and thought, "Next year it will be you." I met her afterward and said, "Hey, that track of yours, 'Like a Virgin,' is unbelievable, it's so great, congratulations." She was nice but it was a really short exchange. I never could have a conversation with her because she always had lots of people protecting her. My whole life, I lived the opposite way.

After the show, I continued with my nonstop life: The American Music Awards ended at around nine or ten P.M., and I had to go straight to a recording studio in Los Angeles to shoot the "We Are the World" video for USA for Africa. There was no time to get ready. I was so upset that I couldn't wash my hair from the art piece I did, so I had orange and yellow paint flakes coming down from my head. I wore this Italian waiter coat because I had a white shag blouse underneath it with overalls and I thought the coat would make me look thinner. Then when I got there I saw Michael Jackson in his bandleader jacket and it looked too similar to my jacket. So I took mine off. Besides, the flakes from my hair were starting to fall on the jacket, so it wasn't the best look.

Quincy Jones, the producer, told everyone to check their egos at the door, but they didn't really do that. I wanted to mingle, but I was like the monster. I had the big orange and yellow hair flakes that looked like dandruff. I said hello to Michael Jackson. Not a big talker, but he was fine. Then I talked to people like Huey Lewis and told bad jokes, and laughed, because I think if you tell something that's not funny and then laugh, it's kind of funny. But even in that situation, I felt like an outsider. Always. I was always like the Rodney Dangerfield of rock. I did the wrestling, I was weird, and then all of a sudden I was singing these big hits.

I went up to Bette Midler and told her that I loved her. Then they fuckin' relegated Bette Midler, whose voice I've always loved—*Bette*

Midler—to some corner to stand with the nonsinging Jacksons in the chorus! Then again, Billy Joel was there, and they didn't ask him to sing solo, either. But I kept looking around and thinking, "Where are the women with the big voices? Where's Aretha? Where's Patti La-Belle?"

I got a good part in the song that Dave really vied to get for me. I knew the line but I didn't know how I was going to sing it until I started singing. It was the pivotal point of the bridge and I had just been watching one amazing singer after another—fuckin' Steve Perry's voice is amazing, Daryl Hall's voice is amazing. It got around to me and the line just came barrel-assing out. The best things I sing are sung when I'm not in control, when I just allow everything to come through me. But I think I scared the hell out of Kim Carnes, who was next to me. Then Quincy kept going, "What is that jangling sound?" He stopped everything, came over to me, and said, "It's all of your jewelry." I thought, "He said to check your ego at the door—not your jewelry." But I didn't say that—I just gave him the jewelry and moved on. For me, it's not really just what you wear that's important, it's how you accessorize what you wear. Hey, we were being filmed—I wanted to look good. Without that jewelry, I felt like a plain Jane. Except for the bright yellow and orange paint in my hair, that is.

The session went on for around ten hours. I thought it was interesting that the first verse and bridge *included* women and the big finish *excluded* women. It was a long night. We walked out at dawn. I felt like I was tripping.

Then the Grammys were the following month. I was nominated for seven of them. Janet Perr won for Best Art Direction on the album, and I won Best New Artist, which is the kiss of death. (Look at the artists who have gotten it in the past: Rickie Lee Jones. Christopher Cross. Arrested Development.) I felt so embarrassed because the year before, Michael Jackson won everything—there were pictures of him carrying an armload of Grammys—and I think the record company people expected me to do what he did and clean up. But I was up against all these big heavy hitters: Springsteen, Prince, Tina Turner, and Lionel Richie. I was the little guy.

"Time After Time" was nominated for Best Song and Phil's "Against All Odds" won. But here's the thing: I haven't heard a lot of covers of "Against All Odds" but I never stop hearing covers of "Time After Time." So maybe it's not the award that counts. It's wonderful to hear what other people embrace about a song that was so personal to me. Tuck & Patti did an especially great version of "Time After Time." So did Patti LaBelle. It's been covered by dozens of artists—I can't even keep track of how many. But the most honored I ever felt was when Miles Davis covered it. I never wanted him to meet me either, because I thought if he didn't like me (like most of the old-timers), he wouldn't play my song anymore, and the way he played it was pure magic.

Between dates on my tour, I'd come back for other awards shows like the very first MTV Video Music Awards, where I won for Best Female Video (and during the 1987 MTV Awards I got to perform "Change of Heart" as I was lowered down on an acrobat bar, which was pretty great). I worked very hard with MTV. I loved video and music. I love the visual age I live in.

So that first year after releasing *She's So Unusual* was nonstop, and a lot of it was a thrill. It was the kind of crazy year where my mother did a television show on celebrity moms and became friends with Cher's mother and Stevie Wonder's (who said she was tough).

But I had a rough time, too, because I started to get sick from endometriosis. Worse, my friend Gregory started to get sick. I loved Gregory and always felt protective of him, because of everything he went through. He was thrown out of his house at twelve when his mother walked in on his stepfather raping him. She kept the step-father and threw out the kid—a sad story I will never forget. Gregory had not had an easy time. Once, he and I were talking about what he would do with his life and he said, "Oh, what does it matter? We're crazy, anyway." And from that, I understood what it felt like to have a terrible self-image—to feel like trash thrown out into the street, hoping that the wind would just blow you away so that you wouldn't have to hang around anymore. It's hard to explain to someone who wasn't abused as a kid how that abuse can screw up your head—how you feel it doesn't matter what you do because the worst was already done to you. And I know in my heart that Gregory must have felt that way.

I also watched Gregory's cousin Diana, a transgender woman, be ridiculed for even trying to be the woman that she felt she was inside. You have to remember what a frightening time it was in New York City in the eighties. There were marauders, young brutal men, coming from New Jersey and Brooklyn, driving around the West Village look-ing to beat whoever they thought was gay.

When Gregory got sick, we had just shot "She Bop" together. Once again, all of my friends, including Carl and Gregory, were in the video. They played the robotic customers at the fast food place. Soon after that, the two of them sat me down to tell me that Gregory was ill. They made it sound as if everything was going to be okay, but re-ally, AIDS was a death sentence then. I was devastated. During my time in the apartment on Seventy-seventh Street, I had come to think that my little Seventy-seventh Street family and I would grow old together, and at one point we would be sitting at a pink hotel some-where in Florida sipping mint juleps (whatever they are) on a veranda and reminiscing about old times together.

Carl was strong at first but it's hard to watch the guy you love go down like that. Gregory had had unprotected sex when he worked at a bar when he was younger, and that's how it happened. But people just didn't know that there was a risk of AIDS then.

When folks ask me why I work for the community, I say it's because of my friends and my family. My work with the True Colors Fund—and my work with Colleen Jackson on the True Colors Residence, a shelter in Harlem that she had built for LGBT youth who have been kicked out by their parents—is, of course, directly related to all of them. How could it not be? (More on that later.)

I saw AIDS change and then debilitate friends, like my hair and makeup artist Patrick Lucas. He's still alive but he fights all the time because the disease doesn't make it easy and you have to take so many drugs. He once told me that the drugs are so hard that AIDS survivors say among themselves that this one or that one is dying of "old AIDS." Patrick was a huge part of the creation of my makeup and hair in the beginning. We would come up with these ideas and he would execute them to perfection. I'd say I wanted the checkered pattern on his shirt on my eyes and he would paint checkerboards on my lids. He also colored my hair for "Money Changes Everything" when we were on the road and I couldn't go to Vidal Sassoon. He made my roots blond and my ends red like a flame. He also did my makeup for the *Rolling Stone* cover. The two of us were in perfect sync. One of my eyes is shorter than the other, though, so I would drive him crazy about making them look the same.

AIDS also took my good friend Louis Falco, who created the choreography in the movie *Fame*. I hope that one of these years we'll wipe out the disease for good. But until then, I quote Nancy Cohen, former executive director of the MAC AIDS Fund and former head of the Viva Glam campaign to fight AIDS, who said, "AIDS is 100 percent preventable, and 100 percent noncurable." You can live with AIDS, but it ain't easy. And if AIDS don't kill ya, the meds can. So I'm committed to fighting it and committed to helping the LGBT kids who are on the street.

While Gregory was in the hospital, dying at the impossibly young age of twenty-seven, he asked that I write a song for him. He wanted me to release it in the spirit of "That's What Friends Are For." I thought, "What, like Burt Bacharach? Yikes, that is a tall order." Most of my life I've been able to deal with the notion that there will always be people who are better and greater than I am, but I can't concentrate on other people. So I wrote "Boy Blue." I poured out my heart, and my liver, into that song, but unfortunately it wasn't right for repetitive play on the radio. It was tangled up in so much of my sorrow and so cloaked in my sadness that I don't know if it was good enough for him.

And the True Colors Residence has a plaque on the building with a dedication on it to the memory of "Gregory Natal, Boy Blue." We couldn't save him, but maybe we'll save a few others. I've said it before: God loves all the flowers, even the wild ones that grow on the side of the highway.

CHAPTER NINE

In 1985, LIFE got weirder. Dave Wolff had heard that Steven Spielberg was doing a project with Huey Lewis, and he thought, "Well, why not do something with Cyndi?" Steven had written a new movie, *The Goonies*, which was a kind of a *Raiders of the Lost Ark*–style adventure film for kids. Richard Donner was going to be the director. And one day Dave came to me, all excited, and said, "Oh my God, we got a meeting with Steven Spielberg in LA. He wants you to do the soundtrack."

I was a little frightened. I'd never met him. I knew he was really creative and brilliant and I was such a huge fan but he was also, from what I'd heard, kind of a strange dude. And I was concerned about keeping the integrity of what I was doing. I wanted to stay true to the fan base that I had built.

It meant so much to me to meet Steven, but then when I got to his office in Hollywood, it seemed like such a sexist place. There were no women except this one producer named Terri, who was awesome. You can't believe how they were all talking about women; like they'd start talking about casting an actress and make gross comments about her body. It made me wonder, "What am I doing here?"

But we stood around and made small talk. At one point Steven said, "Streisand sang to me once." I thought to myself, "Yeah, but I'm here now. Maybe we could talk about that?" Then he ordered lobster for everyone for lunch, which seemed strange because it just delayed the meeting even more.

But then we finally started talking about the movie and how he was going to direct my music video for the soundtrack, which was so exciting. His idea was for me to perform in front of an old film projected onto a green screen behind me. I was crushed. What I should have said was something like, "You know, I came all this way to work with you, and I was just hoping to work with you on a real set—working on a green screen is kind of disheartening for me, even though it's you."

But did I say that? No. I just didn't know how to be diplomatic. So I blurted out, "That's not very creative." Everyone around me choked on their lobster. And of course, I just had to keep going, so I added, "Maybe we could do something a little more inspiring." And he got up and said, "I think I was told I wasn't creative." Then he said he wasn't going to work on the video anymore—I would work with Dick Donner. Fine, I said. And he walked out.

I never got to tell him what I really meant to say, but that's me: I always say the wrong things to the right people. I had no filter, and I was just thrown into these situations. I didn't know how to mix with the big guys. I only know how to do what I do. I don't have many famous friends. I work every day of my life—that's all I do. I live for my work.

And although at the time what I should have been working on was my next record, I threw myself into the *Goonies* soundtrack. I was working twelve-hour days in Los Angeles, living in motels and getting sad, because it was lonesome and LA was very cliquish. But I got all these artists like the Bangles and Teena Marie on the soundtrack, and it was going well until Spielberg went in and stripped most of the music from the film. Apparently he felt like there was too much music, so the soundtrack was meaningless because most of the songs weren't in the movie. The only thing that ended up in it was my voice here and there.

But we had a blast shooting a two-part video for the *Goonies* single, which no one had ever done before. I got all these wrestlers to be in it, like the Iron Sheik, Roddy Piper, "Classy" Freddie Blassie, and Andre the Giant (who saves the day at the end of part 2). The Bangles played pirates, and the night before the shoot, I dyed their hair crazy colors in the bathroom of the Sunset Marquis Hotel. There was an ant trail in the room, in a perfect line like a marching band—these were Catholic-school ants. The videos were a lot of work but I really cared about them. That was maybe the problem—I focused on each little thing I did too much, and it slowed things down and drove me crazy, but I couldn't help myself.

After the videos were done they wanted me to change the song title from "Good Enough" to "The Goonies 'R' Good Enough." And I didn't want to, because I thought if I put the word "Goonies" in, it would sound cheesy and no one would want to play it—and that's exactly what happened. Even though they squashed it on commercial radio, it became an underground hit, at least—because there are so many kids who are just Goonies. But I was so bothered that they ruined the name of that song that I refused to sing it for years. I finally started again a few years ago.

In the summer of 1985 I went to Nashville for a radio convention and that's when I found out I had endometriosis. I had a tumor in my stomach the size of a grapefruit, along with all these other little ones. I went into the hospital, and the doctors were saying scary things like "We need to operate now." But when they gave me the consent form they always give you to sign before you get operated on, outlining the potential risks and stuff, I went through it, saying, "I'm not doing this, I'm not doing this, and I'm not doing this." I said to this poor doctor, "I want you to write down exactly what you're going to do and initial it. You can take out all the endometriosis, but you can't take out anything else—not one tube, not one ovary, nothing." She said, "That's pretty severe—what if I have to save your life?"

I said, "Then wake me up." I was being cautious because my aunt went in to have a lump removed and they fuckin' took everything: her breast, the flesh under her arm. She was scarred for life. I don't think they ever saw a patient do what I did, but I knew what happened when you signed away your rights. I still held out hopes for having a kid, and I felt like, "This is my body." It sounds extreme but I had my own beliefs and convictions, and I was going to live by them—or die by them. So the doctor went in and took the endometriosis tissue out (there were no lasers back then) and there was a lot of scar tissue. I stayed in the hospital for at least a week, and then I was flown to Boston, where I was wheeled to a car. Dave took me to my friend and producer Lennie Petze's house on Cape Cod to recover. Lennie was so sweet and his whole family took me in.

After two weeks, when I was starting to walk, Bob Geldof invited me to participate in Live Aid. I really wanted to go, and Boy George was encouraging me, too, but at that point, my stomach was still distended and I could hardly pull myself up. It took a while to fully recover, and endometriosis caused me to be in and out of hospitals for the next few years.

After *The Goonies* sucked up so much of my time, and then my illness, I didn't even start working on my second album until the fall of 1985. And then I had another operation, and no one was supposed to know I was sick so it was very difficult because I had to first come back health-wise, to have the stamina to work on the album, and then get myself together creatively.

And then Gregory died.

He gave me his beaded Miss Piggy when he died. He loved Miss Piggy. Gregory and Carl bejeweled almost everything they touched—even me. After his funeral, Carl and I, Diana, and our friends Miss Aida and Bobby came back to my apartment in the Thread Building downtown. We were all dazed with grief, and then the piano tuner arrived. I was crying a bit—we all were—and through it all, there was the piano tuner tuning up the piano, note by note. It was the most bizarre thing, but I couldn't tell him to leave, because I needed the piano for work the next day.

It was the saddest time. But at that point, my album was late. So I had to get going on it. To me, music was this: You take everything in your life, you put it in your work, and then it transcends and transforms.

I was wearing black all the time then. I needed it to hold myself together emotionally while I was working. It was then that I heard a little song on a demo that Anne Murray had turned down. It was written by Billy Steinberg and Tom Kelly, and it was called "True Colors." It was kind of a country ballad with gospel overtones. I heard the lyrics and the melody and thought, "Well, if it's a kind of prayer to feel better, then it should be sung like one." So I asked Peter Wood (my keyboardist who also did a lot of arranging with me) to simplify the chords and play the kind of chords we play, which is open fifths, gently—we don't play every part of the chord. I wanted to sing it softly to Carl and all the folks who loved Gregory. I knew it was special, that it was a healing song, and I wanted us to heal a little.

As for the arrangement, it was important to create an archaic drum sound, to penetrate a person's inner being—to call out to that archaic imprint that was created when cavemen first heard a drumbeat. I sang the words almost in a whisper, and we kept the music spare because if the sentiment is that strong, you can't overdo it. I had to give the song depth so I could really speak to a person's soul (as opposed to singing my guts out, which would have been the easy way to go). I wanted to create an otherworldly feeling on the radio and I worked to make my voice sound like it was whispering in your ear, even if you were listening to it in the car. For that, we used a Dolby processor. It brings the air out and makes more of a *sssss* sound.

By singing quietly and using that effect, I tried to resonate with the smallest and most innocent part of a human being, to convey this heavy sentiment in the most delicate way I could. I used the power of being still and not singing out but singing in. From that experience, I learned that the weight of a feather sometimes can topple a mountain, a lesson I've remembered all my life.

We recorded the song live. I had many visions while I sang, one of which was of angels on the ceiling—the whiteness and the wings. I also saw the audience in front of me. With these visions surrounding me, I sang this healing song. I had to get out of my way and know that it was not about me. I had to stand there and wait for the spirits to come, and allow them to go through me. I always want to create music that beckons the spirits, whether it be rock or hip-hop or whatever it is. Some rappers smoke pot to put them in a state to make them them forget, so that they can remember—ya know what I mean?

Later, when "True Colors" came out, it was very hard to perform, because I'd be standing there in front of all these people who were keyed up, and I was keyed up too, and I'd have to sing from that place of emotion. When I did get to that place though, this radiance would come from my heart and travel to my arms and hands. It made a bow that encompassed me, like a hug, and it would go out in the world and do the same thing to the audience.

And when "True Colors" became a hit, I realized that I had fulfilled Gregory's dream—I sang something about him that became popular, like "That's What Friends Are For." I didn't know it would inspire so much activism until later on, in 1994, when I sang at the pier for Gay Pride in New York City. At rehearsal, when I was sound-checking the song, a sweet-looking man handed me a rainbow flag. He said he was inspired by the song to design it. When he told me that, you could have knocked me over with a feather. I wasn't sure if it was true, but I wrapped that flag around myself that night and told the crowd about how Gregory wanted a famous song for him—and this was the one. I saw him in my head so clearly. I sang into the breeze where I imagined he was and told him he got his wish because his community had taken the song I sang for him and for us. It had become an anthem. Ever since that night when I sang "True Colors," I never heard the song the same way. Not ever again. It had become a song of healing, of inspiration, for the community.

Originally I had talked with Rick Chertoff about producing my second album, but he wanted to control everything, while I wanted to coproduce, so that I could grow. So I ended up not working with Rick, and because I didn't work with him, I couldn't work with Rob Hyman, either, because they were affiliated. So there went the band and the sound that I created with them.

Anyway, for *True Colors*, I coproduced the album with Lennie and this time we hired session guys. I was always used to being in a band and felt amiss that I wasn't. And even though we were working with really good musicians, I didn't know how to articulate anything to them. I mean, I had Adrian Belew on guitar, who was the greatest player ever, and the fantastic Peter Wood, and Lennie brought in

Aimee Mann, who was on my label, to sing background. But you can't tell Adrian Belew to play like the Four Tops or get in the funk—it's Adrian Belew, motherfucker! He was in King Crimson! Get with the fuckin' program!

So I wrote with a bunch of different people and just felt kind of lost. When you're on the bottom and everything changes, it's good because it can only change from bad to good. But when you're on the top and everything changes, you worry that the other shoe will drop. But I wanted to continue my work. I didn't want to stop.

I teamed up with Tom Gray (he wrote "Money Changes Every-thing") and we started writing a song called "A Part Hate," because I felt strongly antiapartheid and was very upset about Nelson Man-dela's imprisonment. The problem was that I had also covered "What's Going On," because I loved Marvin Gaye. And with those two songs and the title track, all of a sudden *True Colors* became a very heavy, serious album. So the label didn't want "A Part Hate" on it because they thought it was too political.

I couldn't believe it. They said it was too much of a change—that the Girl Who Just Wanted to Have Fun couldn't suddenly become political. I said, "'Girls Just Want to Have Fun' *was* political—don't you get it?" They didn't. They were frightened. They were fuckin' pus-sies. They paid lip service to being politically aware, but they weren't really activists. So I couldn't put "A Part Hate" on *True Colors*. (In fact I didn't put it out for seven more years.) Me, I still believed rock and roll could change the world and I had seen how it had been done. I made a big impact on Japan and opened up their minds, and what I didn't do Madonna and Janet Jackson went in and did.

The label kept saying, "Where the hell is the *music* on the 'True Colors' single?" Because that single was very spare. I guess they wanted more upbeat pop. But you know what? Unlike a lot of people, I lived a lifetime before I was even twenty. And I had been through so much that year. I had been in the hospital; I almost thought I was going to die. No one at the label except Lennie knew I was sick. I should have let them know—let them feel like they were going to lose me. Then maybe they would have welcomed my second record a little more than they did instead of fighting me all the time. Of course, there were a few lighter moments on the album, too. Paul Reubens— you know, Pee-wee Herman—was a telephone operator on the track "911." We met in 1985 when he was the MC at the MTV New Year's Ball and we became fast friends. He was so easy to be with and funny and we had a similar sensibility. We would figure out things to do together on television, like we went miniature-golfing together on *Entertainment Tonight*. Then when he developed his own TV show, *Pee-wee's Playhouse*, he wanted me to sing the theme song. I told him I would, but I couldn't have it under my name because I was going to put out *True Colors*, which had a serious tone. In our superficial world, people couldn't accept both at the same time. So I sang the theme song using the pseudonym "Ellen Shaw." And then Paul sent me back a tape that was so hilariously funny, of me singing the theme with him in between saying, "Oh no! My career is ruined, oh no!" He's a nut. I love him.

Patti LaBelle, who had become a friend, was supposed to be on *True Colors*, too. But she wanted some royalties, and Lennie and Dave wouldn't do it. I didn't give a shit but then I agreed with them and I lost my chance to sing with my friend on a record.

I met her when I was in LA, when I went to one of her concerts after my "Fun" tour ended. I've always been a huge fan of her voice, and she was awesome, as usual. I got backstage and I remember sitting there just crying, because her performance was so moving. Then she invited me up onstage—talk about totally unprepared. I think she was doing "Stir It Up" and I ended up singing background. Then later I just started singing and jamming with her and we became friends.

Then she had a Thanksgiving TV special in 1985 and asked me to be on it. She invited some other people too, like Luther Vandross and Amy Grant. Poor Amy—she was like a deer in the headlights onstage. Patti can sometimes just run you down with her singing when she gets caught up.

On that special, when I heard Patti sing "Time After Time," it made me feel like, "Okay, I've arrived." We sang together: She called, I responded, and lucky for me I could do whatever she wanted me to. Until I did that special, I had no idea how my work actually affected the African-American community (I heard a lot that black radio was "not my market"). Years later I'd be on the street and African-American people would come up to me—postal workers, all kinds of people—and tell me that they remembered me from that special. That always moved me.

We also sang "Lady Marmalade" together. Like I said, in my first band, that was the go-to song if everything was going amok—my bandmates would go, "Get out there and sing 'Lady Marmalade'!" Being able to sing with someone whose songs I sang as a kid, whose voice I connected with, and who was singing one of my songs was one of the more remarkable moments of my career. That was a big one for me.

While I was finishing work on the album, Annie Leibovitz shot the album cover. I would go do shoots and come back and work on the album. I stayed up all night sometimes and then I'd work out because I had to look good. I tried not to eat past six P.M., ever, because I had lost a lot of weight when I was sick and wanted to keep it off.

Then we shot the video for "True Colors." The concept is that I'm a storyteller beating an African drum while a girl is shown moving through childhood and adulthood. A shell symbolizes the turning of the tides. The video and the song are about learning to love yourself and accept yourself. I was supposed to codirect it but once I put that stupid headdress on I couldn't even move. So Pat Birch, who also directed "Money Changes Everything," was the sole director.

And once again Dave was in the video. I wanted to show the spiritual connection between people and to convey an angelic vibe, so we became solarized when we kissed. (But I don't think I should have had him in that one scene with his bare chest, pulling the white sheet up from me like he did. Everyone made fun of him for that.)

When I had the *True Colors* listening party in New York, I invited a bunch of wrestlers, because they were part of my family, as fucked-up as they were. But the whole wrestling thing had gone to shit because Vince and the World Wrestling Federation crew had turned into these weird, greedy people who pushed Dave and me out, so not too long after the party, I decided to end the whole wrestling thing. I got a lot of shit for being involved in wrestling from the critics, because it wasn't serious. So somehow it made my music less serious. But I don't think that was the case at all and I stand by it.

After the album came out in late summer 1986, I went on *Late Night with David Letterman* again to sing "True Colors" and I was so freaked out. I kept thinking, "Oh my God, how am I going to perform? I have to win all these people over and I have to do it quietly, without singing my guts out." I remember my hair was bright yellow with some red extensions—it was very exciting. I had on a Vivienne Westwood skirt and a hat from the World's Fair and this really beautiful vintage cowboy shirt that was all kinds of green, so pretty.

To capture the spirit of the song, I made everything dark on the stage. And because it was a healing song, I held a little amethyst that was shaped like a heart in my hand, which I didn't show anybody. I was so frightened on that stage and holding on to that amethyst soothed me. And I went to a place that was otherworldly, that allowed me to express my message: You want to heal. Go *heal*. And so, I learned the power of a whisper.

People picked up on that message pretty quickly and the song went to number one. Starting with the "Girls Just Want to Have Fun" tour, some runaways started showing up on the road. They'd follow us in their cars and sometimes we'd take them in and feed them or talk to them. There was one I remember well: a fifteen-year-old girl named Donna who wanted to join our tour. Her parents were very strict, very Christian, especially her father, who was really radical. When you're like that, all you're going to do is chase your kids away. So our production manager, Robin Irvine, who was very kindhearted, brought her to my dressing room and told me, "You gotta talk to this kid." So I talked to her and she told me how her parents were so fucking strict and had forced all this Bible shit on her. I think the Bible is the raciest book you can freakin' buy. It's got murder, incest, rape, stoning, pillage, war—every kind of treacherous, horrible thing—with a very sexist tilt. Which is why I can't stomach reading it. (I'm like, "Are you kidding me? That's what you say about women?")

I was raised a Catholic, like I've said, and my mother was thrown out of the church because she was divorced. It kind of puts a damper on your opinion of the religion when they tell you your mother is going to go to hell, and they don't even know her. So when I was younger, I believed in that stuff with a grain of salt. I knew that there were people who used religion to control other people, and I decided a long time ago that that wasn't happening for me. I was eight around that time. (Yes, that young.) I follow my own basic code of conduct that can be found in every religion, but mostly it's a commonsense thing—do unto others as you would have them do unto you. I told Donna that she needed to communicate with her parents more and that when she was eighteen, she could live her own life. So I spent hours talking to Donna and let her stay the night, but then I sent her home. She was a kid. I met her again in the nineties and she was doing well.

But even though I had become an inspiration to others, I was still me. I still said the wrong things to the right people. For instance, the next spring, in 1987, Dave and I were invited to a seder in Los Angeles that was hosted by a couple of record-company guys, including CBS Records executive Walter Yetnikoff. There were a bunch of famous people there, and power brokers with their trophy wives who barely spoke (and when they did it was about their husbands). It was hellish because I had to sit with people whose values were so dynamically different from mine. They were so Republican that I wanted to kill myself. I definitely felt the hierarchy of who was who. The husbands were all kowtowing to Walter so they wouldn't get stepped on by him in front of everyone. That year the seder fell on Easter Sunday and I was sitting there thinking, "This is how we're spending Easter?"

Conversation included subjects like Warren Beatty only giving parts to women who gave him a blow job. I thought, "Has every woman gone completely nuts?" Then Julio Iglesias leaned in close and said to me, "You are so clever, but you do not like me." I was like, "Hon, I don't not like you, you seem like a nice fellow, but why are you hitting on me when you can see I've got a guy here?"

I also saw Bruce Springsteen and his new wife Julianne Phillips, the actress/model who had no career after him. Big mistake to marry him. Big fuckin' mistake! She was going somewhere, and after that relationship, not so much. I always say, "See a famous man, run the other way." The only person who was never hurt by being with a famous man was Madonna.

I was so relieved to see Bruce. I went over to him and said, "Oh my God, I can't even believe I'm here, I don't know these people. The women just talk when they're spoken to and when they do talk, it's just about their husbands." Julianne nodded and said, "Yeah, I know." But Springsteen just gave me a dirty look. He might as well have taken a fuckin' knife and cut my heart out because at that moment, I thought, "*Et tu*, Bruce-ay?" And then I felt so duped that I became the annoying American to him because I thought that was the worst thing I could do to get even. Like the person you want to get rid of but you can't lose and they talk too close and say obnoxious things and they don't stop. I'm the kind of person who if I know you don't like me and I think you're being a shit about it, I'm going to get even closer just to fuckin' upset you. And if you get upset I turn it up even more.

Bruce obviously wanted nothing to do with me, so that's exactly what I did. Bruce was sitting at a table, so I stood at the edge and said, loud enough for everyone to hear, "Bruce, why don't you do a duet with Placido Domingo? You and Placido could do 'Born to Run' together." At the time, they were pairing up strange people to do duets so they could sell a bunch of records. I just wanted to annoy him, and it worked. He hated me, and I gave it to him tooth and fuckin' nail because I felt in my heart, "How could you pretend to be okay with these people?" In the seventies, while I was a housekeeper or a mother's helper making beds, I sang along with him on the radio. I heard the way he wrote and sang about women and knew that he understood them—understood us. Instead it was like he condoned that whole horrible, sexist scene. Patti Scialfa, his current wife, is very intelligent. Not a bimbo. Not that Julianne Phillips was a bimbo— I just thought there wasn't enough light for the both of them.

I haven't run into Bruce since then. I don't want to meet anybody anymore. I don't want to know what people are like beyond their art.

When you meet somebody and they're wonderful, it's such a genuine surprise and it's so nice. But I don't want to be disappointed. It's too much. And that extends to me, too. That's why I tell people, "Listen, don't confuse my work with who I am, because you'll be disappointed." I've tried my best to do good work and good things, but I'm not necessarily always fantastic as a person, and like I've been saying, I do and say a lot of things that are wrong. I'm human. But that's not what a fan thinks. I know, because I've been that fan.

CHAPTER TEN

I STARTED GETTING SCRIPTS from movie companies, because at the time they were really gunning for pop singers like Madonna to star in films. They wanted me to be in *Girls Just Want to Have Fun*—remember that one, with Sarah Jessica Parker? It was about girls who enter a dance competition. When I read the script I thought, "How dare you take what I've done, dress characters up like me, and then write this stupid, inane script about nothing, when everything I've struggled to do was about something?" I couldn't believe it.

Then I got a call to do a movie called *Vibes*, which was a Ron Howard film. I was—and am—such a huge fan of his. I thought it was awesome the way he used actors like Don Ameche and Hume Cronyn in *Cocoon*. But I said, "Listen, I would love to do the movie, but I may actually suck. So why don't you do a screen test and see if I'm good enough? The last thing I want to do is be in a movie and stink." They said okay, and Ron Howard came to see me in my New York City apartment. He was so nice and down-to-earth. When I was doing the screen test, I kept thinking, "Oh my God, I'm being directed by Ron Howard."

I mean, I had no acting experience aside from my videos. I just listened to everything he said, did what he told me, and he liked it. He made me watch it, too, and I didn't think I looked terrible on-screen. So I signed up to do the movie. I played a psychic named Sylvia, who, with another psychic (to be played by Dan Aykroyd), gets hired by a rich guy to find his son in South America. But as it turns out, we're really hired to find a hidden Incan treasure where all the world's psychic energy comes from. To me, right off the bat, that was so much fun.

I tried to figure out what the hell this girl Sylvia would look like. She was a beautician as well as a psychic, and she was supposed to have pink hair—like, you know those girls who mean to bleach their hair blond but turn it pink? I fell asleep after I bleached it though, and my hair turned white and kind of burned off in spots, so I couldn't process it again to turn it a different color. So I just let it be white-blond. And then I saw that Madonna was doing a movie called *Who's That Girl* and she was a bleached blonde too. I was like, "Okay—nice. We can never get away from each other."

On the topic of hair dye, I knew about it: I've been dyeing my hair since I was probably nine, when I used food coloring to make it green for Saint Patrick's Day. Then at twelve, I used Sun-In, then Nice 'n Easy, before I moved on to the hard stuff. I once tried to dye it back to brown—my natural color—but it turned red by mistake. I liked it though, so I kept it.

I wanted to be good in the movie, so I took classes at a beauty school to learn how to do finger waves and brush up on my other beautician skills. I also started to study with psychics to find out how they did their thing. They all told me, "You are going to be a spiritual leader," and I thought, "I sincerely doubt that. I won't be doing any yogi whatever any time soon."

I met this one psychic, Ginny Duffy, who my vocal teacher and friend introduced me to when I told her I was studying psychics. Ginny was different from the others because she did past-life regression, where you use hypnosis to recover what they believe are memories of past lives. Ginny connected people to their angels, too. I used some of her mannerisms when I was communicating on-screen with the spirits.

I was always having interesting dreams that seemed to dip into my own past lives, so the whole idea of it didn't seem that outlandish to me. Like once when I was sleeping next to Dave Wolff I dreamed that I was a contessa in the New World, in a very hot place, and I rode in a carriage up to a fortress. When I got out to walk, I was smaller than normal. Then someone grabbed me, a kind of dark Zorro figure—it was Dave. Another time I dreamed that I was Dutch, from another time, and I had gotten a small army to chase this rascal thief but I really liked him—that's why I was chasing him. Again, when I woke up, I realized it was Dave. So then I thought, "Okay—past-life regression, that's interesting." That's how my head was explaining everything. I was always drawn to the fact that Dave was a rascal who could talk you into anything.

Ginny also connected me to spirit guides—entities who teach, heal, and help you on your journey into spiritual awareness—and that influenced me a lot. In fact for the next decade, I was very connected to another level of consciousness and became a more spiritual person. I remember when I was promoting *True Colors*, I met a kid through the Make-A-Wish Foundation who had spina bifida. He was around twelve or thirteen and in a fucking wheelchair; he couldn't even move. And I kept saying, "Why, God? Why come to me? I can't fix him. I can't do anything for this kid." It really bugged me, and then I figured out a way to help all these kids that wouldn't be overbearing. Ginny did this thing called Reiki, a Japanese technique using touch to reduce stress and promote healing. So I studied it, because I thought it would be a good thing to learn, because when I performed for kids they always touched my feet and I always liked to hold their hands. I felt that if I studied Reiki, I would be able to give them healing energy, something more than just entertainment—something that would really make them feel better.

The movie company also gave me this acting coach who was amazing. Her name was Sondra Lee and she was a kind, wonderful teacher who really guided me. Sondra was an actress all through the fifties and sixties. She played Tiger Lily in *Peter Pan* and the young girl at the party in *La Dolce Vita*. In her 2009 memoir, *I've Slept with Everybody*, she said she lost her virginity to Marlon Brando—can ya imagine?

Anyway—as it turned out, Dan Aykroyd liked me but felt uneasy about my acting abilities. We did a reading together, where we rehearsed the script, and I was struggling, thinking, "Am I supposed to read it like I'm acting or am I supposed to read it with no feeling?" I was totally green, and nobody told me how to do it. And when Dan saw what I did, I guess he felt my approach was just wrong and he kept saying, "How are you going to talk to your spirit guide?" I couldn't answer him at first because I was lost in the script, and I could tell he felt like I didn't have a clue. He became uneasy about working opposite me, which I understood, but what he didn't realize is how much I always learn on my feet. For instance, I remember once I went to perform without my band and I had to learn how to play "Money Changes Everything" on melodica. In the end I learned the part, but it's always nerve-wracking for everyone around me to watch me try to figure it out. Like, recently I played "True Colors" on the biggest morning show in Japan, and I had to figure out how to play it on dulcimer on the way to the TV station. The Japanese TV promotion guy was there watching me and getting unbelievably nervous, going, "Oh my God, does she know the song?" But I did it. Even though it's sometimes last-minute and drives everyone crazy, I'm usually able to figure it out.

Anyway, so it's understandable that Dan Aykroyd felt that way. For whatever reason, Dan decided to drop out, and Jeff Goldblum was in. Then all of a sudden instead of Ron Howard directing, they took on this other guy whose big motion picture was *Follow That Bird*. So, I was being directed by Big Bird's director. Which kind of made me feel like Big Bird. (I kept thinking to myself, "Just make sure your hair's not too big.") We started filming in California in February of 1987 and went through the summer and fall, including two weeks in Ecuador.

Unfortunately, Jeff Goldblum, who I just figured would be easy to work with, turned out to be a little different and did things that I felt were really upsetting. I don't know why he had to be that way, but he was really awful. He was a strange fellow who, if he knew what you were going to do on-screen, would do something to stop you from doing it. Like we did a love scene, and suddenly he put his big fat hands all over my face. So I took his hands and pulled them down, and he got all upset. I said, "Let me tell you something—I don't like nobody touching my face, okay? That's one big no-no." He also had some sort of odd acting process where before he went into a scene, he would flip through a book, quietly rant, and get twitchy, like he was having a nervous breakdown. Well, one time we had a scene with this older character actor named Bill McCutcheon, who played the museum curator. Before we got going, Jeff stood there and did his whole nervous-breakdown thing again. I asked Bill, "Do you find this very distracting?" He said that every time Jeff did that, he couldn't remember his lines.

So I turned around and said to Jeff, "Look, I can see you got your whole process here going on. I respect it, but do me a favor, take a fuckin' walk to have your nervous breakdown, and then when we start the scene, come back here. Because you're distracting this guy, and you're distracting me. Okay? And I'll tell you something else: If you keep doing this, this movie won't be a murder mystery anymore, because I'll kill you right here in front of everybody." Everyone sort of took a step back. But you know what? Some people push you and push you, and they expect you not to say anything. Well, it ain't gonna happen with me. I'm always going to say something. And when I get angry, I get arrogant. Arrogance is probably my biggest fault.

Jeff was an interesting guy, and filming the movie could have been really great. You'd think we would have gotten along. I mean, he's an art dude. I'm sure he felt like, who the hell was I to have a lead in a movie when he worked all his life to get acting jobs? But he was the other lead, so what was the problem? Maybe something was going on in his life. His behavior seemed to reflect some kind of emotional frailty, but I couldn't understand what was making him unhappy. At the time, he was with the most rockin' chick, actress Geena Davis. I thought she was awesome. She taught me a Swedish song that I sing in the movie, because she has a Swedish background.

Anyway, I fought to get Peter Falk hired as the third lead because I thought it would look good to have two guys with dark hair next to my light hair, and we speak in the same rhythm, but when he showed up on set, I found out he was a little eccentric. Like the camera operator would call me over and say, "Cyn, I got a nice light on you. Hit that mark and do that line for me." Then Peter would come up and say, "Don't listen to him. You don't have to hit the mark. Just do it." I'd think, "But if he took the time to light me and position everything, shouldn't I stay on the spot?" But acting with Peter Falk was extraordinary, as crazy as he was.

Other crazy things happened on the set too. Like one time, a producer came down and I heard him say, "Would you fuck her? Is she fuckable?" Or sometimes I'd start to work and one of the producers would get right in my eye line, looking right at me, watching, while the camera was on. It was incredibly distracting and strange, so then I'd have to say, "He's right in my eye line—hey, could you not do that?" Then this whole time Jeff was going through whatever it was he was going through. And Peter Falk—this totally anarchist rebellion guy who I adored in the end—teamed up with Jeff against me. I was heartbroken that they shut me out. But maybe that was better for the role—you know what I mean? My character was supposed to have a little tension with Jeff.

The power struggle and the trauma that went on underneath the movie overtook what could have been a fun and happy, funny film. You know how I talked about how you want to create music that will beckon the spirit? I always thought that acting was going to be similar to that; it would be like call-and-response—someone would say something to you, and you would respond, right? Make a connection? Not. At the time that I started to work in film, acting became about the close-up and about these actors who basically seemed to want to act alone. There was no sense of unity, and it was really disheartening for me because that's what I was used to as a musician. I wanted them to be my friends but instead they were competitive assholes and I just couldn't help but think, "I did this so I could work with Ron Howard, and he's not even here, he's working in New Zealand, and I wish I was in New Zealand, too, instead of here."

Not everybody was that way, though. The costume designer and the makeup and hair people were wonderful. And the woman who sewed the outfits was incredible. I learned so much from her, and from the camera and lighting guys. I always would watch them if I could, so I could see the monitor that they looked at, because that was the place that you were going to step into, and it was always magical. When you stepped into it, you became the picture and that was like painting. It was just like when you're framing for when you paint a picture. I was so excited about absorbing everything on the set that it made everything kind of bearable.

And there was plenty of stuff that was pretty unbearable, like when the film's writer wanted me to take my clothes off in one scene. I said, "First of all, I don't have that kind of figure. And second of all, why don't you have a guy take his clothes off?" I finally figured out that I could wear a camisole thing so that I looked kind of cute and naked, but not completely naked. And I loved doing physical comedy. Like in one scene I went into a trance and started singing, and Jeff and Peter picked me up and carried me out while I was still singing. I tried really hard to stay absolutely stiff. I loved it because it was like a Marx Brothers routine. You know what else was nice? I got a cat while I was filming—my wonderful cat Nick, who gave me many years of joy and love.

Unfortunately while working on the movie, I got endometriosis again, so I had another operation in Los Angeles. And then Columbia Pictures, the movie company, wanted me to write a song for *Vibes*, so I stayed in LA to figure out what I was going to write. At first I wrote a slower-tempo song called "Unconditional Love" with Billy Steinberg and Tom Kelly, but the head of Columbia said, "This movie is a comedy—you can't have a ballad." So Dave Wolff proposed that I do "Hole in My Heart (All the Way to China)," which was written by a guy named Richard Orange. I said, "But this film isn't about China." He said, "Yes, but that's the joke. It's so nutty." So I rearranged the song and made it sound like the music I liked—kind of punk and tough and fast. But when it was released, radio stations felt it was too hard for them, and they wouldn't play it. They were much more into playing ballads. And here's the thing: They would have played "Unconditional Love." Every time I failed, it was because I didn't listen to my initial gut feeling and instead tried to appease other people. (That's why when I met Lady Gaga to do MAC's Viva Glam campaign, I said to her, "Don't listen to anybody. Whatever creation you have in your head, do it, because now is your time, and if you give it up, you're not going to be able to do it.")

When *Vibes* came out in 1988, they killed me in the reviews. They called it *Bad Vibes* and said my career would never recover. But now when I look at the movie, honestly, I don't think I was bad. To tell you the truth, I really think I did a good job. My acting was very natural. The movie had a lilt to it, it wasn't stiff, it was really entertaining, and it had heart. It was funny and quirky. It wasn't supposed to be Shakespeare. It was just supposed to be a lighthearted comedy, a little somethin' somethin' to get your mind off your humdrum day. You know? But the movie was a flop in every way. Probably I was never meant to work in movies. I was meant to walk the path I'm walking. But *Vibes* really hurt my career, which some people would take in stride, but I couldn't. And it affected my relationship with Dave as well, because he wasn't just my boyfriend, he was my manager.

And while *True Colors* went to number four on the album charts, the record company wasn't happy that it only sold three million copies. The title track was a number one single, and "Change of Heart" was number five, and "What's Going On" went to number twelve. That one didn't do as well as it should have. When I promoted it on the radio, I said that if Marvin Gaye had a wife who promoted his music like Yoko Ono promoted John Lennon's we would remember "What's Going On" as much as we remember "Imagine." Obviously, that came out more abrasive than I meant it. I always felt that people didn't care enough about Marvin, because the drugs had taken him over and maybe turned him into a person who wasn't Marvin anymore. The man could sing and write, though, I can tell you that.

I had to visit radio stations all over the place and do special events for them. I busted ass, and it cost money to do everything, but they didn't pay for a thing. I had to do it though—otherwise, I'd be on the shit list. I also had a long list of stations to call, and every fifteen minutes I'd call another one. That would go on for a couple of hours. In the morning, I'd talk to deejays who were trying to be funny because their listeners were just getting up and grumpy. And because some of the deejays had been awake since three A.M., they were grouchy, too, and they would say stupid things because they were winging it. A lot of them had a bug up their ass and were nasty about having to push my album. And because I never had a filter, I'd be nasty back. It was not a great situation. I still call up radio stations, but before I call anybody, I make sure they want to talk to me and I build in some breaks.

The first "True Colors" tour didn't sell as well as the "Fun" tour, either. I felt really bad about that, even though a lot of people weren't selling tickets in the winter of 1986. And on top of that, my accountant told me I couldn't go into the audiences anymore because I could be sued. So all of a sudden there was a barrier between me, "the star," and "the people," and that was the point of seeing me—that there was no barrier.

I decided that if I couldn't touch the audience, then I'd try to touch them visually and make colors across the stage. So I wore clothes that had one color on top and layered it with more color underneath. As I swirled, other colors popped out, so I painted as I sang. And I moved more, and I sang my ass off. I tried really hard, but I had the sophomore slump. I remember Jon Pareles of the *New York Times* did an article comparing me again to Madonna and how I was going to do better than her, and blah blah blah. I didn't think that was such a good idea because you never know what will happen. And after *True Colors*, Madonna proved him wrong. She is brilliant at selling, and she didn't fight her record company the way I did. I think the secret behind her success is that she would find someone who was really successful at what she wanted to do—a writer or a producer—and do it with them. I never did that. I never wanted to call up people I didn't know. And she also had Warner Bros., and their VP Seymour Stein, behind her fighting the fight with her, and I just didn't get that kind of support from my label. I was always fighting *with* them. Even Dave got caught up in the "Madonna rivalry." One time he said, "Don't you want to compete with Madonna?" I couldn't believe it. I was just trying to stay focused and do my own thing.

Then Don Dempsey, general manager of Epic, was fired, and I was devastated, because I loved him and he was a big supporter of mine. I remember one time in the beginning of my solo career, in 1983, I had to have a promotional dinner in the south of France and I was sitting at the table and didn't know how to behave. He said, "Eat to the left, drink to the right." (He also pointed to one of his ears and said, "I'm deaf in this ear, but you'll notice that sometimes I put people who talk the most on this side, and I just nod.") I started to get really disillusioned with record companies when he was fired. There was a lot of changeover at Epic because Sony was buying CBS and Epic was under that whole umbrella. In the meantime, Dave Wolff was feeling a lot of pressure to make me successful because now that Don was out and Al Teller was in, everybody had something to say about my career. It was not a great atmosphere.

They were all trying to control me and I didn't want everybody telling me "Do this, do that." I was a little full of myself, too—as we all get when we get famous. I was so frustrated that I couldn't go out because Dave Wolff was afraid of me being alone, and when I did, I was impatient. I never called before going to restaurants and then I'd get mad if they couldn't seat me.

And as my relationship with the record company was getting more tense, things were getting more tense at home. Dave had done a real good job of keeping me isolated. That was his method: Keep Cyndi so busy that she never knows what is going on. Even at the height of my fame, when I would hang out with my friend Katie Valk, it would torture Dave. He would call her and ask, "Are you guys okay? What are you doing now?" He'd make calls like that a lot. For instance, if I was working with people in the studio, he'd call the producer and say, "How did she do today?" As opposed to calling and asking me directly.

That's how he controlled me. And that was frustrating because my whole life had been an adventure and now I was trapped like a bird in a cage. I believe that he didn't mean it in a bad way. But I guess in his mind, I was out of control because I had a vision of what I wanted to look like, sound like, and be like. And as we started to grow apart, there was a power struggle. When I was promoting *True Colors* on TV, he liked to have me say that we were engaged but that we weren't going to get married until I was really successful, because he thought it was funny. I went along with the joke but I felt it was very humiliating. Yeah, yeah—the joke's on me. And it only added to the pressure that he was feeling because of the new crop of muckety-mucks he had to deal with at the record company.

And there was also tension between Walter Yetnikoff and Al Teller, who was the president of CBS. Lennie felt that Tommy Mottola would be a better fit for us and Sony because he was a manager and he knew artists and he would be more personable. So somehow Dave, Lennie, and Tommy orchestrated this meeting between Walter and Tommy so that they could bond, and hopefully Tommy could take over for Al when Walter got rid of him, which was looking like a possibility. By then, we had had a long history with Tommy. The idea was for all of us to stay at our house on Cape Cod, which I had bought in 1985. It wasn't that big; it was just a regular house in a nice upper-middle-class neighborhood. It had a dock that I never fixed up, and we got a speedboat that Dave wanted, but he didn't know how to drive it. (When I got some money I decided to buy some real estate: that house, a little piece of land on Cape Cod, and the downtown apartment in New York.)

The house wasn't fixed up, so I had to scramble to do it real quick because everybody was coming in a couple of days. That's my life: I have these bigwigs and their wives coming over for a big shindig and I'm driving around with the neighbor kid picking up furniture. And all I kept hearing on the radio was U2's "I Still Haven't Found What I'm Looking For," and I kept thinking, "Yeah, you could say that again. I need a sofa." I was in such a hurry that I'd just go into a store and say, "I love what's in your window—can I buy it?"

Plus my cat Skeezicks kept pissing on the comforter upstairs where Walter was going to sleep and then she disappeared. I found her burrowed into the wall of the house. I should have realized then that if the cat was pissing on the comforter this wasn't a good idea, but no, I just kept going along, trying to get everything ready for them.

When everybody showed up, I tried to treat Walter like a regular person. I took him out on the boat and scooted around the bay with him so he could forget about everything for a minute and just be a person.

Tommy Mottola brought the two little kids he had with his first wife, and when we were on the beach, Lennie's wife, who was very good with kids, turned around to the one named Michael and said, "And what do you want to be when you grow up?" He said, "I'm going to be my mother's lawyer." He was maybe eight years old. I was like, "Okay, I guess things are rocky at home." By that time, Tommy had discovered Mariah Carey.

Well, the get-together turned out to be successful because Tommy got the gig at my house. Afterward, I rued the day. You can't get involved with this shit because these people are very dog-eat-dog. Walter had an idea to separate CBS broadcasting from CBS music but he needed someone to buy the music division from Larry Tisch, the CEO of CBS (he didn't even like music). Walter wanted to have the Sony executives run things instead and he felt that I would be the perfect person to build up relations with the Sony executives from Japan—working as I did in the Japanese piano bars. So I schmoozed and took a photo with Akio Morita, the cofounder of Sony and inventor of the Sony Walkman, for the cover of *Time* magazine in 1988 for an article they did. I was being a good soldier. Then as time went on Walter and Tommy had a rift. We sided with Walter, which was a whole big mistake, because after that my life went to shit.

Tommy never forgot and never forgave what we did for Walter, and when he took over, the word at the label was that my stuff was being put on the back burner and that it wasn't going to be promoted like it had been. At that point, I should have walked and contacted Seymour Stein, but he already had his girl. Don Dempsey had really understood the qualities that made me famous, and after that, I had all these knuckleheads come in and tell me things like I should dress like Katrina of Katrina and the Waves. One time I had a meeting with Tommy about my musical direction, and he said, "What records do you like that are on the charts?" I picked out the cool stuff, like what U2 was doing. Then he fuckin' said I had to work with this other guy who used to be in Canned Heat! And then the head of A & R—Don Grierson, a nice guy, but he didn't have much of an artistic thing going on—kept trying to make me into Heart. I was like, "I've already been in a cover band, thank you very much, and have no intention of doing it again." Then one of the new heads at Sony turned to me in a meeting and said, "What is that you're wearing?" I thought to myself, "Are you kidding me?" I should have said, "This is what your daughter is going to wear next year."

All of them were trying to remake me after the perceived lack of success of *True Colors*, and I didn't want to be remade, I wanted to do what I did. But because they thought they were more important than the artist, they wanted to make the sounds, and I didn't want to be part of that machine. I wanted out of my contract, but if I sued my label like George Michael did, I would lose, and if I made a record, I'd have to put up with one knucklehead after the other, and I was incredibly frustrated and depressed. Let me tell ya, it was not a good situation.

In the meantime, *True Colors* was nominated for a Grammy for Best Female Pop Vocal Performance, but Barbra Streisand had her big comeback with *The Broadway Album*, and she won. I was always put against the comeback people, like Tina Turner two years before. I don't know—I think it's my karma. I'd rather be awarded for my work than for sentimental reasons. Or maybe it's God telling me that it's nice to be recognized but awards don't make the person or the singer.

And then while all this bad stuff was happening, I was talking to Dave about our plan to get married. We had talked about it for a while. I had the engagement ring on my hand. And my manager, who was also my boyfriend since 1982, said to me, "I don't want to get married on this downswing here. I'd rather get married when we're doing better."

CHAPTER ELEVEN

THE ENGAGEMENT RING Dave gave me was a yellow canary diamond. I saved that yellow canary diamond ring for a long time, but it might as well have just been a gold watch for ten years of service. Dave wasn't going to get married. I wanted the picket fence: I wanted a piano in the living room, everybody sitting together on holidays with dogs and cats, playing music, singing, laughing, eating, drinking. Even if it was some kind of fantasy, I wanted that.

Dave and I would talk about our future together, and he wouldn't actually say he *didn't* want it. He would always just say, "One day we'll have this," and "One day we'll have that." I remember that when he said that one time, I looked at him and thought, "*One day?* What about now?" And I had begun to think about having a kid. Three generations of people would come to my concerts, and the little kids would come dressed like that punky girl from the Art of Noise video that I mentioned earlier. I would see them and think, "Look at them— they're going to grow up listening to my music. In a way, I'm raising them. So why can't I have my own kid?"

But Dave wasn't into the idea, because how would we live our lifestyle while I was pregnant? And also, I wasn't famous until I was

191

thirty, so I was older, which could present some problems (his mother always held that over him). And God knows what else he had lurking in the back of his head. He loved us jumping in and out of limos and being "the couple."

Well, that was what he loved in public. At home, he'd play video games all the time and shut me out. He needed to unwind because work was such a pressure cooker. He was caught between a woman who wanted things her own way and a record company that changed hands among the biggest, most sexist, most macho guys in the world who married trophy wives—women who shut the fuck up because the man is king.

During the late eighties, all of these powerful men seemed wildly out of control. So many of them were on coke, and everyone was sexist. It was really fucked-up and I had a hard time dealing with that shit. I was surrounded by it—surrounded by men. And I had gotten sick again and had yet another operation.

I did not fit in anymore at Sony, and Dave and I weren't fitting, either. I'd cry all the time because I couldn't believe how we had grown apart. And the record company was torturing him. They'd say, "You're the man—*you* tell her what to do." Like, "You're the man of the house, why can't you control her?" I knew it was the end when he and I were having a fight and he said, "They're right. You shouldn't make your own decisions." I was a famous woman at that point. I looked at him and thought: *"Wrong answer!"* But I just said, "Okay, that's it." It was the saddest thing in the world for me, because I loved him. Those interfering record company guys really broke us up—they were just pigs, thick-headed with gold chains and hair coming out of their fuckin' shirts, white shoes, and those fuckin' golf pants—really wrong, you know what I'm saying?

The breakup with Dave took a long time. My relationship and my work had been everything to me, and I always thought that if I only tried harder, I could overcome the trouble. The truth is, hard work couldn't overcome it; it just went too deep. And in the meantime I had Sony breathing down my neck. I originally wanted my third album to be a project called *Kindred Spirit* that was inspired by an old recording. This recording made you feel like you were stepping into another time. I was very much taken with the otherworldliness of it (time being a rubbery thing, anyway). I wanted to create the same kind of feeling on my record, so that's why the song "Kindred Spirit," which did make it onto the record, had that old scratchy sound. I played a dulcimer (which I had taught myself) and my voice sounded like it was from another time, too.

I wanted the album to be called *Kindred Spirit* because all those old recordings were kindred spirits. But the label, big surprise, was more interested in commerce than in art. There's a way to mix the two, but I never did it the right way. I just thought about the art and the magic of the music.

And then what happened was, they switched label heads again. The new guy in charge just loved Diane Warren, who had written so many hits, like "If I Could Turn Back Time" for Cher and "I Get Weak" for Belinda Carlisle. She had originally written a song called "I Don't Want to Be Your Friend" for Heart, and they brought it to me. But I didn't want to sing like Heart. Like I said, I wasn't in a cover band anymore. So I took it and lowered the key and had the zydeco player Rockin' Dopsie play button accordion, and I made it into a Cajun march. Then I also got Baghiti Khumalo, the South African bass player who worked with Paul Simon, to play on that track, so it had a sort of New Orleans jazz-funeral sound. And Phil Ramone helped me produce that track (I think it's a beautiful rendition, but apparently Diane later called up the record company and bitterly complained about it).

In the late eighties, the A & R guy was the genius, not the artist, and because the album wasn't their creation, and because I wasn't doing exactly what those knuckleheads wanted, it was wrong. Lennie and Eric Thorngren, the poor guy who was producing and arranging some of the tracks with me, kept looking at me and going, "Cyn, what's wrong with you? You're the Vinnie van Gogh of rock, do your thing, don't listen to them, come on!" But I was so used to being a good soldier that I didn't know when to say enough was enough (even now, that happens).

At one point some of the Sony executives even made a special trip from Japan to meet with me. They took me to dinner and said, "Cyndi, we believe in you, and we want you to make music again." But nobody in New York said that to me. There was no communication. So I tried for a more commercial album and did 1989's *A Night to Remember*. Which I call *A Night to Forget*, because it was one of those albums destined to be doomed because the record company was changing again. Then Lennie fell on his boat and broke his leg and was in the hospital. After that he left the company, which was devastating to me. So I had to deal with the new heads of state. I couldn't please the new A & R guy. No matter what I played for him he said, "That's nice ear candy." Never "Oh, that's a good song," or "That's catchy." I'd be like, "Fuck you and your ear candy." With all of them, I really felt like I wanted to say, "Get out of my face." And the whole time I was breaking up with Dave.

I should have gotten out when that record executive asked, "What are you wearing?" He was in his own private Idaho. They wanted me to conform, and unfortunately they hired a nonconformist. You can't get a chicken and turn it into a duck. The corporate world was standing on top of everything and that's why the music went south. If you look at music in the early eighties, it was artist generated. So were the looks. The company didn't say to Flock of Seagulls, "Why don't you wear your hair like that?" That came from the band.

In the studio, I was stuck with this guy Lennie had hired who was a total alcoholic. It was so awful that even the musicians were looking at me going, "Cyn, this guy, he's drinking at fuckin' ten in the morning." And I couldn't get him to do anything because he had his own opinions. At one point he was talking about the sound of something, and he said, "It's just a cunt-hair off." Big surprise that I took real offense to that. I was like, "You know what? I'm paying you to collaborate with me, and I don't want to be talked to like that." And while I was trying to make the record, the promotion staff was *in the studio*. Imagine having the promotion staff in there telling you what to do while you're trying to make music! The atmosphere got so bad that I had to stop production. I had heard about this event in Russia, a kind of writing summit between Russian and American songwriters, so I decided to go.

The Soviet Union in 1989 was a real different place from what Russia is now. I took bottled water with me, and toilet paper. I was also careful about sitting on the toilet because the toilet was one length and the toilet seat was another. And I felt like I was being spied on all the time, so I used to try to look good when I got into the tub at the American Hotel, where I stayed. Then I remember I lost something, jewelry maybe, and I couldn't find it, so I said out loud, "Where is it? I know somebody took it. It was right here." And then later, after the maids came in, it was back on my bed. That's how I knew everything was bugged.

Russia was a strange place, because it was so hard to do what you loved to do. People just wanted to create, but at that point, it was against the law to make a video (and some of those musicians were dying to make videos). There were a lot of really fantastic underground bands.

Dave Wolff was still my manager so he came with me, even though we weren't together anymore. But he didn't come along when some of us took a trip on the midnight train to Leningrad and I ended up sitting next to an Italian guy from Jersey. Laura Wills, my stylist and friend from Screaming Mimi's, was with me, and she started calling him "French Fry," so I called him that too, and the name stuck. We were all feeling pretty loose, because we were all artists and that's the way artists are. Anyway, French Fry was so funny. He had pockmarks on his face, but he had touched them up on his passport. He kept making me laugh, and one thing led to another and we had a little affair. While I was doing that, everybody else was having their little flirtatious moments, too. (Diane Warren was on the trip, and even though I was mad at her because she badmouthed my version of "I Don't Want to Be Your Friend," I gotta say, she was funny and she was after the Secret Service guy. She thought he was cute.)

I also met this Russian guy Igor, who was a riot. He took me all over the place to sightsee and Laura was always looking for me (David made her responsible for me). I think Igor had a crush on me. I remember I had brought food from a health-food store at home and Laura goes, "There's no food here, and you bring over food that tastes like dirt?" Which was true—I did. In Russia, you could choose between mystery meat in gelatin or caviar, which made your tongue swollen, but to them, that was very expensive food. Listen, they gave us the best of what they had. They were really very sweet to me, these big, burly guys, even though they weren't used to women doing this kind of work. There wasn't much drinking water available so they kept saying to me, "Drink this. Vodka."

I was there for two weeks, and the trip woke me up a little. I had a moment of clarity when I was on that train. I was really, really lonely and Dave had already left to go back to the US I looked at the tracks and I thought, "Why don't you just kill yourself? You thought that this would be the pinnacle of your life, and now where are you?" I was so tired of being told what I couldn't do by the record company, of being isolated and having people tell me what they thought I was. My relationship was ending. The movie I had done flopped. I was like, "I can't take this life anymore. I can either jump off the train or have an affair with this guy I don't know, get on with my life, and just break ties with Dave." So I had that affair with French Fry.

When I came back from Russia I moved into the Mayflower Hotel for a long, long time, and I left Dave in the loft. Hotel life is very sad. And after the Russian trip, I was still going around with French Fry even though he was seeing his old girlfriend and they were moving in together. I couldn't understand why he was moving in with someone and still calling me. My housekeeper Ann didn't like him, and she finally ended it with him. When French Fry called she never told me, so I thought he lost interest. I kinda felt like I loved French Fry, but then I realized I was just still heartbroken about Dave.

When you start out and you have nothing, and you make it to that pinnacle of your life, you think that your fame and your success are a redemption for everything that ever happened to you. It's not true. Because at the end of the movie, the credits roll—but in your life, that doesn't happen. Credits don't roll. I had to continue living. My whole life up to that moment was about getting there, but now that I was there, it wasn't so rosy. I wanted my life to go better, and I thought it was gonna, but it didn't. Because what I gave up along the way to get to that pinnacle was my relationship. I thought that that was the most important thing to me, and that's why I was still a good soldier about everything Dave had me do. He continued to be my manager, and even though I was worried that the record company was a complete mess, I thought that no one else would really want me as an artist. I never felt that successful, because I was always working so hard.

I got one Grammy that year, but I disappointed the record company because I didn't come home with an armful like they expected. It
was always like that—it was never enough. I had come so far but felt
like I had failed.

There was this idea out there that I was rolling in money, but let
me tell ya, I wasn't. For instance, I really busted my ass touring and
promoting my records internationally, but I got a penny a record in
Europe. I remember asking my accountant around that time, "How
much money do I have?" He said, "You have a million dollars." I felt
like Ralph Kramden. I was like, "I'm rich!" What he neglected to tell
me was that half of that million would go toward taxes. I was never
good with money.

It was such a dark time for me. When I was living in the Mayflower, I was two steps off of that balcony. I would go to the studio
and make my record, and then sit in my dark room and drink vodka
(which I didn't even like). The moon would shine into the room past
the balcony, through the window, and onto the floor. And I'd sit on my
chair and talk to the moon. I would toast her and tell her I was named
Cynthia, after the goddess of the moon. Then I'd just cry while gaz-
ing up at her. I didn't call anyone; I was so upset I couldn't even talk. I
would see my family occasionally but I had to spend most of my time
making my record. I was alone. But I wanted to be alone. I was griev-
ing. I thought the sadness would never go away. I must say the only
thing that always prevented me from suicide is that I never wanted
a headline to read, GIRL WHO WANTED TO HAVE FUN JUST DIDN'T.
That's how stupid and ridiculous I thought the press was, and I didn't
want my life to be reduced to that.

My friend Katie Valk had introduced me to her friend Tracey Ull-
man, so I hung out with her a little bit. I told her that thing about how
I'd jump except for the headline, and Tracey looked at me and said,

"That's the second time you said that to me. I think you should start seeing a therapist."

So I went to a therapist for a second, but it seemed to me that she agreed with me too much, and you can't have somebody just agreeing with you. You have to have somebody who will listen and be objective and ask you, "Has that ever happened to you before?" and "How do you feel about that?" You need somebody to help you climb back up. I just collapsed. The rape, the dark parts of my past—everything caved in at that time and I was lost. I'd go to the studio stoned and Eric would look at me and go, "Cyn, what are you doing? Make your work. Come on." But I would see him working with Robert Palmer, who had this really young girlfriend. It was just like everywhere I looked there was a form of weird sexism. Then I'd watch his "Addicted to Love" video and see a girl swinging her tits around, and none of them could play instruments. What the hell is that?

Dave was still my manager, but I knew that wasn't going to last forever. I thought next time around I should really get a female. I really wanted to work with Sharon Osbourne, who was so cool and always spoke her mind, but people (usually men) told me all this shit like, "Oh, she's crazy." But I see now that what really happened was she stood up to them and they didn't like it.

I lost my relationship, I lost my work, I lost my focus. And I had no one to go to, really. I came into the music business with good intentions, with honesty, and everything I made was organic. Nothing I did was preconceived. I believed that music could lift people up and make them happy. Then I was just sucked up and considered disposable trash, and I felt like, "That's not what I came to do."

In the meantime, Dave said, "Cyn, listen, I feel ridiculous. I'm supposed to move out, not you." We always stayed friends. So I came back and he moved out. And Dave arranged for me to do an interview for the cover of *Details* magazine, and that's how I met Annie Flanders, the founding editor, who became a friend. We'd meet at the Russian Tea Room. She was one of the few people I could talk to. Annie was so creative and so cool. I did some research for what I thought would look nice for the cover. Then Laura Wills suggested Alberto Vargas's style to me (he painted all those pin-up girls in the forties), so I went to the bookshop and found a Vargas book to bring to Annie.

When I presented it to her I told her that when I thought of the cover, I imagined a painting. And she said, "I know a guy who could maybe paint it." So the cover was a painting of me, Vargas-style, with a very classic-Hollywood, platinum-blonde look, like Jean Harlow, and I was framed by gardenias. That was going to be my new image for *A Night to Remember*.

A Night to Remember came out in 1989, and "I Drove All Night" went to number six. It was huge all over the world. (This time Dave didn't play the guy in the video—I got someone else.) But again, the record company was disappointed. But like a good soldier I toured the world in support of that album. The record company wanted me to work Europe and the rest of the world while they broke their new acts in the States, so they could just live off of whatever I had left in me. That's how they are. I remember I went to Italy to do this wild, crazy show in Bari. It was a festival with about thirty acts, one after the other, and it was all televised. When there are that many acts, it's easier, and the sound quality is better, to sing to track (where the track plays without the vocal and you sing along to it) rather than to do it all live.

There was a mix of well-known acts and then Italian acts that I didn't know, which was fantastic. I traveled to the show with Justin, my hair person, because I was going to be on TV. Justin had a beard and long hair down to his butt. Then there was Jodi, my makeup artist, who was tiny, and Laura Wills, too, who was five foot ten, and

Dave. And me, I was right in the middle. The car was stuffed so full with all the luggage and the crap that we needed for the television show that the trunk wouldn't close and we had to use rope. So when we arrived at the festival there were kids waiting around and screaming as each artist emerged from their car. When we all got out the kids started singing the *Addams Family* theme! I laughed so hard. I could not believe that this was happening in Bari. I thought, "We *do* look like the Addams family."

Then a little Italian kid ran up to Laura Wills, looked her right in the face, stamped on her foot as hard as he could, and ran away. They were out of their minds. We just started laughing all the time because our lives were so ridiculous. After we did the TV show, we were brought to this restaurant where all the Sony artists from all over the world were. The Italian artists were sitting on the left and they started singing as the waiters brought out this incredible food. Then everybody started drinking and singing. I listened to this guy, Massimo, from the record company talk, and he said, "In the seventies, we had the Beatles and the Stones, and now we have Duran Duran and Spandau Ballet." And I kept thinking, "I don't think so. Those aren't the new legends."

There were other artists from Australia there called Noiseworks, and they started playing, and we started playing, too, and I just fell in love with what was going on—eating, drinking, and singing. So I started singing with them—harmonies, whatever I could. Then the place went a little loony. They were pouring vodka around, and I found myself on a chair at the end of the night singing "True Colors" with the singer from Noiseworks and the dishwasher, who was playing harmonica. I thought, "What the heck—this is great. This is what it's about, this is rock and roll at its finest." It was well worth the trip. In that moment, the joy came back to the music for me.

I always had fun in Italy. The first time I went there I had to go on another Italian TV show to perform "Girls Just Want to Have Fun," which, if I remember correctly, was a lip-sync. Before I went on, I was telling a producer that my family came from Sicily. He was Sicilian, so that was a big thing. And then I heard a chicken.

"Excuse me—is that a chicken?" I asked.

"Yes, that was a chicken."

"Let me get this straight. I'm opening for the chicken?"

"Yeah, you are," he said.

Hey, why not? That was crazy European television. (When I was promoting *Hat Full of Stars* there, some sheep opened for me, but they peed on the monitors, which wasn't a good thing.)

Another time I went on French TV to sing "I Drove All Night," and I wanted to do a performance-art piece where a car driving along a road is projected onto my naked body, like in the video. So I worked with this lighting woman Carol, who recommended that I get this stretchy, reflective material to wrap around my body. We couldn't get the fucking projector to work though, and my tour manager, Robin, started sweating profusely because it was live TV and we had to go on soon. And these fifteen French guys were standing around the projector, smoking cigarettes and speaking French, trying to make the thing work. At that time Simply Red had that rendition of the song "If You Don't Know Me by Now" and Jodi kept singing, "If it ain't working by now, it ain't never gonna work." I was laughing, thinking, "Oh, my God." The clock was ticking and finally Robin just pressed a button and it worked. I thought, "Ohhh, the on/off button. Excellent." Things like that happened so often. Hey, as long as I could make an art piece, I was happy.

The "Night to Remember" tour took me to many places, including all through Mexico, which I loved. The only problem was that I was playing in bullrings, and I kept losing my voice. I realized that I was sucking in the dirt that was being kicked up from the dirt floor as everyone got excited and started to dance. Once we figured that out we got a fan to blow the dust away from me. I got sick in Hong Kong too because of the air-conditioning (they didn't always clean the filters) and I got bronchitis. It was so bad I had to cancel dates, and then I went to Australia and the Philippines and sang the best I could, with me having bronchitis. In Japan I took every vitamin known to man and started getting better. (And I started to have an affair with another guy, a really handsome Australian journalist who interviewed me. I had no clue that he was going to hit on me. I kept talking and talking and talking about my art, and finally he just picked me up and headed to the bedroom and I said, "Oh.")

I started wondering if maybe I should stay in Australia and make my next record. It would mean leaving everyone I had worked with for eight years to make music. But at least it would be a fresh start. Noiseworks was there, and maybe I could do some work with them. It could be fun. I stood at Bondi Beach looking out at the end of the earth. I realized I might be very lonely. I would be really far away from everything I knew. I had done it once before in my life, but I wasn't sure I was up for it again. And I wasn't sure I could make the kind of record I wanted in Australia. Plus, I couldn't drive. I'm a New Yorker and I never got my license. So I returned to New York. But I always wonder what my music might have been like if I'd stayed.

I had been away for three months, and when I got home it was near Christmastime. I had shopped and shopped for all the presents. Dave came over and packed them all up in his car so we could go visit Lennie and give everyone their gifts. He and I almost reconciled before we left. We made love and then went down to the car, which he left parked in front of the building with all the presents stacked up to the roof. Of course someone broke in and stole them. What a surprise! And what might my old friend Aesop have had to say about that? "Don't be lame and leave the fuckin' car filled with presents for people who might want to steal them!"

I was worn out from touring, when I got an offer to do another movie. I had gotten a couple of other offers before then—for *Steel Magnolias* and *Working Girl*. No one explained to me that it would be a good idea to work with Mike Nichols but I didn't want to do *Working Girl* because I couldn't stand to be in an office again, and I didn't want to play a beautician again. Then I turned down *Steel Magnolias* because I didn't think I'd be good enough.

But I decided to take the role in *Paradise Paved*, which was then changed to *Moon over Miami*—which was then changed to *Off and Running*. But it never really got off and running. It was the last film Orion Pictures made before it filed for bankruptcy in 1991. Here's the thing: Whenever a project has three names, you know it's not going to work. But I thought, "Let's stop with the music for a while and do a movie." It was another crazy-girl story, a quirky film that tried to be serious, too. *Vibes* had a better premise. I played an actress named Cyd Morse who wasn't getting much work so I danced as an underwater mermaid at a Miami night club. Then I got caught up in a murder mystery after two guys killed my boyfriend and tried to kill me too. It was supposed to be like a dark screwball-comedy thing. But it was another sexist set, and in my opinion, I felt the director was overwhelmed. And after a while I felt like I was in a boys' club. And once again, I never felt like I could talk to anyone except my acting coach.

My new acting coach was into the whole "Method acting" thing, which I could never grasp. She gave me all these exercises, like jumping up and down on one foot while singing "Happy Birthday" out of time. I felt tortured during that. I'm a singer/musician. Repetitively saying words over and over again in a scene helped me find the rhythm of it. For me, everything is rhythm. We have a heart, we have a pulse, we have brain waves. We are rhythm. Once I hear the rhythm of a person's speech, then I learn the person who is behind it. That's what I understood. The other stuff I didn't get. I always was trying to figure out what the scene was about, but I didn't know how, and I couldn't understand what they were telling me. I was told not to behave like myself. They would say, "You'll need to talk lower, and don't use your hands when you talk." So I tried my best, but the "why" was missing. I was just desperately trying to please everybody after being dragged over the coals in *Vibes*.

Louis Falco, the movie's choreographer, became a good friend. He had a dance company in New York and I went to see him when he was choreographing the underwater scenes. He said, "Cyn, you have to undulate." Undulate? What the hell is that? Then he saw me trying to undulate and said, "Uh, never mind, that's okay." Then when we actually did it in the water, he told me to twirl around, and I twirled around and twirled around like a drill, until I hit my head on the wall of the pool. Again, he said, "Uh, never mind." I also had to learn how to swim. I don't like to get my face wet so it was kind of difficult. Then I had to learn how to scuba dive. Sometimes I would freak out, and the swimming teacher would say, "If you freak out, rest, become really calm, remember that you can breathe, and think, 'What am I afraid of?'" I still use that now when I freak out—as long as I can breathe, I can remain calm.

The costume designer liked the whiteness of my skin and wanted me to have black hair in the pool to make me look different from the other mermaids. Then they decided I'd have a black top too. But the black top did something strange to the underwater visual: It sucked all the light in. All the other mermaids had on light-colored tops that made their breasts look even bigger than they were—not that they weren't built like brick shit houses in the first place. But my black top made my breasts look smaller, so that I looked like a twelve-year-old. Just before I went into the water, the guy who worked for the producer came running over to me and started yelling about the costume. I said to him, "Why are you yelling at me? Is this the first time you looked at my costume? Why didn't you check it before? I'm petrified of the water, and now that I'm about to get in, you're stressing me out?" Everybody was freaked out because by the time I got to the end of the conversation, I was yelling.

After I went into the water a bunch of times, I realized that not only could I work the air pipe and breathe by filtering the water with my tongue, but I could also lip-sync. All of a sudden, I was performing underwater. Not for nothing, but I was like Flipper. Who knew you could lip-sync underwater? That was fun. At first, they had a stunt-woman doing some of the underwater shots but the director felt I had more personality. The frustrating thing was that after all that work learning how to do this, they only filmed a little bit of the song. They didn't even do one complete take. If they filmed the whole song, even just once, then we could have created a video with clips of the movie in it. Which I thought might have been why I was cast, so that they could have cross-promotion in two different worlds, music and film.

While I was shooting that movie, I found out I was nominated for another Grammy for Best Female Rock Vocal Performance in "I Drove All Night." The funny thing was, when we were compiling that CD, I told Don Grierson "I Drove All Night" should be the first cut on the album, because this song would be nominated for a Grammy. I remember how he looked at me like I was a bit delusional. But this time, I was going against Bonnie Raitt's comeback and she won for

"Nick of Time." (Like I said, the first time I was nominated for best vocal, I lost to Tina Turner's comeback. The second time, with "True Colors," I lost to Barbra Streisand's comeback. The problem with me is that I either keep coming back or I don't go away . . . I'm not sure which one it is.)

The producer of the film would not allow me to take a day off to go to the Grammys. It was just a really difficult time. I felt really beaten down. But then my assistant, Paul, who was on the set with me, kept saying, "You gotta meet this guy David Thornton—he plays the murderer. He's really funny. I can't tell if he's straight or gay but God, is he cute."

CHAPTER TWELVE

DAVID, DAVID, DAVID: that was all Paul kept talking about, because he had a crush on him. ("If he's gay, then he's my new boyfriend," he said.) Then he did some investigating and found out that David had a girlfriend, but he didn't get a vibe that things were goin' good. So when we were going to dinner one night and *Off and Running* did not supply any transportation for David, I said, "Maybe we should call the murderer and see if he wants to come with us."

During filming, I didn't want to stay in the fancy hotel in Miami Beach with my costar David Keith and the director. The room was on the water, but it didn't even have a view. So I asked if I could stay at the nearby Eden Roc, where I could have a nice, big penthouse with a patio and a beautiful view for less than the cost of the room they got me, and they said yes. The only problem was that sometimes I found palmetto bugs in my room. Ya ever seen a palmetto bug? Their faces are so big, you could still see the expressions on them when they keeled over. (I said that once in the elevator, and the manager was there too and he got mad because I said it in front of some guests.)

When David Thornton came up to meet me, he did a really silly thing. He pulled his pants all the way up like Urkel and shook my hand with rounded shoulders and said, "Nice to meet you." So I knew he was funny. We started hanging out in a little group with Paul and Louis and Marilyn, my acting coach, and I really loved our times off the set together. David is this fuckin' sensational actor (he went to the Yale School of Drama), very creative, and also very sweet.

When we all did our first script reading together, we went through a scene where my boyfriend lets this room-service guy (who was played by David) into our room and he karate-kicks my boyfriend out the window and kills him. After the reading, I called up David's room and said, "Listen, pal, not for nothin', but don't you be kickin' my boyfriend like that. I'm going to tell him not to answer the door." And I hung up. After that, he started to send notes to Paul that were supposedly from Madonna, telling him that he should go work for her instead because he wouldn't have to taste her food like he had to do with me. He wrote all this funny stuff, and then it was on. One time I was out with Marilyn and I took all the shrimp tails from my dish and stapled them to the bottom of a piece of paper. We got into it and we were both laughing. Then I cut out letters from the newspaper and glued them to spell out, "Dear murderer, please don't kill me—from the mermaid." Then I put that by his door.

Back and forth, back and forth went these practical jokes, which were so hilariously funny. Then I found another crazy letter in my dressing room—only this one wasn't so crazy. It was written just before the first day of shooting, and it said that I had all the beauty and knowledge within me to do this. How generous was David to say that to me? Louis was reading it, and he turned around and said, "Cyn, you know what this is?" I said, "Yeah, it's a card." He goes, "No. It's a love letter."

I was the one who made the director hire him in the first place. I sat in on all the auditions because I was supposed to be involved; we were all going to be a team. We saw all these guys who wanted to play the murderer, and then this one guy came in who was so intense that he scared the script reader so much that she just dropped the paper. I looked at him and thought, "Yeah, he's a little good-lookin', but isn't that what makes a murderer really menacing?" His energy just filled the stage. I looked at the director and said, "You know, it's that guy, what's-his-name." The director pulled out his headshot and said, "No, he's too good-looking." I said, "Listen, you can always make a person look ugly. But you can't make an ugly guy act good, the way this guy can. It gives the story weight."

Unfortunately, David Keith, who was to play the lead male role, was going through a rough time in his life, I think. He just didn't seem to be himself, because before I worked with him, I met a musician who knew him who said he was nice. But he wasn't so nice during filming. Like, I'd be soaking wet after a scene and he'd take the portable air-conditioning unit and put it right by me. And I found it abusive that he made the kid in the movie cry. The kid was really a great little actor, and instead of continuing to act after that movie, I think he went to military school and then into the army.

This was my second film and it had the same strange atmosphere as my first one. I could never seem to get away with an easy set. And I never found a way to shut out the people who were trying to distract me on purpose. It's like, where are the fuckin' rules of etiquette on a film set? I did that movie to get away from the tumultuous changing of the guard at the record company and all those corporate heads who wanted to put their stamp on me and wanted to be the celebrities instead of the artists being the celebrities.

So I thought, "Okay, I'm going to go to Miami, and I'm going to live these pages for the next few months. I'm not Cyn anymore, I'm Cyd. I'm not a blonde anymore. I'm going to do something different." And when the director told me to dye my hair black like Louise

Brooks, I jumped. But when the producer saw it, he flipped out, so I put an orange glaze over it so it would seem dark brown.

Then I started filming and realized what a pain in the ass it was to be with those people. The movie actually had a good script, but like I said, I felt the director was overwhelmed. He'd yell on set, and then if we looked upset he'd go, "Come on, everyone, this is a comedy! What's wrong?" He reminded me of actor Eugene Levy in one of those old *Second City Television* skits. I'd think, "This can't really be my life, can it? Is it always gonna be a comedy of errors?"

At least I had fun with my friends, and with David. He taught me how to shut out the idiots around me by listening to music on my headphones that was connected to the scene I was about to do. After a while a few mermaids started to pounce on David like cats on a mouse. And one day he told me about a girl who was a model, who gave him a lift to town because she was going to her exercise class. He said she changed into her workout clothes while she was driving. She must have let go of the wheel once in a while, too, which, considering he was in the passenger seat (or what they call the "death seat"), must have been quite a ride. He would stand behind me when that model came around, and he'd say, "Oh, no, here she comes again, that's the one that took her clothes off in the car. Come on, just do me a favor, please just pretend you're talking to me." I was like, "Okay, okay, I'll talk to you."

After I watched all these girls hitting on David, I thought, "You know what? I'm Cyndi Lauper, goddamn it! If somebody's going to get this guy, why can't it be me? So what if I look like a twelve-year-old under the water with my black top on? That's just the light. Let me shine a light on *this*!" So I put on this cute sleeveless tunic that I wore for a TV appearance once in Madrid—it was vintage, orange with a green paisley print on silk with yellow trim, with a little bodice. I zipped up the back zipper, looked in the mirror, and told myself: "I'm Gumby, damn it!" I fixed my hair, put my lipstick on, put on my clear Frederick's of Hollywood pumps, and went out the door.

All of us crammed into the car to go to a restaurant, and of course we couldn't all fit, so we had to sit on each other's laps. All of a sudden I started feeling something on the back of my calf and I was like, "What the—?" Then I realized it was David's hand, and I thought, "Why, you sly devil."

We had dinner and then walked on the beach. The moon was full that night. The moon always seemed like some big ol' lantern hanging over the waves that washed up on South Beach. David and I were standing in the surf. It was really windy and I had my arms out, and the wind was blowing against my dress. I stood at the edge of the water, lifted my arms straight out at my sides, and said, "I wish I was a kite." He asked me why, and I said, "Because then I could fly. But it wouldn't be so good, because somebody would always be pulling my string." So he looked at me, and looked out at the water, and said, "Why not be a wave?" And all of a sudden I stared at him and thought, "How many times have I talked to people who don't even hear me? Here's a fellow who not only heard me but was able to answer me back in a poetic way."

We walked back to the hotel, and David kissed me good night in the elevator. I went back to my room and thought about it, because we were friends and had a lot of laughs together. Then I called him up on the phone and said, "Excuse me, did you just kiss me?" He said, "Well, you know, I usually never do this." He sounded a little nervous and like he was putting his clothes back on or moving around the room or something. So I said, "Why don't you come upstairs and finish what you started?" I think that was a line from an old Mae West movie. Hey, it worked for her.

So he came upstairs. And we made love for the first time on a bed drenched in moonlight, against the sound of the ocean waves. It was Valentine's Day 1990. That's why if I'm ever working and not home on Valentine's Day, it's such a heartbreak for me.

The thing was, he still had a girlfriend. But like I said, at that point, they weren't doing so good—if they were, I don't think anything would have happened. So I said to him, "Listen, I'm crackers for ya, and I don't do so good as the other woman. So you gotta make up your mind here. Talk to her." So he did. David's not really the cheating type anyway. But because of my experience with French Fry, I decided to be very clear about my boundaries.

In the meantime, I was so happy because they brought a beauty makeup artist onto the set. The guy before had a specialty in blood and special effects and he made my eyes look a little uneven. You know, the "One eye looking at ya and the other for ya" look. The new makeup artist was an older woman named Marie, and I loved her. She was funny and supportive and knew when I was trying to remember lines. And she loved David, too. I talked to her one time about him and said, "I don't know about this, I just met him." Because after two weeks he started saying, "If we're going to do this, then I want to either move in together and be serious, or not. I just have to know." I was like, *whoa.* The night after he told me that, I had a dream that we were Neanderthals, and we were walking across the continent toward the sun. (When Africa and South America were one continent.) We had to get to the sun, because something was happening to the ground. In the dream, we had spent our whole life walking to the sun, and I realized that the man I spent my life with in that dream was David. The first thing I did when I woke up was check my face, because I was so upset about my Neanderthal facial hair. I mean, how much electrolysis would that take, anyway?

David and I did move in together. We needed to see if it was just one of those movie romances. And at first it was a concern of mine that the last serious relationship I was in, the guy's name was David. When I first became friends with David Thornton, he was the murderer in the film. So I called him "the murderer." But when things changed and we were not in the movie, I started worrying that I was collecting Davids. So I went to see a therapist, the one I saw while I was making *She's So Unusual.*

In the end, the therapist said something like, "Okay, let me get this straight. You met a guy you love, but his name is David. And you're willing to break it off with him because his name is David?" Yes, I said. And the therapist said, "Then you've got a problem." And I realized, "Yeah. Right." I mean, what the heck? As Shakespeare once said, "What's with the name?" (I mean "in a name," of course.)

We got married in 1991. We didn't wait very long since we had both just had long engagements. We figured, what the hell, if it don't work out, it don't work out. So we gave it a shot. David bought me a few different rings. One was an 1840s crystal that had belonged to a Hindu princess. I believe in reincarnation and the past, so he thought that would be a good contender. There was an antique Roman ring with the stamp of Eros, too, and a Victorian English regards ring with gems whose first letters spelled "regards" across the finger. That was the one I picked.

The ceremony was in New York, but we had a hard time finding a place to get married. I was going to lie about my religious beliefs and everything else just to get married in a church. But David said, "Why even bother?" Instead, he wanted to get married in our favorite Italian restaurant, Siracusa. I thought it would be great for the reception, but they had a little grocery in the front where they sold spaghetti and sauce and stuff, and I kept thinking, "I'm going to walk down the aisle next to the homemade spaghetti?" I waited my whole life to get married. Were we going to play "Volare," too?

So David kept looking, looking, looking, and he came up with this place called the Friends Meetinghouse. It was Quaker, and it was perfect, and the thought behind it was beautiful too. We would invite our friends and family and join as friends and lovers. But when we met with the muckety-mucks of the church, we did have to lie. David did most of it, while I stayed out of sight. And when I went in, I was very plain, in a running suit and brown hair. (I look very Italian with brown hair, like you can hear the organ grinder.)

And then David and I talked about who would marry us. I said that if I believed in anything, I believed in the Church of Voice. I'm a singer, I told him, so let's get married by a singer/minister. So we asked Al Green, but that did not work out. Then we thought of Little Richard. (Those were the only two guys I knew of who were reverends.) He was from my community too—the rock and roll community—and I happen to think that Little Richard's voice is one of the greatest in rock and roll. So my tour manager Robin contacted him and Little Richard said he would do it. It was exciting.

I wanted to wear white hot pants and go-go boots but David didn't want to feel like he was at a rock show. So I went straight. I went to Saks with my friend and then-stylist, Laura. We got an A-line satin dress that went to the knee—very sixties—with embroidery down the front. My hair would be a soft blonde, and I had long white gloves, a pillbox hat with an A-line veil down to the chin, and satin shoes with an A-line bow. My aunt Gracie told me I looked like Grace Kelly. I figured that was as conventional as I could go. But I lied to the woman at Saks and told her I needed to dress like a bride for a rock video so I could get married in private. My grandmother was the maid of honor, and I didn't want her to have a heart attack.

To help with the wedding, we hired Robin, and my friend Annie recommended a florist named Dorothea. She did the most beautiful arrangements I had ever seen in my life. The flowers were all white and pale pink. My grandmother was very down because she had fallen and was in a wheelchair. So I figured, you know, nothing cheers a dame up like a pretty dress and a nice occasion to go out to, so I asked her to be my maid of honor. I loved my nana.

My sister came too. And Katie Valk and Howard and lots of friends, but no business people at all, since it was the business that wrecked the last David relationship. And Rob Hyman from the Hooters was there with his wife, Sally. We had become very close to them. I met up with them again when I performed with Roger Waters at the Berlin Wall in 1990. The funny thing was it was like no time had passed. And now Sally was part of the picture and it was so much fun. She was hilarious, awesome, and she and David got along like a house on fire.

It was nice to start making more friends. Since I was always away, I never had a lot of them. I had my band but that was because I'd spend most of my time traveling with them. In the meantime I never got to see friends like Bonnie Ross, the one I mentioned who worked for the Red Cross and was dressed as a nurse in the "Girls Just Want to Have Fun" video. I met her at a gig and just adored her—still do. I always remembered her telephone number because it spelled out "MADLOVE." I love seeing her in that video. Like I said, I tried to make a photo album of all my friends and my family, and extended friends and family, in my videos. Then I could always go back and see them—"Oh, look, that's my aunt Gracie, what a pisser! Look at my cousin, look at my brother!"

I had a wonderful time at my wedding, and I was so in love with David. I wondered what David's parents must have made of having me as a daughter-in-law. David's father taught English at Harvard and wrote books about Robert Burns, the famous Scottish poet. I saw him twitching during the ceremony because Little Richard was murdering vowels all over the place. The night before I had put my arms around him and lifted him a bit and said, "Don't worry. You're not losing a son—you're gaining somebody who don't talk English that good."

We were on Long Island for our honeymoon for only a day because David was an understudy in a play and they called him back to be on standby. Years later we finally had a real honeymoon in Hawaii. After the wedding, I took a minute to have a life, because I felt like I didn't have one. And if you're an isolated artist, what the fuck do you write about? How it's really tough to live in an ivory tower? Or how my bodyguard looked at me the wrong way and so now I'm feeling depressed? I wanted a real life. So I bought Dave Wolff's half of the house we bought in Connecticut. My new husband had already moved into my loft in New York City and we spent weekends in Connecticut, or sometimes we'd go to the house on the Cape.

Just as an aside here, my house in Connecticut is not too far from where that chimp named Travis ripped off that woman's face. You remember that horrible story, right? When the chimp became an adolescent she had to start giving it Xanax. Then it freaked out one day and the woman called her friend to help her and it ended up biting the friend's face. I would have gone to the vet and gotten a tranquilizer gun or to the zoo to ask for help.

So anyway, my mother, who now lives on Long Island, called me, all upset, and said, "Oh, I was so worried, because that chimp was near your town."

"Ma," I said, "had it been me, I swear to God, the headlines would have read 'Chimp just didn't want to have fun.' Okay? That's how you would have known it was me."

Anyway, after David and I got married, we stepped back for a bit and went up to the Cape for a month. I just wanted to be alive. I had to get back to why I had started to sing in the first place. Why did I become an artist? What was my story? I was going to write a book but I guess the timing wasn't right then, so I told myself, "Okay, you can't write a book, but you can write your story in songs. So do it."

I started writing after I had been at the Cape for a while. Annie and my other friends and family came to visit me there. And around the time when I began working on the album that would become *Hat Full of Stars*, I traveled with Annie Flanders to go to Alee Willis's birthday party in LA. (Now that I have a kid, I can't even imagine just getting on a plane to see a friend.) Allee Willis is a musician who became a close friend. She would eventually cowrite five songs on the album (Rob and Eric cowrote some, too). I stayed at Allee's house, and it was so wonderfully nutty, it looked a little like my "Girls Just Want to Have Fun" video and Jacques Tati's *Mon Oncle*. Outside her house, her walk curved and had green on one side and blue on the other—it was like an art piece.

I wrote the title track, "Hat Full of Stars," with Nicky Holland, who lived upstairs from me in the Thread Building. The idea for the song came from this hat that I got a long time ago in Vermont, before I went to college. Like I talked about, I was by myself, and very lonely, and oh my God, was it cold. I used to visit the Free Store in Johnson, Vermont, which was for poor people, like a Goodwill. It was a wonderful store with great clothes, and that's where I got the hat, which was kind of a cap.

I wore it all the time. Even though it was cold, Vermont was so beautiful, and I always wished I had someone to share it with. So one night, I took my hat off and put all the stars in it. That way, every time I put my hat back on I could remember that beautiful night sky, and maybe I could share it with someone. When I met Dave Wolff he wore that hat a lot. But what I was also saying in those lyrics, metaphorically, was to create a magical feeling around yourself. That's what it was always about for me, to make myself feel brighter, more alive, taller, with bigger hair, to wear flashes of color that invigorated me, or to paint my hair with them, or my face.

Even though "Hat Full of Stars" is a sad song, it's also uplifting. There's a line in there that goes "You could've seen far / You should've seen the magic / In my hat full of stars." It's "coulda, shoulda," because like I said, in the neighborhood I came from, everyone always said, "I coulda been this, I shoulda done that," but they never did. Well, I made sure I did—that I wasn't one of the "shoulda, coulda, woulda" people.

I also wanted to write about social issues, about real people. There's a song on the album called "Product of Misery" (remember, that was Bob Barrell's phrase) about a woman who is broken down, whose life is drudgery. That was a response to the George H. W. Bush administration, who sold us a bill of goods. And I put "A Part Hate" on the record, which I wasn't able to do for the last one. The timing was right because the Rodney King riots were spreading across our country. In a lot of ways I saw apartheid in my own country.

"Sally's Pigeons," which I wrote with Mary Chapin Carpenter, was about a girl from the neighborhood who died from a back-alley abortion. With that kind of story I needed to hypnotize people with the music. I made all different little sounds part of the story: the synthesizer, the loop, the rhythm of the street, of the people, and for the first time in my life (except for "Time After Time") I was singing my songs, singing my stories. It's so important to me to write songs that are taken from my life so that they have real meaning.

I always felt that the paths that people took were worn into how they walked, how they lived, and I know it's romanticizing things, but the important thing for me is to portray the richness of their stories in sounds and words. Even the album cover, for me, always has to be a painting of the stories put together.

When I was looking for a coproducer, I talked with Run-DMC's producer, and I told him how I wanted to take loops from hip-hop and mix them with pop but that I didn't know how to be successful at it and appease the record company, too. He said, "But you're Cyndi Lauper—you could do whatever you want." I thought, "I wish." I didn't go with him because I wasn't sure if he would be able to keep the record-company guys happy. Instead I went with Junior Vasquez, who ended up pissing them off anyway. But I loved Junior and had a good time with him.

When the record-company people heard the songs, they wanted to remix some of them before they were even finished. They had all these nasty-ass mixers that mixed things into shit, so they could be tailor-made for each fuckin' radio station. Compartmental radio was starting to happen, so now if you wanted to hear a specific genre you had to turn to that kind of radio station, because they split up rock, hip-hop, and dance, as opposed to just turning on Top 40 and hearing it all. I told them, "If you touch my record before I'm done, I'll gonna have to kill ya." Unfortunately I said that to the president of the record company. And again everyone choked on their lunch. What I didn't understand then was that them remixing my music had nothing to do with my album. It just had to do with how they had to make it sellable to radio stations. I had no manager—no one to translate that to me. If they had explained it that way, I would have understood and listened, because I was a good soldier.

But instead I got all emotional and knee-jerk and pushed everyone away. I should have talked it out in a reasonable way. Plus, I looked like a fuckin' alien to them. Could you imagine Lady Gaga coming into a meeting in 1993 and getting anywhere? It was a different time then. I even tried to tone down my look, because everyone tried to sell me a bill of goods that it's all about the inside, not the outside. If you can believe it, I even went through a hip-hop clothing phase. Imagine me in those baggy clothes.

I was proud of that album, and it got nice reviews, but it didn't sell. There was no single off of it at all and yet I thought it moved music forward. I put so much into it and tried so hard to make it great, to do something different. When it was released in June of 1993 and I saw the sales figures, I went home and cried my eyes out. It was my first real big flop. The record company didn't bother promoting it. They just threw it away, while Tommy Mottola was up on top, putting every dollar into his new bride Mariah Carey's career.

I fought with Sony for years, but ya know what? The good thing was, because they didn't give a shit, they allowed me to grow.

CHAPTER THIRTEEN

I FINALLY GOT THE home life that I had always wanted when I married David, but when you're a musician, you can never stay home for very long. One of the lowest points of my life was the end of 1993, when I was promoting *Hat Full of Stars* and I was shipped off to the East. (I do pretty well there and my management at the time was like, "Let's milk her, because she's big in Japan.") So I was in Japan on Christmas, not with my husband, and I was so heartbroken. I remember I told Yoko Ono before I was leaving that I was depressed I would be away, and listen to this: She found out where I was staying and she put a fuckin' Christmas tree in my hotel room. She had her brother do it. I'll never forget that.

I toured for the album in the US, too, and I had this idea to make a road documentary called *Cyndi Lauper Discovers America*. I would talk to people across the country to find out what's on their minds—current events, their families, politics, music, whatever—which would be kind of funny and kind of great, too. So I met with TV people about it, and I was told I had to raise the money myself. But my lawyer and my film agency weren't interested in doing that, so I couldn't get a director. I even met with Michael Moore, the guy who did *Bowling for Columbine*. In the meantime, I spent a lot of money trying to film it when I was on the road (a club tour with two buses and a ten-piece band) but it never panned out. That was a real beat-up time for me, even though I was doing great music. (Listen, I didn't know anybody who was doing loops and pop folk together like I did on that album. Had I known someone, I would have had an ally. I wouldn't have felt so alone.) I needed a good manager after the last guy that I had, who was a dope. He was from a management company that also managed really well-known bands, so when I hired him, I felt like, "Oh, these guys will understand being innovative, right?" No. They did not. One time, right before I was going to go on a talk show, he told me he had lost the single, "Who Let In the Rain." You're managing a music act and you lose the single they're going to play? I should have just said, "Well, you lost your job too."

I was going to do a club tour and create a club record, but instead my manager let the record company tell him to go with "Who Let in the Rain," which was a soft ballad instead of modern music. And it failed. I learned that if I want to write anything about politics I'll always cloak it in a relationship to make it more palatable to people. That's why I like the blues, because it's covert. Everything they write about the white man is cloaked in a love song. Their real feelings are under the page, masked. But with a song like "That's What I Think," I was so horrified by what the Bush years were like that I wanted to talk to the people directly and pull them up again. I mean, everything had become so corporate at the time. I remember that everywhere I traveled, every city looked the same: the same cookie-cutter skyline, like the Coca-Cola signs, no matter what country. And that's when I began to understand the gravity of what was really happening in our world. I'm still proud of the song "Sally's Pigeons" and its message. But at that time, people in the music industry were so busy trying to do things that were business-driven and watching profits and the bottom line that there wasn't much room for creativity. I'd go to music panels to hear people in the industry speak and no one would talk about the craft of writing—they would talk about promotion, selling, and the two minutes of fame you might get. All of a sudden the craft part of it was over.

Then the people from the TV show *Mad About You* said they wanted to work with me. I had never done a sitcom before, but they thought I would be perfect for this character Marianne Lugasso. She was the ex-wife of star Paul Reiser's cousin Ira, who was played by John Pankow. I said yes, and I was very glad I did, because Paul Reiser was one of the nicest, most talented people I've ever worked for. He was so funny and a great, great boss. I got so comfortable with everybody during the first filming that I sang to them and started doing my Ethel Merman impersonation, and the fellow who was directing turned around and said, "That's Marianne's voice! That's her personality." So all of a sudden, through the voice, I captured the whole rhythm of the character.

Once the character clicked, Paul wrote great dialogue for Marianne. It sounded like it came right out of my head, like it started in my brain. The rhythm of Marianne's language matched how I naturally speak, because Paul is also from Queens. He was in a better neighborhood, but he was still from Queens, and Queens has a certain lilt whether you're from Jamaica or Ozone Park or Forest Hills. It gets more swingy in certain places, it loses a couple of vowels or consonants, but it all has the same rhythm. That rhythm was created by the people who migrated there during the 1920s and '30s—the Italians, the Irish, and the Jews. I love history, and it's all right there in a Queens accent. (If a French person wanted to learn how to speak English from me, well, you know, it's going to sound a little funny.)

Anyway, the first year I was nominated for an Emmy. My agent really tried to get me nominated because she felt I did a great job. I didn't know if I did a great job, but I do know I tried hard to be good for that role. That was the best I could do.

Then they invited me back for another season and when I returned, it was so much more fun, because I was able to figure out who Marianne really was. She also married a rich person, so I had to dress the part. I went to Dolce & Gabbana and they lent me some clothes. (My big mistake was that I had the production company mail back all the Dolce clothes, and I don't know what happened to them but the woman from Dolce was very mad. I guess I should have done it myself.)

The second year I was also nominated for an Emmy, and I won, do you believe? But do you want to know something? I felt really bad at the ceremony. I didn't know what I was doing and no one was there with me—no manager, no press person. I went with the makeup artist. I was kind of like thrown into it. I guess everybody just thought, "Oh, Cyndi, she can do this." But I was dressed like me, not realizing that I had to dress like *them*—not like rock and roll. I wore a Vivienne Westwood outfit with a corset and tight gold pants with gold platform toe-crippler stilettos. I wore my hair up, and it was a few different shades of blond and black. I mean, it would have been cute for the Grammys.

I went to the press room and they asked, "What makes the Emmys different from MTV?" By that time I had been pushed off of MTV. I mean, you know how it is. It's like they want the next big thing. They weren't going to play anything if it wasn't a hit, and I didn't have a hit. So I said, "I don't know—I haven't been there much lately."

Well. That was the wrong thing to say, so they stopped asking questions. There was nobody from the press department helping me, and I didn't know where to go or what to say or do. The manager I had at that time was a music guy, and he didn't even take a commission for my acting because he had nothing to do with it, so I was on my own. It was time to get rid of him, anyway.

Then I got another manager and he seemed great at first, but I'll never forget the time when we were coming back from a European trip and he said to me, "You know, you're never going to be as big as you were." I was devastated. I said, "What do you mean? You don't know that." Billy Joel, and other people, got to do it, got to come back. Then instead of saying to him, "Okay, I'm sorry but if you feel like that, I can't work with you anymore," I stayed. I'm an idiot.

You know what it is? Whenever I stood up for myself, it always came out wrong, because it was so over-the-top. It would always be a fight, rather than a negotiation. If you want to be successful in anything, you better learn how to reel it in. That said, I've had an amazing manager for many years named Lisa Barbaris who used to do my music press. She is like a sister to me.

Anyway, I was talking about *Mad About You*. The next time I went back, Helen Hunt had been doing well playing Paul's wife, Jamie, and she had kind of taken over the show. She was directing, which was interesting, but there was tension on the set.

Like I said, I wanted to get out of my record contract but I couldn't. Then the company wanted me to do a greatest-hits collection. In fact they wanted me to do that before *Hat Full of Stars*, but I didn't think I had enough hits, so I said, "Let me get this album done and we'll have another hit to put on it." How did I know they weren't going to fuckin' do anything to promote it? At least somebody appreciated my work, because I heard that when Alanis Morissette went in to talk to a guy at Maverick Records about what she wanted to do next, she took some records with her, including *Hat Full of Stars*. It made me feel better that somebody heard what I was doing and I wasn't wrong. I was just there early, and I had a very conservative record company that was going through changes and the executives had their heads in braces.

I remember at that time the producer Jimmy Iovine wanted me to work with him on the *Very Special Christmas* project for the Special Olympics, so he called me up personally. He asked me what I was doing, so I played "Sally's Pigeons" for him over the phone, and he was genuinely interested. All of a sudden I wished I was at his record company. I also played it for Patti Scialfa, Bruce Springsteen's wife. We did a photo shoot together and she said, "Cyn, I love the way you put the loop with that music." And then the next thing I knew Springsteen came out with "Streets of Philadelphia," with his big voice, low music, and the loop. I was like, "Oh, nice. Why do I play stuff for people?"

So in 1994 I put out the greatest-hits collection *Twelve Deadly Cyns . . . and Then Some.* I reworked "Girls Just Want to Have Fun" to give it a reggae feel and it became "Hey Now (Girls Just Want to Have Fun)." The single did well in Europe, and for a couple of weeks I did a European tour with twelve drag-queen dancers. I kind of just wanted them to be there dancing with me, but I couldn't help them put together a routine because I'm not a choreographer. We were basically doing it by the seat of our pants. But they had a good attitude about it. And it was me and twelve drag queens in a bus, which was kind of awesome. You'd think that because they dress like women, they'd be more like women. They were a bunch of kick-ass rockers, though, passing around vodka bottles. There were some hilarious times, especially in Spain. One time we went to this restaurant for dinner and the guys went into the ladies' room dressed like women, which of course caused a big commotion.

The next night I had off, and I was dying to eat early and I said, "Is that place open yet?" so the lady from the record company asked the restaurant if I could go while they were setting up, because I was starved. A woman at the restaurant said, "Okay, but will she be coming with her ... friends?" That made me laugh.

During the tour, I talked to the guys about the discrimination that they faced, and I figured that maybe I should write a song for them. I wanted to make it a dance song to celebrate them. It became "Ballad of Cleo and Joe" on my next album, which I had started writing with Jan Pulsford, my keyboard player on *Hat Full of Stars*.

The Gay Games started in 1982 and had become this international LGBT sports and cultural event, and in 1994 they were taking place in New York City. My friend was working on the committee and I thought, "I'd love to play those games." It seemed to just be an extension of the clubs I was playing at night. My friend Howard Kaplan said to me, "Cyn, you should do the new 'Girls Just Want to Have Fun' mix and have, like, fifty drag queens dancing with you." So I did and that was the first time I worked with Jerry Mitchell, who I'm now working with on the *Kinky Boots* musical. (It still makes perfect sense that I wrote music for *Kinky Boots*, because I still love them shoes.) Jerry was funny and knew exactly how to choreograph the drag queens. So there I was singing the "Girls" remix with them, and their shoes and head-dresses were extraordinary. The problem was that I had to remember my steps and not just stand there and look at them. But I was so struck by how elegant they looked that I got struck by a dancer walking by, and the microphone knocked into my lip. But I kept singing. And when I didn't see them on the JumboTron, it was really upsetting to me. I was like, "Are you kidding me? You mean the gay community is going to discriminate against *drag* performers? What the heck? Why wouldn't you put those amazing shoes on the JumboTron?"

After that I thought, "You won't show them? I'll show them. I'll not only show them but I'll make them all famous." And I made the video for "Hey Now" with all of those fabulous drag queens by the twelve-story Unisphere from the 1964–65 World's Fair, which is in Queens—of course. My friend Kevin Dornan told me about the globe, and I realized it would be a wonderful place to shoot because it's so iconic and putting the drag queens underneath it is a great visual. I sold a million copies of that record in England, but did you know they wouldn't put that video out in the US? The record company decided to squash it here. Apparently there were too many drag queens in it. Then Gloria Estefan saw the drag queens and she put them in her video for "Everlasting Love."

In 1995 I got very sick and the doctor asked me when I was going to have a kid, and I told her, "After this tour." She said, "It's always after this tour or that tour." Then my friend Helena said, "Cyn, just have a baby." So I did. I started trying to get pregnant in 1996 through in vitro (I didn't have time to wait). In vitro was expensive, and after a while I realized that the paintings in my doctor's office weren't prints, they were real—I was paying for them. But it didn't work.

When I was trying to get pregnant, I started spending more time in the Connecticut house. Jan Pulsford stayed nearby and we started writing songs for the new album in my little home studio. It was great. I didn't have anybody breaking my balls, and if Jan went to bed, I could keep working if I wanted to. I had first been inspired by her work when I heard a track she had called "Searching." We made a great team and I had a wonderful time with her. She was just awesome. The reason I called it *Sisters of Avalon* is because Jan is Welsh and loves Welsh mythology and Arthurian legend and all of that. (She has a son named Merlin.)

I started writing *Sisters of Avalon* while doing a promo tour for *Deadly Cyns*, which took me to three continents in six weeks. When I came back from that tour I was on a cane because I had fallen from a stage. I had to dance on top of speaker cabinets, because we couldn't afford the stage that I wanted.

And Jan and I were talking about this book *The Mists of Avalon*, by Marion Zimmer Bradley, which is kind of a retelling of the King Arthur legend from a female point of view. The sisters were the healers, the wise women, and I thought *Sisters of Avalon* sounded really empowering.

The song "Sisters of Avalon" is about a rite of passage. At the time I wrote it, we were traveling during the end of '94 and I read an article about a little girl who was being circumcised, and the family treated it like it was some big party. And that's what inspired me.

When I got the go-ahead to make *Sisters of Avalon*, Steve, my manager at the time, told me to find an old mansion like the English bands did and record my album there. So I talked to a producer that David Massey, who was my A & R guy at the time, recommended. This producer had done some work with Tricky from Massive Attack in an old barn and said if we found the right place I might even be able to sing outside. He said we could record using Pro Tools, Logic, and sixteen-track tape. The album was going to be a kind of first, because we would try and get an old-fashioned tape sound with all the advantages of using a computer. I was excited about the idea.

I had come back from that Japan trip where I was away from my new husband for Christmas and New Year's. I came to realize on that trip that I needed to reassess my career and life. I would need new management and a new me. The one thing I got from that *Hat Full of Stars* project was a wonderful band, which this time I was the real leader of. I talked with and played with and was close to them. I led them onstage the same way I'd seen men like Cab Calloway and Bruce Springsteen and Prince do. I always thought, "Hey, how come Bruce can be boss of his band? If he could be boss, so could I." Besides, I wanted to be able to do music live and on the spot. I wanted to be able, when something came to me during a performance, to just lead the band into that. I have said before that the joy of performance, for me, is that in its best moments, I can be anybody. I was Cab Calloway and Elvis and Tina Turner and Ann-Margret. I was Mick Jagger, too, and James Brown and Edith Piaf. Whoever came to me.

My one hope every time I sing is to sing freely enough to have the spirit come to me. And once I am there, it is truly a gift. I am flying free; I finally get to escape everything. And in that space, whether anyone recognizes it or not, I feel connected to something greater than myself. And that's how it's always been for me right from the first time I opened my mouth to sing. That's why in those cover bands I was in, if I asked someone how I was that night and they said, "It was okay," I never understood. In my mind I was just dancing with Mick Jagger and it was fantastic. I realized eventually that I couldn't close my eyes anymore and just sing. I needed to get the band and the audience to see what I saw and felt inside. I needed to have them escape with me. So I had to go back again and learn everything I could.

When I toured with that incredible ten-piece band for *Hat Full of Stars*, I played live with a loop. But I had the drummer retrigger the loop every four or so bars. That way, if I wanted to try something and make a slight left turn in the middle of the song, it was possible. We weren't so locked in. It made it easier to be spontaneous. And I think you need to have spontaneous combustion sometimes. But to really lead, I needed to learn how to give clear cues and I needed to learn to count well enough to count in and out of the music phrases I wanted to include as we were playing.

So I tried to work closely with the drummer. On the "Hat Full of Stars" tour, I worked with Rocky Bryant and then Scooter Werner. I'd ask, "If I wanted to do this kind of change here, what would be a clear and good count for you?" And they told me. So I'd do that more. I work as close as I can with whatever band I'm making music with. But I think it will always be a process.

Most singers talk in such a cryptic way to these guys it's a miracle the monitor guy can guess what the heck the singer means. So every time it sounded good to me, I'd ask what he added to my voice or took out. Or I'd ask what kind of speakers he thought would suit my voice best. That helped me learn how to communicate with the monitor guy.

Anyway, back to *Sisters of Avalon*. Jan and I, and our producer Mark Saunders, finished recording the album in an old mansion in Tuxedo Park, New York, which had its own spirit. I was tired of recording in studios. They're overpriced and overrated, and with today's technology you don't need them. And in Tuxedo Park we had a great view. And a housekeeper. And a chef. Unfortunately when I was planting the last petunias and putting the gnomes next to each room, my manager told me he was leaving to take a job at Sony. He was my second manager since David Wolff.

There were so many tracks that I was proud of. "Say a Prayer" was about Gregory, and AIDS, and the fight between life and death. "Love to Hate" was about the record company and the too-cool-for-school younger artists who were so rude and stupid that they didn't even realize that half of the shit they did, they did because we did it first. (The eighties have become so big now, and now there are these nostalgia tours with a bunch of acts doing a few hits. I wouldn't go out on tour like that. I just don't want to.) And "You Don't Know" was just about people on television who have no idea what they are talking about, like these so-called political experts—the left suppresses the right and the right suppresses the left.

When we taped the "Sisters of Avalon" video we used a keyboard player who was in a wheelchair. Jan thought everyone would think that was her in the wheelchair, so we never released the video because she was so heartbroken about it. It wasn't a success anyway because people weren't focused on it.

When I was in Europe doing promotion that's when I started trying to get pregnant again. Then in March 1997 I found out that I was finally pregnant. I couldn't believe it. I wanted this little baby for so long. I used to look at pictures of my husband's mother holding him with a triangle mouth, and of course now my son has that triangle mouth. I used to call him "Luscious Louie" when he was little. I was so excited, but I didn't say anything publicly for a while. At first I thought I was going to have a girl, because when I was trying to get pregnant I kept having a vision of twin girls leaving with a suitcase. But as it happens, I had a beautiful boy.

I ended up doing a video for "Ballad of Cleo and Joe" while I was pretty pregnant. It wasn't supposed to be a video. The record company had me doing press promotion in some design place in New York and I looked around and said, "Hey, I'm all dressed up, I've got on a black wig, why not do a video? Just give me a turntable and two lights pointing down on me, aiming for my stomach. You stand up there and film it."

I made a guy glue tiny mirrors on my big round stomach to make it look like a disco ball, and I wore a silver bikini top because I thought it was funny. I figured this was the only time in my life I could get away with wearing a bikini and not worry that I didn't have a good shape.

When I was editing the video, I kept getting Braxton Hicks contractions, and the two video editors were looking at me like, "Oh my God, please don't have your baby here." People were always saying that to me. Then there are the wise guys. "Hey, lady, what are you having, twins?" David said, "The next time somebody says that, just say, 'I don't know what you're talking about. I've been drinking a lot of beer lately, but I'm not pregnant.'" I did that once. It was very funny. And everyone touched my stomach when I was pregnant. I felt like saying, "Get your hands off me before I fuckin' knock you to the ground! I'll show you what a pregnant woman is like! You better back off." People don't bother an animal when it's pregnant. You just don't.

I read fan emails while I was pregnant. You gotta understand, email was new in those days. It was like *Star Trek*, like I was writing in outer space. Many of them were from people who told me about how it was really tough for them to come out and that the song "True Colors" really saved their lives. When they announced that they were gay, they were disowned by their family and friends and lost their jobs. Some were suicidal. But instead of committing suicide, they would sing this song to themselves, in the same way that I would sing "Across the Universe" to myself.

As soon as I started answering those emails, they started coming in heavy. I don't even know how many—I just knew it was a lot, and that every single one was the same. And that's when I realized that the gay community had embraced this song. I immediately called my sister and told her about the letters and said that if there's ever a time that we could help out the gay community we should. And when the time came, we did PFLAG's "Stay Close" campaign together, which featured celebrities and their gay family members, with a message to support your gay loved ones.

I was also the opening act for Tina Turner's summer "Wildest Dreams" tour while I was pregnant. This wasn't an eighties thing: Tina was promoting new material, and so was I. But my mistake was that I did alternative songs from "Sisters of Avalon," and it just didn't suit that audience. The tour helped her but it didn't help me at all. It hurt me. It made me an opening act.

Famed photographer David LaChapelle wanted to take pictures of me pregnant. So I told my publicist Kathy Schenker and she said, "He doesn't want to take a picture of you." I wasn't sure why she was my publicist in the first place—it wasn't like she was bringing me anything earth-shattering. Years later, David asked me what happened with him taking a picture of me and I told him, "Kathy Schenker happened." That's how this business works. It's kind of fucked-up.

The album came out in 1997 and the record company let it fall through the cracks. Jan was surprised; she just didn't expect for it not to achieve anything, but I did, because I knew the record company had no intention of doing anything for that CD. It was on the *Billboard* album chart for a week. We sold sixty thousand copies on tour and it was just heartbreaking. When I was pregnant and on tour with Tina Turner, no one from the record company came to see me.

Tina was nice but we didn't get that close, if ya know what I mean. I connected much more with Cher when we toured together in 1999 for her "Do You Believe" tour. Cher is amazing, just the coolest person. When she invited me on the tour, she said, "Come on, we're gonna do great together." She was right.

Cher would do things like rent out an entire movie theater for everyone on a tour stop and we'd all watch a movie. God bless her, every day she did her yoga, every day come hell or high water. That's a pain in the ass but she could do it all. She was disciplined and she did the right thing and she was pleasant and she's just cool. If there was a problem, you'd hear about it, she'd come up and talk to you, and then it was done.

By the time she invited me on her 2002 tour, I had just lost the label I was at, and I thought indie was the way to go. But a million people saw that show—a million. And it was kind of awesome because we were able to put on a really great performance. My band was incredible. Cher started to have me on the JumboTron, and then she began to direct me. I don't know where she got the time, but she did and at one point she pulled me aside to say, "Listen, when you wear all that dark eye makeup I can't see inside your eyes." She suggested I wear other makeup and put more light on me.

During the day, I did in-store appearances, because I didn't want to just be on the tour, I wanted to really contribute. That's why I recorded "Disco Inferno," too, on producer Jellybean Benitez's label—so I'd have some new material. And I bought clothes to look as great as I could for Cher and for me. My husband had said, "If you want to be successful, you have to look successful. You can't wear cheap shit." So I hired a stylist and she bought me stuff from all over the place, including Dolce & Gabbana. Anna Sui also gave me a suit and a pair of leather pants, God bless her. For in-store appearances I put on white jeans and Etro shirts. Onstage I wore suits and ruffled shirts, kind of what I remember Otis Redding used to wear.

I sang fifty minutes a night and I wanted to do something special for the people who came to see me. I knew that Cher's fans were sitting in the front, but *my* fans were in the back and I wanted to make them feel important, too. So I'd run to the back of the venue and climb up the back stairs while I was singing. I'd rouse the whole place. I had a fantastic sound engineer so it sounded great. And there's nothing like making a whole bunch of people who are very impressed with themselves feel like they don't matter by excluding them.

The tour was a blast, but unfortunately I was working so much that I started to wear myself thin. During our show in Oklahoma, I fell while running down the stairs to go in the audience and I really hurt myself. The metal on the steps dug into my leg, so there was a gash and I couldn't get back up again. I felt so bad because Cher's dancers looked at me and got really worried. They got people to run backstage to get something, anything, to help me, and brought me bags of ice to put on my leg. Even though I couldn't move, I finished the song.

And then I went to the hospital and got it bandaged up and was given some painkillers. But I still wasn't myself, and I said, "I can't do this, I have to go home." When my little boy saw me with crutches he started crying, but he calmed down when I told him I'd be okay.

At first Cher's people totally understood that I needed to rest and one of her people, who I'll call Mr. Smiley, wanted me back. I couldn't go when they wanted me but as soon as I could, of course I did. I only missed two or three shows. At first I had to perform in a wheelchair and one time I almost fell off the stage. And then gradually my leg got better and I switched to a cane, and then I was fully back. But I haven't been able to jog ever since.

One time when we were heading for a show in DC we wound up getting stuck in terrible traffic and we had a flat tire, and I was going to be late for the show. You're not going to believe what happened. They sent a police escort so we could make it through. We quickly got dressed in the back of the bus and walked right off the bus onto the stage. It was so dramatic and wild. But I also felt really bad. Cher was a stickler for being prompt and Mr. Smiley said, "You can't be late anymore. If you are, I'm going to start to dock you." But that experience taught me to be more on time, which I'm so grateful for. (I still am a little late, though. I'm trying. There's a lot of shit to do to pull this old ass together—I do the singing exercises, the eyelashes . . .)

Another time we were in Laredo, Texas, and I was running late after an in-store again. My assistant Jackie and I had to pack up everything (she did most of the packing), quickly get dressed at the hotel, and get to the gig. But someone forgot to have a car waiting. So my assistant Jackie got a cab for us and we started shoving all of our shit in it for the show. We tried to get this poor Mexican cab driver to get to the stage entrance as soon as possible: "Drive on the grass and go backstage. Come on, you gotta go, you gotta go!" So this poor guy who was absolutely horrified drove on the grass, not knowing who the fuck we were. Then we were blocked by a bunch of people who were lined up to see Cher so I stuck my head out the window and yelled, "Please let me through! I'm gonna be late, I gotta be onstage, I'm supposed to be onstage, please, *please,* let me through." Some of them were like, "Fuck you." But some of them just looked at me going, "Oh my God, it's Cyndi Lauper!" and moved over. We finally pulled in backstage and all our trunks were outside because it was a small venue and Miss Thing had everything inside, including the elephant and the kitchen sink. We ran out of the cab, popped open the trunks and pulled out all our shit, and I ran onstage. It was so ridiculous, and again, I was mad at myself because I was late.

Then after we took a break for Christmas, Cher wanted to go back out, but I had to be with my kid because he was such a wreck. He missed his mom. I think Cher understood. After that, whenever she did something good I'd call her up and congratulate her. I think she's awesome. It's just really hard to be friends with famous people because they're really busy.

It's funny—I did the Cher tour, but I was never invited to the Lilith Fair. There was supposed to be a "women in rock" moment at the end of the nineties but it was really a Christina Aguilera and Britney Spears moment. Those two were like me and Madonna, head to head. But Christina was a different kind of performer from Britney— and although everybody says Britney can't sing, it's bullshit. She can sing—she just can't sing like she does on the record, because no one can, really. Those Swedish producers she worked with made her stop at every word. That's why her voice sounds like that—so controlled. I would have killed those producers. They would have been dead.

Here's the thing that's so bizarre to me. When producers contact you to work together, it's because they hear something in your work that they want to combine with what they do. So it's so strange when they make you unrecognizable—unless, I guess, you want to do something unrecognizable. Which I think is very plausible for me—I sometimes wondered if I should just hide my name the next time, so people would just hear my singing without knowing who I was. I could put together a persona like Daft Punk. You don't even know who those guys are or how old they are. That's the wonder and the beauty of it.

The whole idea that young people are the only ones making good music and that older musicians do some form of old-fart music is bizarre to me. A lot of the younger artists now, they sing literally one word, and then the producers piece it together with the other words using Pro Tools. When I did *Bring Ya to the Brink* and I worked with Swedish writers who acted like I was Svengali because I was adding my own input, I just looked at them and thought, "They don't read credits, they don't know what I do, they don't know that I've produced."

When one producer started directing how I should sing I said, "You're a wonderful drummer, why don't you show me how to sing like a drum?" And I directed him on the bridge to make it like an echo. And the song "Echo" really worked; it's catchy and it's fun. It's a great dance record. But it was not a priority. The record company had four other acts that were priorities, and unfortunately there was nothing I could do.

Which, by the way, is what's so great about this musical *Kinky Boots* that I'm doing with Harvey Fierstein and Jerry Mitchell. I couldn't have walked through the world of Broadway with two better guys. They're very gifted. They know the world they live in and they really *like* my music; that's why they have me there. It's not like they just threw me in there because of my name. They're not trying to change me. It's been exciting because I don't have to worry that some-one's going to tell me to do something ridiculous that is not me at all (and if they do, Harvey says, "That's ridiculous").

And like I said, when I sing something, I really want to connect to something bigger than myself. I don't want to just sing. I have always wanted to escape, and when you sing in the right rhythm in the right key and say the right things you can open up that corridor. That is the only place I want to go when I sing. Singing makes you bigger than who you normally are. And thank God for my teachers and all the singers who came before me and who are singing now. We all learn from one another and are connected.

So anyway, back to 1997. Declyn Wallace Lauper Thornton was born in November of that year. We named him after Elvis Costello (whose first name is Declan). It's just like what they say: Your whole perspective changes when you have a kid. After he was born I had a meeting with the record-company people out in New York and they brought in a new A & R guy, Peter Asher. But the head guy was the same guy I met in Paris before I was pregnant who told me everything was going to be good. You can't listen to a lie twice. I had one more album on my contract and I said, "Listen, if you're not going to do anything to promote it you might as well let me go. I don't want to go through that again. I worked really hard, I tried really hard, I gave a really great image, tried to make a really great album cover, but it all doesn't matter if you guys are not going to promote it." And this one guy said, "No, this time we're going to do something. Why don't you go home and sleep on it?" He was trying to placate me. I pulled out my baby's picture and said, "Why don't you go home and sleep on *this?* Tomorrow when you're shaving, look at this baby's face in the mirror and tell him how his mother had to get another job, because you wrecked her career. You can do that to me, but you're not going to do that to my baby." Peter looked like he was going to fall down; he couldn't even believe it.

I tried to leave, and they came after me and said, "Okay, you just have to make a Christmas album." That would be my final album for Epic and then I could get the hell out. I said that I just happened to be working on a Christmas record because I always wanted to make one. I love Christmas. So that's how it happened. Jan came back to stay with me upstairs at our house in Connecticut with her son, who was eight or nine. We had worked together so well that it was a natural next step to keep writing. And Declyn was just born, and a nice woman named Delilah was taking care of him. Dec was the most awesome little kid. He was funny and laughed a lot—just a sweetie. Jan and I wrote in the living room. I made a lot of great music in that house (what I consider great, anyway). I wrote all of *Hat Full of Stars* and *Sisters of Avalon* in that living room. Later I wrote *Shine* in there, too.

The house has a very magical feel to it that makes you forget time and space. It's made like a little dollhouse, so it is fun to write there. David would come by with Declyn once in a while as we recorded the album in the garage. The album has a song called "New Year's Baby (First Lullaby)" that I wrote for Dec, and he grabbed the microphone and just sang into it. So that's him that you hear in the solo. He thought he was singing. He even did a little yodel thing in it.

When the album came out, my great publicist Lisa (the one who eventually became my manager), got me on the Rockefeller Center Christmas tree-lighting television special to sing "Early Christmas Morning." And not just that, but I was accompanied by a kids' choir. All these little kids were in scarves and Christmas sweaters. It was awesome. I started the song by sitting on the floor in a white cape, playing the dulcimer, and then I threw my cape off and I had on a red satin Mrs. Claus–style dress with white crinoline underneath.

When I was a kid in Ozone Park, my friends and I would come into Manhattan at night during Christmas. In the middle of the night, you kind of had the city to yourself. We'd see the store windows across the street at Saks, decked out with all the Christmas decorations, and then we'd go to see the tree. And there I was performing in front of it. I thought that was pretty amazing.

It was such a special time when Dec was little. I remember when he was a toddler, I brought him out with me on Cher's "Do You Believe" tour, with his caregiver, Delilah. Dec was his own guy. He wanted in on everything. During that tour I had a few opening bands before me, including Fergie's band Wild Orchid, before she went on to join the Black Eyed Peas. Dec used to point his chin toward the woman he wanted to be brought to. He was all over Fergie like a cheap suit. He started to have a fascination with drums too so Scooter from my first tour gave him sticks, and he demonstrated how he could use his wrists. Scooter said he had really good rhythm. When he was three we went into Sam Ash Music Store for drums and he sat at a baby kit and imitated everything in a drum instruction video that was playing. One time he went shopping for a cymbal and hit every one in the shop. The guy who worked there looked like he was going to kill me. Anyway, later, when he was three and a half, I included him onstage with me. I'd let him set up his little drums and play with us.

One time I had to leave him for an in-store appearance in Manhattan and he started to cry because he wanted to be with me so I said, "Okay, we're taking him." I dressed him up, and Jackie drew a little mustache and goatee on him. He played drums on a cardboard box with the band, who were all very giving to him. And the people just loved him! He was something. But then at one point the band decided that they didn't want to play with him anymore until he really learned. So he got upset and didn't want to come anymore. He also felt like they took me away from him.

But then he got involved with hockey. Can you believe that I became a hockey mom for a minute?

Little one / little son / All my life I've wished you welcome.
—"December Child"

CHAPTER FOURTEEN

SHINE WAS SUPPOSED to be a dance record. I was moving in that direction after I wound up doing some work with these two fellows from Soul Solution who remixed "Ballad of Cleo and Joe." It became a big dance hit in South Florida because of a fan and friend of mine named Carlos Rodriguez, who was so upset at how the record company treated me that he got a job at a radio station and played my music. (Thank you, Carlos.) And like I said, I had done "Disco Inferno" for the first Cher tour because I didn't want to just be the oldies artist with nothing to sell. It was nominated for a Grammy for Best Dance Recording for 1999 and became a hit in the clubs.

I wrote the song "Shine," and some other ones, with Bill Wittman, a longtime collaborator. I wrote with Jan, too, and I kept trying to go back to writing with those guys from Soul Solution. I felt a connection to them because, like I said earlier, my aunt knew Bobby Guy's uncle and because we had been successful. But time moved on and they changed and I changed.

Anyway, *Shine* started out as a dance record, but when I performed the songs I was working on at clubs, I realized their shortcomings. A lot of them were too complicated for dance. I'd perform something and realize, "Oh, this song has too many chord changes." Dance music only has like three chords, or maybe four at the most. It just doesn't change that much. It has to be simple as hell and not have too many words. Things have advanced a little since then, but basically, I found that dance music was more restrictive than pop, whereas I initially thought it was going to be more creative.

At the time, I would have liked to have gotten input from Junior Vasquez, but he wasn't talking to me because I insulted one of his friends or something, and he was living with strange people who kind of took over his life a bit. I didn't really know what was going on, but we fell out for a little while (now we're talking again). When I started playing the dulcimer on my albums he would say to me, "Nobody likes that hillbilly shit you're playing." So sometimes if he wouldn't return my call, I would just call him again and play the dulcimer on his message machine.

So I had to shift the album away from dance a little and make it right for what it was: an album of pop, rock, dance, and R & B. At that time I also went and did a little something for Tricky. I did vocals for the song "Five Days" for his 2001 album, *BlowBack*. I admire him very much as an artist. I met him in a studio in New Jersey, but it was an odd experience because when I got there, I had to start writing the song with him, I mean literally, everything—the lyrics and the melody. I can do that, but I wasn't prepared and I was so on the spot that I couldn't even think. I felt like a deer in the headlights.

While I was there I also played him the ballad "Water's Edge" to ask him what he thought, and he said, "Cyn, to me, that's a hit song." He liked me a lot because his toilet kept running and running, and it was driving me crazy, so I lifted the lid off and fixed it. When he did an interview about the album and they asked about working with me, he said, "She fixed my toilet."

One song on that album that I always thought was so funny was "It's Hard to Be Me," which I wrote with Bill and Rob Hyman. It just feels like a comedy song even though it's a rocker. We laughed very hard when we were writing it. Like there's the line "You see me everywhere in my underwear / You may wonder what I'm here to sell." That's because around 2000, models were being shown in underwear in their ads, and I kept thinking, "Where are the clothes? What are they selling?" Even though they were in underwear, you didn't know if they were selling underwear, or music, or clothes, or what. The song is meant to be ironic too, like with the line Bill came up with, "It's hard to be me / Nobody knows what it's like to be me / the envy of mediocrity." (He's very clever, Bill.)

Along with "Comfort You," Jan and I wrote "Higher Plane," which I thought would be a big hit. I loved those songs but then when I played them for the record people, they'd say, "It doesn't sound like you, Cyn." I was like, "Isn't that good?" So what if it doesn't sound like me? "Shine" sounded like a hit to me, too, but radio wouldn't play it because of the drums, because of the rhythm. They couldn't tell me what it was that they didn't like about the rhythm, but I paid the guy who engineers for Mutt Lange to remix it. He wound up compressing my voice so much though that it sounded like I couldn't sing. I realized that just because the compressor worked for other people didn't mean that it would work for me. And then I just felt like Vinnie van Gogh trying to make a hit painting again.

The way I used to sell my records was that I would perform dance mixes of my songs in the clubs. I started to wear all the shit that I wore for Gay Pride when I performed in the clubs. So I had on a bejeweled rainbow flag, so when I spun around in the light, it would shine. Then I started wearing these headdresses too. I remember I went to Canada to do some shows, and at the time, the Bravo network was doing a piece on me about the creative process. So they were following me around. I was also eating disgusting diet food again to stay skinny.

Anyway, I had booked a couple of shows in what they told me were dance clubs, in Edmonton, Alberta. I had off during the day and the Bravo people went away somewhere, so I wandered around and found this shop with all these beautiful feathered headdresses. And keep in mind this was Edmonton, okay? Not New Orleans. So I went in, and there were headdresses in all different colors: a red one, a white one, a blue one. I was so excited. But then the woman who worked there kept looking at me and asking, "Do you ice skate?" I said, "No, no, I don't ice skate." But she continued to ask me. Finally I said, "Why do you keep asking me if I ice skate?"

"Because this is an Ice Capades shop."

So I bought some new wide feathered headdresses and I brought them with my bejeweled flag to the club for my gig. I walked in and there was chicken wire in front of the stage and a dirt floor, and there was an opening band for me. And I was like, "Um, why is there a band at a dance club?" But I quickly worked out some songs with them—slash-metal versions of "She Bop" and "Girls." Then I got my headdress on, and I was dancing around with my glittery clothes, dressed up like some crazy-ass witch doctor, and singing songs like "Higher Plane" to a track (like you do in dance clubs), and all of a sudden I stopped and looked at everybody. They were all just staring at me, dumbfounded. So I said, "You all must think I'm out of my mind, but see, I thought this was a dance club, and in dance clubs, you do this kind of thing."

I don't know how I got through that show. It was like something out of a movie. I don't mind getting dirt thrown on me once in a while, but I really felt like I had hit the bottom. I was like, "These people could give a shit about me. I could be dead." The audience was so disappointed, because I wasn't the Cyndi Lauper they knew.

There was one more show I had to do in Alberta and the club owner told me that the next club was more of the same. I called my manager and said, "Are you fucking kidding me?"

"Can't you just get through it?" my crazy manager asked.

"No, it's bad for my reputation," I told him. I got out of that one, at least.

Glamorous, it wasn't. There is this one makeup artist I work with in Toronto and sometimes my life is so ridiculous that when I tell her about it, she starts laughing and saying, "Okay, where are the cameras? It can't be this ridiculous."

You probably won't be surprised to learn that that was about the time I left my manager, because he had really proved that he wasn't doing too much to help me. Then I hired the best manager ever—Lisa Barbaris. I actually knew for a long time, since 1995, that she would be perfect. Like I said, that was the year I did the Gay Games in New York City. My friends Brian Salzman and Howard Kaplan got me into the games, by the way, not the record company. They wouldn't even promote the "Ballad of Cleo and Joe" in the clubs because the head of the dance division thought it was too gay. They were into ballads and speeding them up instead.

So my friend Chris Tanner, who is this wonderful painter and drag performer and an actor, called me and said, "Cyn, Pride is in two weeks, you've got to have a float, you gotta be in the parade." I said, "Are you kidding me? How am I going to get a float in two weeks?" Chris said, "You call the organizers and tell them you're Cyndi Lauper and you want to be in the parade and you take all of us, and we kill it." So I called up Lisa, who was my publicist at the time, and somehow she got me this float. I had all these drag queens on it, and I played every version of "Girls Just Want to Have Fun" there fuckin' was. Then I was told that I couldn't sing "Girls Just Want to Have

Fun" in front of St. Patrick's Cathedral, because it was a no-singing zone, and that if I did they would shut it down. I said, "*Please* let me sing and let them shut me down. Do you realize what the headlines would read? 'Cardinal O'Connor Just Didn't Want to Have Fun.'" So I went ahead and sang, and the funny thing was, the church did not shut me down: they knew what the headlines would have read. So my little Catholic-schoolgirl heart was all a-flutter.

But I knew when Lisa pulled that parade float out of nowhere that she would be a great manager, and she is. She's capable, she's loyal, and I love her and I think she loves me. She works hard—sometimes she works too hard and I want to say, "Hey, come on, we're gonna die, can you just take a minute here?"

But I still had my old manager then. He didn't come to Gay Pride. And another time when I did the Vienna Gay Life Ball for AIDS in Marie Antoinette's white underwear with a wig that had a boat with a guy in it, I remember he looked at me and said, "Why can't you just wear jeans and a T-shirt?" The last straw was when he sent his assistant on his behalf to the record-company presentation for *Shine*. I decided to can him and hire Lisa.

Anyway, *Shine* was supposed to be released by a smaller record company called Edel on September 1, 2001, but a few weeks beforehand, Lisa called me and told me, "Edel America is going out of business. You've got to get the rights to your music." So we fought to get them back, and then I had the opportunity to put out the album with a really small indie label, but I just wasn't sure about doing that. Plus some tracks had leaked to the public. I figured this out when I first performed and everybody was already singing along. So Lisa went to other labels to see if they would pick it up, but the feedback was so disheartening, like, "Who does she think she is? She's not a producer, she should just sing. I can only take her if she does everything I tell her to do." They wanted me to work with the songwriter David Foster. I didn't want to work with someone whose music I didn't like. Yeah, he's a very talented guy but he makes very middle-of-the-road music and say what you will, but I don't make middle-of-the-road music. I didn't want to do overwrought ballads. How much angst can you sing? Even some of the R & B people came back and said, "She can't produce, this is horrible." The horrible work that they were talking about inspired a lot of the music that's happening now. I can hear "Shine" in Katy Perry's "Firework." And Arcade Fire is a huge fan of mine and a lot of stuff inspired them—so I've been told.

So after that I said, "Let's just produce an EP ourselves and see what happens." Lisa told me to choose five songs, so I chose "Shine," a remix of it, "It's Hard to Be Me," "Madonna Whore," and "Water's Edge." "Shine" is the biggest underground song. When I sing it it's a huge hit, people go wild.

And by the way, the song "Madonna Whore" had absolutely nothing to do with Madonna. It was about the Madonna-whore complex. I was just writing about my experience as a woman: "Every woman's a Madonna / every woman's a whore / you can try to reduce me but I'm so much more." But of course because of the thing with me and Madonna, that's what people were going to think. Dopey me.

But Madonna herself brought that concept into her greatest, most provocative stuff, such as "Like a Prayer," which, not for nothing, made me love her. When I saw that video I said, "All right, she's fuckin' great." She pushed all the buttons with that one—brilliant. And when Pepsi dropped her after that video, not only did she wind up taking money from them, but she used that controversy to make the video even bigger, and everyone saw it—everyone. When Pepsi pushed her down like that, what they really did was push her up. She just knew how to work that. And like I said before, I always put my best foot forward but I didn't know how to manipulate the press. I had no business sense.

So I sold the EP on my website and Lisa worked really hard to get it sold through Borders. I would not give up, and I had a lot of help from my friends, who really stepped up. It was a little indie EP, and I think in the end I sold sixty-eight thousand of them. Which I think I sold one by one. The whole thing wasn't what I had originally planned for the album, but those were decent sales figures and that made it all a little easier. I'll never forget getting everything ready for *Shine* and finding out that Sony was putting out yet *another* best-of collection, the *Twelve Deadly Cyns . . . and Then Some* DVD of all my videos up until "I'm Gonna Be Strong." That kind of sucked. They were cannibalizing my sales. You can't have two things out at once. But what could I do?

During the *Shine* period, I went to Transylvania to do a TV show on a stage across from "Bad Vlad's" castle. (He was Vlad the Impaler, the inspiration for Dracula, but I think "Bad Vlad" is a much better handle.) So I went to Romania. It was 2000, maybe 2001. My hair was white-blonde and black. It's funny, I always remember the year and album from my hair. Anyway, it was presented that it was a big deal and that *I* would be a big deal in Romania. Who knew? It was another great adventure. I didn't have a crew that I was used to, but my band was killer. I had Sammy Merendino on drums, Bill Wittman on bass, Knox Chandler on guitar, Steve Gaboury on keyboards, and Allison Cornel on violin, viola, and sometimes dulcimer, too. (Two dulcimers are better than one, if you ask me, so I played dulcimer as well.) Anyway, I was so excited we were going to play the *Shine* CD along with some other songs.

I had gone to Trash and Vaudeville before I left. I had been scouring the city to find an Edie Sedgwick look. No one was doing that.

I kept going to showrooms and showing them pictures, but no one carried anything remotely like what she wore. Of course, the following year, and the year after, Edie made a big resurgence. Her look just wasn't available when I needed it. But in the end I changed what I wore and went more downtown.

So when I went to Romania I had a silk blouse that was kind of that sixties type of shirt that started to bell at the elbow, and black leather pants. In the end I was barefoot, but that wouldn't matter because I actually never made it to the main broadcast.

When I arrived we were whisked away by the show promoter's crew, racing through the streets with sirens going. I couldn't figure what the sirens were about, until I found out they were ex–secret police. It became very much like James Bond, all of a sudden. And I kept thinking to myself, "You can't make this shit up." Then I started to think about my three-year-old at home and started to get a little nervous, so I told them they needed to slow down. They didn't—then I got really angry and said I needed to get back in one piece to my kid, and they slowed down as best they could.

I'd never been to Romania before—that was what made it so enticing. We stayed in a mountain village with a big lodge-style hotel. It was very quaint. And there, as promised, was the Bad Vlad Castle. We all went out to eat the first night and Bill ate bear. I couldn't get down with the whole bear thing. I had the venison. I ate Bambi's mother or father instead.

The next day was the press conference. I had on my new look, with red and blue and black jeans from Trash and Vaudeville and my Edie Sedgwick eyes. It was a new me. I was so excited about starting this new chapter of my career—Cyndi as an indie.

Everyone was really nice to us, except I had no idea that homosexuality was illegal in Romania at that time. So during the interview when they asked, "So you fight for gay rights?" I said, "You're damn right I do," and I just started going on about how I think everyone should be afforded civil rights. That caused quite a stir in the room.

While I was doing sound check I told the monitor guy, who was gaping at me like I was nuts, that he had to turn up the guitar, and quick. I was saying, "Come on, come on, you have to do it *now*." I made him cry. I'm not kidding. If you're going to cry, don't take the fucking gig, because it's not easy. I liked him a lot, but there's no crying in monitors. (There will always be glitches in my whole "learning to communicate" thing. I do a lot of "I shoulda said this, I shoulda said that," but I'm still on the path of learning.)

In the meantime, my manager was about to get beat up by this big fuckin' Transylvanian woman who was managing the Romanian Elvis performing before me. This stupid guy played music that sounded like oldies, but it wasn't even cool, like the Stray Cats or anything interesting. But the people of that country probably loved it. We got through it though, even though Elvis decided to eat up a lot of the time. I sang a few songs, including "She Bop."

By the way, if you listen to the very end of "She Bop," you'll hear that Michael Jackson took the bass line and wrote "Bad" from it. Right before he went in to record "Bad" he sat behind me on an airplane with Emmanuel Lewis and he was listening to "She Bop." Anyway, it doesn't matter. I'm very flattered he even thought of that. Nobody was promoting me like they did him. I was also a little jealous of him—he was on Epic. But they treated him so badly. He had a lot of pressure on him and when all the press about the molestation came out the record company really distanced themselves from him—everyone did. I don't know what his private life was like but he was always sweet to me. Then of course when he died the record company was like, "Yay, Michael." They were drooling over all the money that they were going to make because all his records jumped to the top of the charts, just like Whitney Houston's.

Anyway, when we finished the songs and got offstage, we discovered that everything in our greenroom was taken. Everything was gone. It was like that old expression, "Here's your hat—what's your hurry?" Then the Romanian airplane that we took made an unexpected landing at a military base in the country to get some fuel. It wasn't first-class—it was low-class. It was a Fred Flintstone flight from hell. But it was a funny moment, and we laughed a lot. And you know what? We saw the country, and I bought a few glass vases.

Back in the US I did a lot of in-store appearances for *Shine*, which I loved. I met so many people and heard sad stories from sick vets who were coming back from the Gulf War. I tried so hard to sell CDs and to sign as many autographs as I could. The weird thing about in-stores is that it's hard to sign fast enough. You want to shake everyone's hand, to take a picture, make a connection, and be a human being, but the store managers want you in and out of there in an hour or two. But that's impossible. If there are five hundred people, then you're going to be there for three hours.

I always love meeting people, but I miss my family so much when I'm away. I feel like Willy Loman sometimes. I get this feeling of despair, and it gets harder as I get older. It's funny, my keyboard player Archie "Hubbie" Turner says he wants to do a reality show called *The Old and the Useless* because when you get older in this business, you start to feel useless. But you're so not. When I first saw Hubbie perform live, I kept saying, "I hope that young kid is easy and good to work with." It turns out he was older than all of us! He was sixty-five. He gets through life in a magical way. He's a lucky bastard. I think that everyone you meet and see has some magic and I'm always interested to understand what that magic is. I know Allen Toussaint, who played on my blues album, has magic; I know that my guitar player has magic; I know all the musicians I play with have a certain magic about them; and I know my family has a magical quality about them. So I do live a really charmed and magical life—it's just that some days I forget to take that in because I can't see it, or I'm busy looking at something else.

And even though I complain about how busy my manager keeps me all the time, at least after all these years I'm still singing, and I'm still viable. *Bring Ya to the Brink* was nominated for a Grammy. *At Last* was nominated for a Grammy in 2003—although not for singing, which it should have been, but for arrangement. I don't read music for instrumental parts. I arrange by ear. I listen; I know what I want. Sometimes I'll tell somebody to play a completely different song but to change the chords to the chords of the song that we're playing. And they look at me like I have two heads at first. I've gotten savvy with explaining to people now that I have an odd way of working so they need to bear with me. I have always believed that music is like cooking—you take a little bit of spice from this cabinet and that cabinet and you mix it all together and see what you got.

Anyway, after *Shine*, Lisa kept thinking about how the record-company people said that I wasn't a producer and that the only way they'd sign me is if I did what they wanted. Like Clive Davis said, "Do I think she's wonderful? Yes I do. Will she ever do what I want her to do? No." So Lisa said, "Cyn, nobody really understands that you arrange music. Why don't you arrange some classic songs *and* interpret them? This can be about arrangement and interpretation—let them hear the singer you are." I said okay. And believe it or not, I went back to Sony, because they had that idea along with Lisa. There was one guy I kind of really liked there named David Massey, and I signed because of him. I figured, better the devil you know. But when I first met with him, he wanted to hear a tape of what I would do. I said to him, "You want a demo? I've been doing this for twenty years, and you want a demo?" But that's their protocol. They had to put a lot of money up and blah, blah, blah.

When I realized they wanted demos I figured, "Oh, I better find a song to do a circus trick in, because that's the only way they'll do this." So I went and thought about songs that had influenced me when I was younger and influenced the way I heard music. Although "At Last" was not a song that I had originally picked. It seemed like one of those songs that everybody and their mother sang.

So I started thinking about it and I remembered when I was a kid and used to wait for the A train on Liberty Avenue and 104th Street to go to school. I remember a poster in the train station of this beautiful black woman with blonde hair, Etta James. And I used to stand and look at it, and at the other women on the platform all dressed up to go into Manhattan. If you lived in Queens, Manhattan was the mecca—the mecca of style, the mecca of art, everything was in Manhattan. It was your dream. So everyone who went to work in Manhattan dressed differently. (This was around the time I was studying fashion, because I was going to the High School of Fashion Industries.) They stood differently, too. It didn't look like they were staying in Queens, where all the mothers were going to the A & P supermarket—it was like these women were going to the *city*. Watching them, I felt this otherworldly thing like I always did. Like I said, I've always had one foot on this planet and one foot . . . I don't know, somewhere else, that enabled me to see things and feel things like that. And I was also painting at the time, so it all looked like a painting. Sounds are like a painting to me, too—the clotheslines in my neighborhood sounded like music, with the sheets flapping in the wind. Or the pigeons flying overhead, that sounded like music, or the mothers calling their children from a distance, planting their feet firmly down and yelling around the corner, and you'd think you heard your name so you'd go running home.

So when I interpreted "At Last," I tried to put all of that into the music and then I remembered how you could feel the sway of the train's trestles when it was approaching, so I asked my accompanist and the person I arranged the music with, Steve Gaboury, to re-create that feel with the rhythms because piano is a rhythm instrument. It almost seemed that he breathed with the piano—in and out to the rhythm of the trestles that moved against the wind as the train came into the station. And at that point I stepped off the platform to sing the first line of the song.

I just kept singing and he just kept playing. And at the end of the song, I did the circus trick by holding a big note out for a long time so that the record company guys would say, "Oh yes, she can sing, let's sign her."

I also did "Walk on By" and "Unchained Melody," which were very popular when I was a kid. All these songs were covered by a multitude of artists, so I figured the only way that people would hear my interpretation was if I rediscovered them and found a new soul, a new path, a new story within the story. Which is always how you should interpret a song: What's the story? Where are you? What's around you? Is it cold? Is it hot? Is it nighttime? Is it daytime? And what just happened? This is the storyline you start from. When I was a young girl looking at the Etta James poster, it was the time of Janis Joplin, and I saw Janis Joplin and the hippies and the juxtaposition of these two cultures in a swirl, rock and raw blues and a changing culture.

And listeners will feel the story, whether they're aware of it or not. Because a lot of this wasn't overt and spelled out—it was an interior rhythm that I needed to connect to. In that space, a story has more richness and an otherworldly quality. And instead of singing out where everyone else would sing out, I would sing in. And where they would sing in, I would sing out. Then I would wrap my head around the story of whatever spirit was coming to me. When singing ballads I always feel that you have to turn yourself inside out and most of my work on *At Last* was a combination of singing with power and revisiting the power of a whisper.

Every sound is a character. The story of "Walk on By," which I told before I would sing it live, was that there was this young girl in my neighborhood who became pregnant when she was twelve and wound up raising the kid alone. Her boyfriend went on to other things but her life was radically changed and she was not prepared financially or educated enough to really provide for herself and a child. Her life stopped right where she was and she began a totally different life that had less financial opportunity and less educational opportunity.

I was so glad that Russ Titelman, who has worked with everyone you can think of, from Eric Clapton to George Harrison, was the producer. I knew that Russ would understand this stuff, because a long, long time before that, he sent me this old Richard Rogers–Lorenz Hart song "Little Girl Blue," by Nina Simone. In the beginning she does a bit from the Christmas carol "Good King Wenceslas." This, too, is all interior—it's very quiet and almost stark. Because Christmas is the saddest time for a lot of people, and the loneliest. That kind of thinking colored my version of "La Vie en Rose."

That whole album was a story about the women in my life. There was one housewife in the neighborhood who was very large. I would see her when I worked in my grandmother's garden, which was surrounded by those metal fences that squared off your piece of land. You can see through and look straight down and see other people's backyards. It was the most amazing thing to see all those people during their daily struggles and joys. So this heavyset woman would make her spaghetti sauce on Sunday, and I could smell it from my grandmother's garden. While it cooked she sat on a little chair with her accordion and played "Volare," to the point where I would think, "Oh my God, I'm going to kill myself." The bat wings on her heavy arms swung back and forth as she squeezed the bellows of the accordion, and later, when I was an adult, I realized that *"volare"* means "to fly" and it all came together. This was a woman with a life of toil who found joy playing a song about her heart taking flight while her bat wings followed. And all those metaphors from *The Old Man and the Sea* came back to me.

So these kinds of images came up a lot for me when I was making the *At Last* album (although I couldn't sing "Volare" because that would have really killed me). I felt strongly that I wanted to tell these stories through the orchestration and arrangements of the songs chosen for the album. When Russ played "Stay" for me, I remembered being at my older cousin Linda's house, in her bedroom listening to her 45s. She played "Stay," along with a lot of Four Seasons and songs sung by girls with girlish voices, like Lesley Gore. Meanwhile Linda's mom, my aunt Gloria, and the other grown-ups would be listening to Latin music, cha-cha music that had these wild album covers with women wearing fishnets and colorful lipstick. And if I stood in the middle of the house, maybe in the kitchen toasting marshmallows on the stove, I would hear a song that was like "Stay" playing over a Latin rhythm. It was basically a mash-up, before its time.

That whole period when I was growing up in Queens and visiting my aunt on Long Island was filled with Italian music, and women wearing muumuus in the day and cocktail dresses and cha-cha heels at night. And in the backyards they'd have middle-class garden parties that were lavish to us, because they would have a stereo blasting out the bedroom window filling the yard with music. If it was a special occasion like a birthday party at my aunt Gloria's, they'd hang out Chinese lamps. We lived large in a way that people who *really* live large don't—there's a spice, a richness, a joy that working-class people have. And even though we were kind of products of misery, we still had a vibrance.

So this whole album was about my growing up and the stories around my childhood. I added "On the Sunny Side of the Street" because I grew up listening to Louis Armstrong, and I needed another up-tempo song. There were too many slow, deep ones, and if we didn't pick it up we'd have to give out razor blades with the record so people could cut their wrists. Anyway, here was a song about being positive instead of negative, about taking everything that was sad and just saying, "Okay, all of this is sad, but I can deal with it, and I'm going to choose to walk on the sunny side of the street anyway." And that's how my life always was.

Another up-tempo one I included was "Makin' Whoopee" with Tony Bennett, but I got in a little trouble with Tony. I was looking for a way to do the song differently, because it was so straight. I listened to how Ella Fitzgerald did it with Louis Armstrong, and I liked the way Louis talked a little in between singing, so I figured I'd do that. He got mad at me though, because he didn't understand all the speaking stuff and he wanted me to be like k.d. lang, his frequent duet partner. He also wanted me to know the song really well before I got there. I didn't want to, though, because I wanted to learn it with his band before he got there so that I could perform in their rhythm instead of just singing on top of it.

So even though I didn't write any of those songs, it was very autobiographical, because I was taking bits and pieces from my life when I felt crushed or saw someone was crushed. Or who was having her little garden party and being joyful. Growing up, we still had this color, the different people and ethnicities, and the different fashion they wore, the different things they said. It was like Shakespeare to me. In the meantime, like I said earlier, my mother was always taking us to the Delacorte Theater to see Shakespeare. I always felt I could find Shakespeare right in my neighborhood, when I'd watch everyone walk down the block from the factories to where the trees started on our block. It was tree-lined after our place because my grandfather chopped down the tree by our house. So the trees didn't start until Mrs. Schnur's house next door.

Mrs. Schnur was friends with my grandmother, and these women were very much a part of my journey and my awakening. I saw this generation of women before me have all their hopes and dreams dashed, ripped up like my aunt Gracie's photographs. I saw all these women, the lady across the yard, my mother, her sister, my grandmother, who had no shot, who didn't go to college, the girl who was twelve years old and pregnant with a kid who everyone passed by. All of these stories moved me to make a change in any way I could. And I'm sure I changed things in just a little way, but it was something, and for one second, it was cooler to be different than it was to be your normal conservative person.

At Last was never meant to be a radio album, and then all of a sudden the record company wanted to play it on radio. I kept saying that my voice was loud in the mix—you couldn't even play it in a club because if you turned it up, my voice would kill you, but they didn't listen. I felt like it was the kind of album you could have playing at a dinner party.

Art is interpretive, and it's important to take inspiration from your life. The album cover is a painting of the stories put together, and you'll see that on the cover of *At Last* I have on a black cocktail dress, with the city in the background, and I'm in a manhole, coming up out of a barge. In the video for "Hole in My Heart (All the Way to China)" I came out of a manhole cover, too, and I wore Chinese pajamas. I wore a black wig that I put in pigtails, and I had on glasses and a hat. (It was pretty funny, but I don't know, now that I look back on it, I think it's a little racist.) My mother was in the video in a rickshaw, and my aunt Gracie too, which is kind of sweet.

Anyway, it's funny about the sewer, because I did come from the bottom; I did feel like nothing before I felt like anything. Through the years, I've always studied a lot of self-development stuff, which has sometimes helped me and sometimes not. I'm intense because the work I make is intense and because when I sing I'm intense. I'm just an intense little motherfucker, what can I tell ya? I try, I listen to the Buddhist CDs, the Abraham CDs, to the point where I had one assistant say, "Oh my God, not again, please don't." Those CDs are maddening after a while, because you just feel like, "Shut the hell up and get on with it. If you want to be successful, just fucking do what you need to do. If there's a wall in the way, fine. Let me take a step back, let me make my way around it and get to point B." That's how I try to do things now.

Years ago, my husband would walk in and look at me while I did spirit dancing with my friend Marion. We would burn down our villages and build them back up again in our heads. The Honduran housekeeper and the nanny, who were sisters and I think were also Jehovah's Witnesses, were really freaked out—I'd see these two heads through the door, watching me. Before I met David, during the *Vibes* era, I also did yoga, and with Ginny Duffy I did creative visualization, which made me understand how I got to where I wanted to be: I always saw myself there. If you can't see yourself doing what you want, how is it going to happen?

I don't mind being this intense. When things get to be too much, I space out, I pop into a different reality where I see things differently— that's been how I've lived my life. I always felt like I had this guardian angel, one I talked to my whole life. But now I feel like, "You know, maybe you got a guardian angel, maybe you don't. But be here now, be compassionate, try and open your freakin' mind and your eyes to what is happening now."

What maybe adds to my intensity is that I'm often alone. I'm in hotels a lot, and I'm home by myself when Dec is in school. But I have my dog, and I leave the television on sometimes just to have a talking voice in the background. I keep looking for a job where I won't have to leave my kid, but I don't know if it's possible. Someone said to me once, "Why don't you just do private events, and then you can be home and make the money you want?" But the whole idea of not making music for the public anymore really freaked me out. And when I write, I have to be by myself, but I want to be with my family. So often I write late at night. I don't mind getting up in the middle of the night to do that. It works for me, and then I can see them. And of course, I have my imagination, so I'm never totally alone.

During the year when I worked on *At Last*, my father told me that he went to the doctor and he had skin cancer. And I said, "Dad, skin cancer is easily cured, did they take it out?" He said they got it all, but then he said it had spread to his lymph nodes and I didn't really hear that part at first.

With my first experiences with the health-care system, I was lucky—when my mother got ovarian cancer, she got great care. I wanted my dad in Memorial Sloan-Kettering Cancer Center, one of the best places in the country, but he couldn't go, because his AARP insurance wouldn't pay. But they would pay for Columbia, which didn't have as good care as Sloan-Kettering. But I just didn't have enough money to put him in Sloan. There was a very kind nurse at Columbia who helped me find a hospice for my dad to die in. And that's what I did. I put him in a really nice hospice, the best I could find.

But when my father was dying, I blamed myself for never selling out—I might have had integrity, but I didn't have the money to do anything for him. Instead of investing in preventative care, the medical system invests in "you get sick, we take your money, honey." They don't want doctors who take your blood and prescribe vitamins, because then that would keep you alive.

I tried a lot of different things when my dad was sick in hospice care. I brought a qigong woman, I brought a healer, but they weren't having much luck with him. I tried doing reiki too, while the qigong woman worked on him—his head was hot and his feet were cold, and I drew the heat down to his feet. I got all kinds of rocks and stones, and brought another Reiki healer named Michelle, who works with doctors. I also brought all kinds of music, and when one high-pitched vocal played, my dad looked at me like, "What, are you kidding me?" That made me laugh.

I kept telling the doctors and nurses, "Just give him more drugs, because I don't want him in pain." My stepmother was not okay with that, probably because she didn't want to let go. She said, "Why do you want to keep him so doped up? You don't want him to die, do you?"

When my father did pass, my stepmother said she would send him to be cremated and then we would get the urn back. But I felt like, when he gets cremated, it's all over, and there he is, just sitting on the friggin' counter in an urn? So I decided to go to the cremation, and I was surprised when my husband, who was fearful for his own dad's health, came with me. Earlier I kept telling my father, "When you get better, I'll take you to the Great Wall of China." So I brought a silk scarf from China to the cremation. When I asked to see him they said, "That's extra." Fine, I said and they showed me a cardboard box. I put the scarf around him and pink flowers over him—over his heart, to heal any sadness.

I called Elen while I was there, and she said, "What's that music in the background? What are you playing?" I said "Requiem for a Death" or something. She said, "Why don't you play some Hawaiian music? He played Hawaiian guitar." So I made them put on some Hawaiian music when I said good-bye to him. As my father was going into the fire, this one song came on, a classic Hawaiian tune called "I Like You," by Sol Hoopii, and David said, "This is like a Woody Allen movie." I played the whole album, *Master of the Hawaiian Guitar, Volume 2*. My dad liked that music. He always brought the world home to us, my dad, and I loved that about him.

CHAPTER FIFTEEN

In the seventies, I was so afraid all the time for the people I knew who were gay, like my sister, Elen. People were so fuckin' crazy. At first, in the seventies, you thought life was going to get better—especially with Harvey Milk being a city supervisor in San Francisco. That was a time you felt like, "Oh my God, we're living in a new time where people will finally just let people be who they are." And then the guy was killed, and it was awful.

Even the police were really cruel to the gay community. They'd raid gay bars, and arrest people, and the whole thing was wrong. I was very worried about my sister because people act so stupid with someone who is different, and gay bashers were coming in from out of state (which still goes on to this day). I'd think, "Oh my God, my sister is a small woman, what is going to happen to her in New York?" I worked with this one musician, a really talented kid, who was beaten because he was gay. The attacker got away with it, because when he went to the hospital, he said, "I'm fine, I'm fine." Yeah, he was fine, because it was like, what was he going to do? He didn't want to go to the police. Some people think they're not going to be taken seriously, so a lot of times, this stuff isn't even reported.

Elen went to CUNY Queens College but dropped out when she was a freshman to find out why the world was the way it was. So as I said earlier, she had a lot of different jobs. She was a ship's plumber; she worked on the railroad fixing boxcars; she worked in a garment factory; she was a carpenter, a masseuse, then an acupuncturist. And there came a time when she joined the socialist movement, and she was going to go help poor people fight in Nicaragua. She was still pretty young, and I was like, "Are you shitting me? Why are you going there? Just stay away from that." But she didn't listen. And then she went to live in Phoenix, where she saw all these injustices against the Salvadoran refugees and the poor, and a ton of corruption in the local government. Ya know, our mayor, Michael Bloomberg, gets a dollar a year for a salary. He insists on it and he doesn't take bribes from anybody. But these other guys were corrupt. So she ran for mayor of Phoenix as a Socialist Workers Party candidate. One reason was to help the Salvadoran refugees get sanctuary. At the time she was working at the Marathon Steel Company in Phoenix, cutting hot steel with a blowtorch. And I happened to be really famous at the time, so *People* magazine did an article on her in 1985. Dave Wolff went wild, saying, "She can't even balance a checkbook—how's she going to balance the city?" I told him, "You don't understand what she's talking about doing there. She's talking about corruption. She's talking about standing up for people." She didn't win, but she called attention to what was important to her. And years later, the same guys she said were corrupt were indicted for corruption.

Me, I don't think socialism really works. And communism is a load of crap, because every country that has it has communists . . . and a couple of people who happen to be doing really well. Politics is about power. And power corrupts. There's always someone at the top of the food chain living large.

Elen worried about me, too, which is why she introduced me to Carl and Gregory, so that they could watch over me when she wasn't there. She really thought society was going to fall apart because it was so evil in the seventies. People were buying Nixon's and Agnew's lies. I'd get depressed because my friends and I all thought, "Wow, Americans believe everything they're told. What happened to the generation that was going to change and save the world?" Elen has always been very upbeat, positive, and compassionate. And in the end she went back to school to become an acupuncturist and an herbalist, which is what she is now. It's the perfect job for her because she really cares about people.

She came out in her twenties. It took a long, long time for her to come out to herself, and at first, she was bisexual. Later, she was fully out. Elen always wanted to be Peter Pan when we were playing—she always wanted to be the guy. When we made music, she'd play the drums, which none of the girls wanted to do. She was really good. My mother used to try and dress her in girly clothes but Elen would never wear them. Never! We all wore jeans, but we'd have to go into the men's shop and be fitted for them because they didn't sell girls' jeans at the time. I'm sure she was very comfortable like that. My mom even gave Elen a Toni perm. Poor Elen. In the meantime I used to look at that perm and beg Mom to teach me how to do it. I was always cutting my Barbie and Pollyanna dolls' hair. I lined them all up and put a cloth around their necks, like they were at the beauty parlor. Barbie was a real heartbreaker, but then all of a sudden, Barbie was freakin' bald. That was a shocker.

So Elen was always a huge inspiration for me. And my involvement with trying to bring an end to AIDS began when Gregory told me he had AIDS in 1985 (after he was in the "She Bop" video). Then he just got sicker and sicker, and he was in the hospital and he couldn't swallow, so the doctors had to puncture his stomach with a bag thing so they could feed him. It was so messed up. Since there wasn't much information about AIDS at the time, I didn't know if he would get sicker if I visited, but I couldn't stay away. And then when I came back from seeing him, all my friends and everybody were so freaked out and frightened of me, like I was carrying something. I remember one time I cut myself and I was bleeding when I was around Gregory and thought, "Oh my God, I'm bleeding, what about germs? Is he going to get something from me? Am I going to get something from him?" It was just bad.

It was heartbreaking. I just wanted to have our life the way we had it. The whole thing was awful. I saw firsthand what AIDS does to people, so I wanted people to know that they gotta use a condom, they have to have safe sex. Is it worth your whole life? For me, getting involved was the right thing to do. There were other great singers who were loved by the gay community who did not come out to help, and I decided I wasn't going to be like that. I do remember, though, that Liza Minnelli, Yoko Ono, Kate Pierson, Jean Paul Gaultier, and tons of others spoke out.

So I did things like the Gay Games and the Pride Parade, and my activism was reflected in my music, like everything else in my life. I played the first AIDS benefit in 1985 in Los Angeles. And when Rock Hudson died later that year, Elizabeth Taylor spoke out, and I was like, "Okay, that's good, because we all need to speak out." And MAC, the cosmetics company, helped in the beginning, too. We were losing a whole generation of great designers, hair people, and makeup artists.

In 2002, when actor Harvey Fierstein was getting a Human Rights Award, he asked if I would sing "True Colors" at his award dinner, and of course I said yes. I brought my violin player at the time, who was touring with me for the *Shine* CD—her name was Denny and she was new. I asked her to play "True Colors" with no accompaniment. I thought in this echo-y old bank the sound of a violin and a voice over might be really beautiful. So I sang for Harvey and then he accepted his award and Harvey, being an advocate for the LGBT community, spoke with eloquence and reason. That night it really hit me that I needed to do something, too. I had been working and singing in the clubs promoting *Shine* and seeing everyone in the audience with no shirts on, and high on cat tranquilizers and ecstasy and speedball, just having unsafe everything. The drugs made them lose their inhibitions.

And as Harvey spoke of new infections among young gay men and the rise in deaths from AIDS-related complications, he said that happy people don't self-destruct. There was a new expression in the late nineties and early 2000s: "barebacking"—not using a condom when you have sex. They thought you couldn't die anymore, because people were living with AIDS. But as I said, people were dying from "old AIDS," because the drug cocktails were so harsh.

So I thought, "Why don't we make a pride T-shirt and use the proceeds to help fight AIDS?" So on the T-shirt, I put a picture of me from the Cher tour holding the rainbow flag with the words "pride" and "respect." Because if you respect yourself and your partner, then you won't put them or yourself in danger. All the proceeds went to the American Foundation for AIDS Research (amfAR). During the Cher tour, I would wrap myself with the rainbow flag at concerts and tell the story of how when I was growing up, my mother always said that no matter what we did, we'd always be her kids. We were lucky that way. On Cher's tour, everything was timed for the visuals she had, so I only had a certain amount of time to talk between songs. That would drive me out of my mind (you know me).

That's also the time when I heard of the Stay Close campaign through Carmen Cacciatore from FlyLife, a company that does press and promotion in the dance world and gay clubs. Carmen connected me to PFLAG (Parents, Families, and Friends of Lesbians and Gays), who came up with the campaign. I was on the PFLAG fire-engine float for the Gay Pride Parade in the summer of 2001—I had on a headdress and my sister was also on the float, dressed as a fireman. Elen wanted to wear a T-shirt that said "Butch" on it and we looked everywhere but couldn't find one. Finally I said, "Elen, you're dressed as a fireman—people are going to know." My mother was also on the float with a little sun hat, waving. It was the first time that we had done Pride together as a family.

In 2002 I was also in the Los Angeles Gay Pride Parade, and I sat in a champagne glass. We were sponsored by a fantastic gay bar called the Abbey. I sang all my dance songs over and over and over.

So that's why I did the T-shirt. We created it and sold it at the Prides, and the money went to gay nonprofits. I thought that maybe if we promoted gay pride and gay respect, we could put the message out that we're not trash. The thing about being gay that my sister told me is that you're made to feel dirty, like you're having dirty sex, not regular sex. So there's self-hatred and shame. But an inclusive society is much stronger than an exclusive society. If you keep cutting yourself off at the knees, you're never gonna stand strong. You can't just weed out people because they're gay. You never know who it is who's going to have the brilliant idea to cure cancer or fix the economy. How ridiculous are we going to get here?

At the time, I was touring for the *Body Acoustic* CD, and I stood onstage and I said, "Listen, you can ask lawmakers to do whatever you want, but basically, I don't think they're in it for us. We're in it for us. We're the people that really change things."

So I decided maybe there was a way to inspire people without exactly telling them what to do, and instead just bring everyone together. I was inspired by doing PFLAG's Stay Close campaign with Elen and by my meeting with Judy Shepard, the mother of Matthew Shepard. So we started to think about doing a "True Colors" tour.

Matthew was the University of Wyoming student who was murdered in 1998. He was picked up at a bar by homophobic kids and was beaten and killed. The night he was killed, we didn't just lose Matthew; three lives were absolutely ruined—Matthew's and those of the two men that killed him. And why? Because if you raise your kid with fear and hatred, that's what wins in the end, and it's a lose-lose situation. I have a kid, and sometimes he gets bullied, like a lot of kids, and I wrote this song for him called "Above the Clouds." The message of the song was something that Pat Birch told me once. She is a wonderful choreographer that I met when I went on a show called *Friday Night Live*. (They never put me on *Saturday Night Live*, for one reason or another.) She said that when she worked with Martha Graham, Martha told her something like, "When you walk with your head above the crowd, you can see far, but then you are also a target. You stand out." I always remember that when I want to do something different and I get grief for it.

Jeff Beck wrote the piece of music for "Above the Clouds," and I wrote the song over it. Jeff had been working in a little studio that was in the basement of the Sunset Marquis with keyboardist/writer/producer Jed Lieber. As soon as I heard the music, the lyrics came so fast I almost couldn't write them down quick enough. My friend Kevin was there with me too and if I stopped, he'd say, "Just keep going, shut up and write it as it is." The chorus is what I tell anyone who's going through something like being picked on for being different. "There's a place where the sun breaks through / And the wind bites cold and hard / Stings my ears and tears my eye / When the day starts to shout out loud / Stand tall / And glide / When you're all alone in the crowd / Don't fall / Don't hide / When you walk above the clouds / When you walk above the clouds."

The thing is, when I was made fun of in high school, it was hurtful. I felt totally like an outsider. Although everyone is different, for me the outside started to feel otherworldly—more thoughtful. And after a while I didn't give a hoot what anyone thought about me, just what *I* thought about me. In that space I could educate myself. I walked around a little crazy sometimes. You'd be surprised how afraid people get if you look a little crazy. Maybe I was mad at some of my schoolmates, but I wanted to experience a bigger world rather than the tiny-minded one that laughed at me because I was so different. Was I weird as a kid? Hell yeah. But I wanted to grow and change into what I wanted to be, not what I was told I was suited for by someone with no imagination, especially because all I had was imagination. That's how I lived. And I got through by imagining living the life of an artist. Hey, Walter Mitty had nothing on me. What can I tell ya?

All I want to convey to anyone who is suffering while they're young is that sometimes you get a reprieve when you're older. Maybe it's just your perception that changes, but somehow it eases up, because life ebbs and flows. When you're ebbing, maybe you're strengthening your perspective on the world. And when you're flowing, maybe you can use everything to create, to write, to sing, act, and eventually stand taller and see farther. I guess it's up to the individual if they decide to rise to the occasion. For me, being part of the fray might have made my vision a little shallow. So I don't regret my experience.

When I performed that song in a live show, I would go out into the audience and stand on the arms of the seats. I stood on the wrong end of one of those folding chairs once or twice and fell. After that I stood on the arms of the chairs. They were much more stable. And after a while I learned to move side to side and use my legs for balance. I moved my body and arms while I was singing as if I was surfing above the crowd. I felt that had a nice effect to it with the spotlight on me in the dark.

I'll never forget in 2005, when I was presented by the Human Rights Campaign, the nation's largest lesbian, gay, bisexual, and transgender civil-rights organization, with their highest honor, the National Equality Award, for my advocacy for equality for the community. When I accepted the award I decided to sing "True Colors" because I'm not a speechmaker. Afterward, I went backstage and there was a woman just sitting and staring. And she looked at me with her big eyes and roundish face, and it was Judy Shepard. We locked eyes, and Judy started crying, and we hugged for a good moment. When we were done hugging I said, "You look like you could use a drink. Hey, you got any vodka here?"

Like I said, it had been so profound to hear her speak about the son she had been robbed of. We started talking and what we eventually did was take the Matthew Shepard Foundation's purple "Erase Hate" bracelets and put them on special cards that shared information about Matthew and the foundation, with a special message from me. Matthew had said he wanted to get into politics, and in the end, through his mother, he did.

I've always been a strong and engaged supporter of LGBT equality, and of course I always knew that the community was not equal, but I didn't know the full extent of how bad it was until I heard some of the hard-core facts. By 2006, Lisa and I started working closely with the HRC and we listened to stories of how gay couples' lives were impacted by still being denied the opportunity to marry. In fact, my sister raised her partner's two sons with her before anyone was open about doing that. They had no rights. We heard how people can still be fired in thirty-eight states for being LGBT, how hate crimes continue to take place at an alarming rate, and how these crimes aren't covered by hate-crime laws.

So when it came time to do my own tour, I decided it would be nice to bring everybody together. If the tour was going to be the "True Colors" tour, then damn, let's make a real rainbow. Let's include everyone—straight, gay, transgender, black, white, Hispanic, Asian, young, and old. I remembered when music was mixed like that when I was a kid. I kept thinking, "When I have my own tour, I'll mix it up, too." I have a friend, Iffath, a brilliant doctor who delivered my son. She's Muslim. As part of her religion, she gives a portion of her salary every year to charity. So I thought, "That's not a bad idea. Let's have some fun, do some good, and raise some money for charity, too."

The "True Colors" tour raised money for the Human Rights Campaign, the Matthew Shepard Foundation, PFLAG, and CenterLink. We never made a profit from the tour, but we did raise a lot of money and awareness for those nonprofits. And I think we changed some perceptions about the community by talking about what was going on. You see, the only thing that the LGBT community wanted and still wants is to be full-fledged citizens, with the same rights as any straight American. They pay the same taxes but they don't have the same rights.

In the 2007 "True Colors" tour we showed a short HRC film in between setting up performers. We also had postcards at every show in support of the Matthew Shepard Hate Crimes Prevention Act for people to send to their senators and congressmen. If they felt strong enough about it they could use the postcard to urge that hate-crimes protection be extended to the LGBT community (it wasn't then). And we would mail them. That year we toured sixteen cities and collected over fifty thousand postcards.

We didn't have a lot of money for the tour. My partners were me, my manager, and my agent. We had to put up money for production and stuff, but we didn't have squat. I'm not rich (people think I'm loaded, but I'm not—I didn't do the Cyndi dolls and clothing line when I maybe should have). My manager isn't rich because if I'm not rich, then she's not either, right? Poor bastard. So we had to think of things that looked visually good for cheap—which is what I feel like I'm always doing, by the seat of my pants.

So my agent Jonny Podell said, why don't we make the stage look like the Delano, the Miami hotel that has these sheer white curtains that float when the wind blows? It's very sensual and pretty and picks up the light well. I thought it was a really good idea but I wondered how we could keep the sheets away from the musicians. What if they wafted in their faces?

Rosie O'Donnell got on board with it too, because it just so happened that she had a falling-out with *The View* and she had some time. I first met her in 2002 at a Cher show and she was in the audience taking pictures. I remember thinking, "Oh my God, she's under my chin, I hope those pictures are okay." Because sometimes you're bent over yelling, pouring your guts out, and that's just not a pretty picture. And I think after that I went to her house for something, around 2004 or so, and I remember being nervous.

But I felt a real connection with her. Because she's a bit of a misfit, like me. There is a sadness in her heart, as funny as she is. And also, even though she grew up on Long Island, we have similar accents. We speak in the same vernacular. We aren't from fancy neighborhoods, we are from the lower middle class, and I understand and relate to her based on that. I can't relate to her about losing your mom, but my sadness comes from feeling so alienated as a kid that I didn't even know why I was fuckin' alive. I used to think, "Why did God make me so weird, so in another world all the time?"

I find it really extraordinary that I feel so close to Ro, yet there are a lot of things I wouldn't share with her. I'm afraid to, because deep down inside I think people who are very successful think that other people just want to leech off of them, and I don't want to ever freakin' be a part of that. I want to have relationships based on equal ground, so wherever I'm not equal, I kind of hold back a little bit—especially with famous people, because you don't know what's in their heads. Although Ro is the most down-to-earth famous person I've ever met. I thought Ellen DeGeneres was like that, too—very funny, but very down-to-earth. But I never struck up a really deep friendship with her like I did with Ro. There was just something about Ro, and she loved my music—like when I'm writing stuff, I send it to her before I put it out, because she asked me to.

So she went on my tour, and I did some performances on her cruise for gay families. This is how much I care about Ro, because I can't swim that good. And I don't like to get my face wet and God knows I don't want my hair wet—I don't want it changing to a color I don't put in there myself. The cruise went to Nova Scotia, and I froze, of course. At one point, we got off the boat to go on another boat to go look at whales. There were no whales though, and the water was rough, and I thought, "Why am I on a boat, when I just got off a boat?"

The second time I did it, we went to Alaska, and Lisa thought we should bring our families with us to show them that there are all different kinds of families. So I brought my kid. We got to Seattle and it was all going good. My son met the captain and he was being the cutest, funniest kid. Then he had to walk across the gangplank, and the ship was like a tall building and he has a fear of heights, so he said he wouldn't do it. Well, Rosie happened to be on the other side so she called, "Declyn, how you doing?" to distract him and got him across. Anyway, my kid's a hockey player and a lot of kids on the teams are homophobic—adolescents and preadolescents like to quote from *South Park* and say, "Oh, that's so gay."

Here's another thing Ro did. The first night there was a party on the boat and there was liquor around. So Dec looked at me laughing and picked up a closed bottle of alcohol to make believe he was drinking it. I said, "Dec, that's not funny, put that down." And Ro walked up behind him and said, "Actually, Dec, that is kind of funny, but I could see how your mother would be very upset by that." She has such a way with children. They love her. Another great thing about Rosie is that she initiated having my sister, Elen, come onstage and play guitar with me on that trip and a few times on the "True Colors" tour. It was awesome, because it was like when we used to play together when I was eleven. Rosie was very open to my sister, very nice to her, even though she wasn't famous—some people who are famous are only nice to famous people.

The "True Colors" tour was timely because at that time, you gotta understand, things were really tough with George W. Bush. He and his administration were saying hateful things, to the point where my gay friends were talking about leaving the country and I was like, "Wait a minute—this is our country, what are you talking about?" The first time the issue of gay marriage came up, the Republicans shot that down right quick and I thought, "Gay men do all those batty old Republican ladies' hairdos and dress those women up, but when it comes time to give a little support, those women don't open their mouths." The Matthew Shepard and James Byrd Jr. Hate Crimes Prevention Act passed the House and the Senate, but Bush wouldn't sign it. In his mind, God didn't create the gays. But that doesn't change the fact that hate crimes go on every day. The guy who did my makeup and hair on *The Celebrity Apprentice* once took a train from the set to his home in Spanish Harlem, and he was surrounded by guys yelling at him not to look at them. All the other riders just turned their heads and did not say a word.

I felt it was important for parents of gay kids who just couldn't handle or understand it to talk to other parents of gay children. Because who were they going to talk to? They couldn't go to the church because they'd just tell you you're going to hell and your kid's going to hell, or they'd try to "cure" you. You're either born gay or you're not. It's not something that you decide to be. If you could decide, why would you want to be something that makes people act so horrible to you? Hatred comes from ignorance and fear, and the gays became scapegoats for the Bush administration, which diverted people's attention from what was really going on, like the war in Iraq.

So I was so happy when Ro got on board the "True Colors" tour, and then other artists started jumping on board, too. The British group Erasure was right there ready to go with us, and I thought that was just amazing. On the 2007 tour we also had Deborah Harry, Boston's the Dresden Dolls, and the Canadian band the Cliks, who were awesome. There was a lot of speculation about why straight people were putting on a tour for the gay community, but I wanted it to be inclusive, like I said.

Margaret Cho was the MC, and Judy Shepard and a lot of other people had a problem with her show. Mothers would leave during her set and say, "Cyn, I think the subject matter is just not right for my kids." Margaret's material is about fucking and sucking and blow jobs. It's funny, but it's mature content, and the problem is that my music is cross-generational. So they brought their kids because of me. But I wasn't going to censor her because that wouldn't be right—that's her act. She did a great job transitioning from one musical act to the other. She moved that show forward.

What I wanted to do was to make it a festival, a one-day destination where we could all have fun together, where we could have a tea party and dance with DJs. And just be able to feel that we're all family and then have a concert at night.

It was so much fun for me because I could pick all the cool artists that I liked, and all night long I was able to listen to their wonderful music. When you have your own tour you can set the tone, and I wanted to make everyone comfortable. I sat in the cafeteria with the performers. If they needed hairspray, I had it. The door was always open, you know what I mean? And then at the end of the night I would sit with the Cliks or the Dresdens and we'd all hang out and have a beer or whatever, and talk about music, about art. It was the kind of thing I always wished I could do. I loved the camaraderie.

The Gossip performed at some shows, too, and they were so great. Before lead singer Beth Ditto went onstage, I'd run around to help her, saying, "Okay, what do you need? Come to my room, I got this, I got that." One time I told her, "Look, you get out there and you take no prisoners." That night she pulled her dress off and sang in her underwear. I was like, "Okay, she threw off her dress like I throw off my shoes. How awesome is she?"

Sometimes younger artists like when you give them advice, and sometimes they don't. When Lady Gaga and I did MAC's Viva Glam campaign together for MAC's AIDS fund, I tried to help her out. If I saw her leaning on her thigh, which would make your thigh look bigger, I would tell her to come up and lean on me. We spent one whole day together working our asses off getting our photos taken, and she helped me too.

I saw a little of myself in her. I said, "Wow, I even dance like you," and she looked at me and said, "Cyn, I used to study you." A lot of people say that older artists inspire the young, and I thought especially after working with her on the campaign that it goes the other way too. Gaga woke me up to the fact that I was making myself plainer and plainer and plainer because everyone was telling me, "You can't do this, your clothes are weird," and to this day I still get grief about what I wear. So now I just wear black. And when I worked with Gaga, I was able to relax and have fun. I could be myself without feeling like a freakazoid, because in a lot of ways we were cut from the same feathered, hot-glue-gunned cloth. We could just be the way we were, because we're artists and that's just the way it is.

When she said she studied me, I imagined this crazy image of her when she was a baby, standing in front of the TV set, putting on and pulling off her sunglasses to "Girls Just Want to Have Fun." I see Gaga is very good at taking inspiration from outside influences and reinventing them in herself. Madonna does the same thing. Hell, we all do that. Maybe my inspirations are from old movies sometimes, but that's what I loved about Gaga the first time I saw her. She looked like *La Dolce Vita*!

So back to the "True Colors" tour. Touring was a lot of work, but we had an awesome time, especially on the West Coast. I never shook so many hands in my life. I felt like I was running for mayor. But I knew I was doing something good. I used to go backstage and do more meet-and-greets because I sold the pictures for charity.

On the San Diego stop, I remember trying out a song of Erasure's called "Blue Savannah." I asked my guitar player at the time, Knox Chandler (a great innovative rock guitarist), if he would play a kind of twisted low-string Duane Eddy part to it. I sang over it and felt like I was in my own black-and-white movie; I was Roy Orbison and Edith Piaf all at once. It was live and then it was gone, but I lived in that moment, for however long it was. Then back to more pictures and handshakes.

And when there were mishaps onstage, I'd weigh the situation quickly and then act. There was an awkward moment once with Knox during "Money Changes Everything." I almost knocked him over, guitar and all. I had tried to crawl between his legs at the end of his solo, but his legs weren't really wide enough apart to crawl through. I guess I was in my own Rolling Stones movie (did Mick ever do that?). Anyway, the poor bastard almost went down, and being under his legs at the time, I pushed his butt up with my head, kind of like a soccer ball. That's a little behind-the-scenes story from the show—really the "behind scenes," if you know what I mean. I kill myself sometimes!

And San Francisco is such a magical city, so I loved when the tour stopped there. And let's face it, there's so much history there: the hippie movement, City Supervisor Harvey Milk, the movie *Vertigo* was shot there, Tony Bennett's song about "that city by the bay". . . . How can I not love it there?

So when Lisa, my manager, suggested we walk down to the water, I said, "Of course." So off we went. At first, it was very invigorating. Then we found a place called the Blue Mermaid Chowder House & Bar, and I thought maybe it was the same one that Joni Mitchell talked about in "Carey" (the song, not the movie *Carrie*). Eh, probably not.

Anyway, Lisa and I had all kinds of seafood chowder there for lunch, which of course threw my whole diet to hell. The two of us love to eat. At first we were going to take the trolley up the hill after our meal. But then we had a chowder sampler, followed by more chowder, followed by a salad (which made us feel as though we were actually following some sort of diet). And of course we ordered white wine instead of red, thinking it was lighter.

Well, after dinner, we decided to walk back. And the thing about walking is that you get to discover new things and places you wouldn't have noticed in a cab or car. So in the same way one might digress in a conversation, one might digress in a walk. And then we just kept walking and said things to each other like, "Can you feel it in your legs and butt yet?" But after about an hour or more of this, we were definitely lost.

After a while I felt like we were in an *Ab Fab* episode. After listening to everyone's directions, we went up and down the hills several times. I felt like crawling but couldn't show Lisa the wimp I really was. So I made jokes and said I didn't mind a long walk—just the heatstroke. I kept calling information to call the Fairmont Hotel to come pick us up and the hotel would go, "Which Fairmont did you want?" They said there were two. I didn't know which one. When we finally made it back, of course it was happy hour at the bar in the hotel. We felt we should treat ourselves to a Bellini. It's Friday, we told each other—what the heck. Oh. Wait. No, it wasn't. Well, it was *our* Friday. Anyway, after a while, we decided to finally get some sleep after the long bus ride we had the night before. But I couldn't sleep, which led me to go online. Which led me to look at an article written about Britney Spears and me and the "True Colors" tour in the "Page Six" column of the *New York Post.* It said that her choreographer told *People* magazine that Britney was going to come onstage with us at the Greek Theatre in Los Angeles and that she decided not to.

So the real story was this: Britney was invited to perform in Las Vegas with us. But no one representing Britney ever responded. So I wrote a blog post that said,

> Here's the deal, Brit: If ya hear this, you are welcome to come to the Greek Theatre. This is a good cause, and I am grateful that the spirit moved ya, doll. And if you are coming, can you contact us? Though I don't know you, you seem like a good kid. You are welcome.
>
> X
>
> Cyn
>
> PSSST . . . sorry I didn't respond sooner.

Well, she didn't come. But she still seems like a good kid.

Even if Britney didn't perform that night, my sister, Elen, did. She came and played guitar with us on "Money Changes Everything." Like I said, when I was little, I was in my first band with Elen. And there we were on the stage of the Greek Theatre, sans the mops for guitars, Mom's old wigs, and her high-heeled boots. And that happened because Rosie suggested that Elen play guitar with me on her cruise.

In 2008, we got the "True Colors" tour up and going again. The lineup was awesome, from Joan Jett and the Blackhearts to the B-52s to Sarah McLachlan to Joan Armatrading, and Rosie came back. I got to meet Wanda Sykes, who is as awesome as you think she is. The MC this time was Carson Kressley, who is a complete doll. We had a few different young groups go in and out. The Cliks only did a few dates, and Hunter Valentine did a date or two. Then I got to meet Tegan and Sara. We were able to get some good momentum and to give a lot of people money. After one show where we did an after-party fund-raiser for PFLAG, Wanda and I hung out and she said to me, "You're a soldier." Then she told me she would always help the cause, that she was inspired. Coming from her, that was humbling. She's funny and smart and committed to the cause. Bless her. I love her. And last year, when I presented her with an award at the New York City LGBT Community Center, she told me that it was her experience on tour that began her decision to come out of the closet.

I've always believed in "Power to the People" (that's the song I'd sing at the end of my set on the "True Colors" tour). I'm glad straight people like Madonna finally spoke up for this community that has worshipped her for so long, and Gaga was right there, too. My feeling is, do what's right. Nobody is asking for more than the other guy—just fairness. Why is that so wrong? I love when Republican politicians say that we shouldn't legalize gay marriage and somehow connect it with pedophilia. Statistically, it's straight people who are usually the pedophiles!

On the tour I also handed out cards that instructed people on how to vote, because a while back, I didn't know myself. I voted for Clinton, but I didn't vote in the Bush election, and look what happened. I don't tell people who to vote for, just how to vote. Because if you want inclusion in the world, you better start with including yourself. You need to participate, otherwise you can't complain. I was very disappointed about the sexist things that were said about Hillary Clinton when she was campaigning. Once in an airport I saw a Hillary Clinton leg nutcracker. And of course the racism that President Obama faced was awful. Republicans pretend they're on the side of the people, but they certainly don't think like poor people because they ain't poor. Sarah Palin got a million for her reality show. And senators get their health care paid for. They should have the same shit as us because then they'd vote in favor of their own selfish asses. I don't know how they do it, but I cannot turn a blind eye to the people standing next to me.

While we were still on tour, Lisa, my agent Jonny, and I started to talk with gay activist Gregory Lewis, who we brought on the road with us to handle the charity part of the tour after working with him at HRC and the Matthew Shepard Foundation. We saw the people at each show energized by the music, by the comedy, and most importantly by the message of equality. We realized that if we could have this sort of impact doing a tour, maybe we could do even more year-round on issues that needed attention. It was then that the True Colors Fund was born. I knew right away that I wanted to continue to get straight people involved in supporting the community.

So then we started the Give a Damn campaign in 2010, with the goal to educate and engage the straight community in the advancement of gay, lesbian, bisexual, and transgender equality. The reason the Give a Damn campaign went in the direction it went was be-cause Jonny got a lot of grief about us being straight and doing a gay tour. I said, "But we're straight people advocating for gay people, and why not? This is a civil rights movement. We need to get *everyone* in-volved." We should come out as gay for straight, straight for gay. It's especially good for straight people to become informed and involved about all kinds of issues affecting gays (which in turn affect all of us): from gay marriage to suicide to discrimination at work and school. Then, to help the cause, I thought we should make it sexy to be an advocate for equal rights for everyone, including LGBTs. So we produced over thirty public service announcements that in-cluded people like Susan Sarandon, Whoopi Goldberg, Elton John, Jason Mraz, Sharon and Kelly Osbourne, and so many other people. I can't even thank them enough. (I can't remember them all but you can look it up for yourself and see them, and it's really fun and visu-ally interesting: www.wegiveadamn.org.)

The campaign made a big splash out of the gate when actress Anna Paquin identified as bisexual for the very first time in one of our PSAs. The news was covered by everyone and anyone. The website was so in-undated it crashed in the first fifteen minutes the campaign went live. And I was so happy Ricky Martin did one, too. It was the first "gay" thing he did after he came out of the closet, and it was a huge deal. I do kind of wish that a straight Hispanic male would step forward to say, "It's okay to be whoever you are," because a large portion of gay kids on the street are Hispanic.

I remember being really struck by something when I was promot-ing the first "True Colors" tour. I did a photo shoot for *Interview* mag-azine, and I wanted to include LGBT youth. What I had in mind was the work of a photographer named Diane Arbus, who in the 1950s and 1960s took pictures of marginalized people. I thought, "If I could do a picture and show young transgender kids, how many there are, the faces of them—the old, the young, the kids—then maybe people could really see a community, yet it would be art, too."

So I scouted for different locations and people to incorporate in the photo. I went down to the Christopher Street Pier in NYC and met so many youth who shared their stories of being thrown out on the street for being gay or transgender. And then I met Colleen Jackson from the West End Residences on the Upper West Side, which Lisa is really involved in. I performed at one of their benefits, and then when Colleen came to the Radio City Music Hall stop of the "True Colors" tour in 2007, I asked if there was something that could be done to help. Colleen came back with the idea of housing for homeless lesbian, gay, bisexual, and transgender youth. She wanted to call it the True Colors Residence and use my name and I said, "Go ahead, and whatever we can do, I'll do." I had already started advocating for homeless LGBT youth and there is no national organization that solely addresses the issue, so we decided that the True Colors Fund would develop that organization.

An extraordinary circle in my life is the building of the True Colors Residence in Harlem. It's New York State's first permanent housing for this group. Many homeless LGBT kids face violence in mainstream shelters, so the True Colors Residence provides young people between eighteen and twenty-four with low-income housing while helping them get back on their feet. The True Colors Fund is a partner on the project and provides funding and support as it grows, and I'm the honorary chairman.

At the True Colors Residence, they teach life skills that these kids may not have gotten growing up—like that you can't get that spangled scarf that you want because you have to pay the rent. So they teach budgeting. (Although some artists will opt for the spangled scarf and not eat, which is what I did.) And they don't throw you out—you can stay as long as you need to get back on your feet.

There's only thirty beds there, so I'm only scratching the surface of everyone who needs help, but if this is my one contribution, then it's okay. But I didn't want to be just a stupid celebrity shooting my big mouth off. I figured if I was going to shoot my mouth off, it might as well be constructive.

For me, it goes all the way back to my friend Gregory, it goes back to the pier and working with the drag performers on the "Hey Now (Girls Just Want to Have Fun)" video and my great friend and a wonderful artist, Chris Tanner. When I committed to doing the True Colors Residence, they came to me and said they wanted to put a plaque for Gregory on the cornerstone of the house. Colleen had heard Gregory's story. I sometimes told it in concert. So now not only did he get a song, but there's also a plaque for him at a place that should have been around when he was thrown out as a twelve-year-old on the street. The plaque says, "Gregory Natale, Boy Blue," and some of the chorus of the song "True Colors." If you look at your life, everything is connected, and we keep going round and round sometimes.

I was so happy when the Matthew Shepard and James Byrd Jr. Hate Crimes Act was signed into law in 2009 by President Barack Obama. Lisa and I went to the celebration ceremony at the White House. Lady Gaga had performed at the Human Rights Campaign dinner the night before, and the president joked, "It's a privilege to be here tonight to open for Lady Gaga . . . I've made it." So when I met him I said, "I heard you opened for Lady Gaga," and he started laughing and said, "She took all your moves! You're the original."

I'll never forget going to perform at his presidential inauguration. I had to get up for it at five thirty A.M. I met Rufus Wainwright, Thelma

Houston, Lisa Barbaris, and Gregory Lewis, who would eventually be the executive director of the True Colors Fund, downstairs in the lobby of our hotel. I really should have been wearing running shoes instead of heels, but I was so worried about how the bottom of my pants would look that I forgot about how my feet would feel. They reminded me after a mile or so though.

But as I watched all the people move toward the National Mall I forgot about my feet. I had never seen Washington so alive. Everyone was rushing along, happy to be cold together. I felt like I was in the midst of the people, in the midst of history being made. It was another "power to the people" moment, and I almost cried but I was trying hard to keep up with my friends. If I lost them I'd be crying for a different reason.

Anyway, my admission ticket was purple, and as I looked at it, just for a flash, I wondered if the color meant anything. I remembered how upset Rev. Jerry Falwell got with that purple Teletubby, thinking it was gay because it had a purse and a triangle on its head. Maybe purple was a code? When we actually got to the purple gate, security said to just squeeze in at the front of the line. So we tried. But then a woman on the line said, "The back of the line is way down there! We got here at two A.M.!" And then bravely, Lisa said, "The security guy told us to come here and wait. I'm with Cyndi Lauper." And then another guy yelled, "I thought we're all supposed to be equal here." I wanted to point out that I was with Thelma Houston and Rufus Wainwright and say, "Of course we're equal, just not right now. And, you know, maybe you want to meet Thelma Houston." But I knew that stuff was only funny on TV, not in real life, so I zipped it and opted not to do my impersonation of Larry David.

Then the gate for the yellow ticket line opened. The gate for the orange ticket line opened. But the gate for the purple ticket line did not. It never did. So I made up my mind to leave. There were so many folks, though, that we almost couldn't move at all, but we finally managed to swim through the crowd and go back to the hotel.

We went to breakfast and then to the HRC hangout to watch the inauguration. A lot of folks were crying and I was too. Aretha sang "America the Beautiful" in her glorious hat, and then I realized that she looked as cold as I had been. But I knew she had to be there, because she was there with Dr. King at the Lincoln Memorial way back when. I had seen that as a child on TV. Rick Warren giving the invocation really threw me, though. When he began to speak, my head just went to an old TV special I used to watch with my son and husband around Christmastime, called *Rudolph the Red-Nosed Reindeer*. I used to think, "Who the heck wrote this? And why is Santa acting so messed up?" Rudolph and the little elf had been thrown out of Santa's workshop because they were different. It seems that different always gets everyone all riled up. Then I started to hear my friend Rosie's words replay in my head. She spoke them to me in our dressing room on tour once: "Cyn, we're on the Island of Misfit Toys." That's where Rudolph and that elf wound up before saving the day for Santa. And I looked around me in the room, at folks watching so hopeful, arm in arm. I couldn't help thinking that love is love and that maybe, someday, everybody will understand that.

Then Reverend Joe Lowery spoke and I remembered how, when I was a kid, I also saw him with Dr. King on TV. I felt in my heart that this must be the real invocation. This reverend seemed to be the genuine article. He asked his God to "help us choose inclusion, not exclusion . . . tolerance, not intolerance." I was thankful that a voice of reason had been put into the mix after all. He spoke directly, and I realized that maybe I was supposed to see the contrast—that to speak your truth, you need to come from a very simple place, without posture. Just simple and honest.

I couldn't believe I was really living this in my lifetime. And I thought, "Maybe 'The Age of Aquarius' isn't just a song somebody made up after all. I guess we just have to never give up on ourselves or stop raising our voices together when we think something is wrong." We don't have to agree. We live in America. And here was the proof; because on January 20, 2009, we got to see Dr. King's words ring true. He said, "The arc of history is long, but it bends toward justice." That day was evidence that one day, it will bend with liberty, toward justice for all of us.

So, back to the True Colors Fund. Inspired by the kids I met on the Christopher Street Pier and by Colleen Jackson and the True Colors Residence, we knew that our focus at the True Colors Fund had to turn to doing what we could to bring an end to gay and transgender youth experiencing homelessness. So, we traveled across the country in 2011 and met with shelters, drop-in centers, young people, community leaders, and many others to find out what the true state of affairs was for these kids being kicked out or running away from home because of their sexual orientation or gender identity. We are going to work to educate the public about the problem and engage them in the solution, just like we did with the Give a Damn campaign.

What we learned astounded us and we realized quickly there was a great need for a national voice on the issue, someone whose sole mission is to address gay, lesbian, bisexual, and transgender youth homelessness, someone to help educate the public about the problem and engage them in finding a solution, someone to help support the incredible people and organizations—shelters, drop-in centers, etc.— helping these kids on a day-to-day basis, someone to help advocate for them in Washington, DC, and on the state and local level, and someone to help ensure that the places these young people seek out help are welcoming environments—whether it be their homes or the social services available to them.

There is a lot of work that needs to be done and we are committed to doing everything we can through our new program, Forty to None. It is estimated that up to 40 percent of all homeless youth identify as gay, lesbian, bisexual, or transgender, yet only 3 percent to 5 percent of the general youth population does the same. The disparity is glaring and the primary reason it exists is because of family rejection. As a mom, I cannot imagine throwing my kid away for any reason, let alone because of his sexual orientation or gender identity. It would be like ripping out a piece of my soul. So, I am beginning a new journey, to do all that I can to get that number of 40 percent to none. It's going to be a daunting task, but I'm confident that we will be successful, especially if we all come together to do it.

CHAPTER SIXTEEN

I WANTED TO DO the dance album *Bring Ya to the Brink* for so long. I started writing it in 2006, but I couldn't get it done in time for the "True Colors" tour. I mean, I could have done it really quick, but what was I going to put out—some piece of poop? (You feeling that alliteration?)

So after the first tour, I got busy. I wrote "Set Your Heart" about the gay community, because I wanted to write something to make everybody feel better, to tell them that I was going to be there for them. A little part of it had a sampling of "Where Are All My Friends" from Harold Melvin and the Blue Notes, because it reminded me of the gays being the scapegoat. If I were gay, I'd be standing there going, "Hey, where are all my friends?" This was an answer to that: "Hey, I'm right here." But when I played it for the record company, they didn't want to release it as the first single because they thought it was too commercial. What do you say to that?

"Same Ol' Story" ended up being the first single in the clubs instead. I kept the "fuckin'" part for the dance clubs, but when I released it for anything else I had to take it out from the title so it wouldn't be totally banned. Rappers do the same thing, and as my son told me,

"Ma, it has a curse word, it will be a big hit." My son introduces me to a lot of music when we're in the car on the way to hockey games, so I listen to Lil Wayne, Ludacris, and 50 Cent. I realized that once I get past the assault on language, 50 Cent's voice is like butter.

Anyway, "Same Ol' Fuckin' Story" came out of a conversation I had with Carmen Cacciatore, my friend from FlyLife. He was standing next to me in the studio when I was singing to track, and we were upset about something Bush did, and he said, "Yes, same old fuckin' story." So I started singing that. I figured, "You know what? You gotta sing what people are saying." He's not the first person I heard use that phrase. The rich get richer, the poor get poorer, one for me, two for you. That's how it will always go, no matter how hard you work. And when you're poor, or even when you're middle-class, all you do is work, and there's no quality of life. I know about that, even though like I said, everybody thinks I'm loaded.

Then Carmen said to me, "Maybe you should go to England. I could introduce you to dance artists and producers like Basement Jaxx and Digital Dog." And my A & R guy Daniel thought I should also check out the Swedish music scene, because in pop history the Swedes stand out as having an incredible sense of melody. So in early 2007 I went to England and Sweden to collaborate with a bunch of dance people. At first it was so much fun with Digital Dog. They were kind of surprised that I was into working with them, but they were up for it. Basement Jaxx were up for it too, for one song, and then we tried to work together again and that didn't work out too good. I think they didn't think I was cool enough.

Unfortunately, a lot of these guys never read the credits so they didn't know I'm a producer and an arranger and not just a singer, and they want to do it all. But as soon as you start telling me what to do, like I'm supposed to listen immediately, I won't listen—immediately.

It's not bad if somebody says, "Oh my God, try this because when you did that, I thought of this." That's collaborating. But not, "Now do this, and do this." I don't need somebody to walk me step by step. Though, in their defense, those guys were very eccentric. Sometimes they'd just disappear and even their manager couldn't find them, which is kind of great when you think about it.

I think "Rain on Me" was good, but now when I listen to the words I wonder if it was too sentimental. Some inspiration for that song came from a conversation I had with my husband about our son, about how your kid can yell at you—he can rain on you, and it doesn't matter.

Then the line "I saw you gather all your hopes with all your dreams" came from the fact that I have met many up-and-coming keyboard players, producers, and writers who I've collaborated with who, again, didn't really understand what I do and wanted me—the singer—to take a backseat, have a lobotomy and just follow. I'm not a silent partner. I'm not going to dumb myself down.

Axwell wrote the track for "Rain on Me". All these guys who write music tracks consider themselves to be producers but I do not. They do have a certain skill but I don't consider what they do to be real production. Sometimes they make these Frankenstein cut-and-pastes, and once you introduce a real singer, it becomes flat; there's nothing left in the track for them to latch on to. You might as well not have the voice there. The problem with some of these producers who write and program and mix is that they get too tied into their gadgets and don't think about what a real record sounds like anymore. And sometimes they are so into their own thing, their trick, it's difficult for them to work with different people. For me, there is an art form to production, so I purposely make them sign a contract as coproducers and cowriters. But I was glad to collaborate. I was sick of my process; I wanted to see how other people did it.

Working well with other artists to create a particular vision that I have, without stymieing them in any way, is a challenge. I'm learning more and more how to do this without ruffling feathers, but I must confess that I don't know how to do it as well as I'd like to. I've plucked a few chickens in my time. I have never been a delicate flower. Hopefully I am getting better. Or, as Yoda would say, "Better I'm getting." I've got to be graceful, and smart, and patient, and secure.

It was hard at first for the Swedish producer Peer Astrom (who has been working on *Glee* from the beginning). He wrote "Into the Nightlife" and "Echo" with me and Johan Bobeck. Peer wanted something very specific. But me being the guy who was going to go out and sell it, made it all the more important that I could get behind it. But I always thought he was a very reasonable guy.

Some of the trouble with collaborating also had to do with the language barrier. Although we all spoke English, I've always said England's English is not what we speak across the pond, baby. And when I stop and think about my lack of command of the English language in my own country—well, it's pretty comical. I speak the Queens English, but the borough—not the person. My experience writing with other artists and producers on that CD was still inspirational though. I always hope to keep learning and collaborating with other artists who inspire me.

Lisa came with me to Sweden, and I was so grateful because we had an awesome time. At first we stayed in a Sheraton in Stockholm. It was new and nice and had a great gym. I would go every day, I told myself, but that only lasted for the first two days. I watched guys working out with big weights next to me as I lifted my measly eight pounds. But when I met Alex Kronlund, the first writer I met there, he said I should move to someplace more inspiring to write. So I crossed the bridge to the Old Town.

That's where Lisa and I went looking for an authentic restaurant to get some real Swedish food, like Swedish meatballs or something. We went down to the big tourist street and passed this place and decided it looked kind of cute and quaint. We saw a guy standing outside and asked him if the place served authentic Swedish food and he said yes. The guy's name was Danny and he was a bartender there. He became our favorite bartender, and the place became our favorite hang. And it wasn't just because the food was good, or because we knew how to get to it. It was because of Danny.

We got to talking about New York and Sweden and things to see while we were there. Danny said we should go up to this square, and he told us the history behind it while Lisa and I sipped aquavit and ate elk meatballs. I was told that aquavit is a very Swedish drink, and apparently the Swedes enjoy a bit of elk, which is drier than beef and tastes nothing like squirrel (which you know I've eaten) but is gamier than chicken.

So back to the square: Apparently in the Middle Ages a very arrogant Danish king crowned himself king of Sweden, too. So this self-appointed king guy pissed the Swedish people off so much that he caused a really big uprising, and the Swedish guys chopped up all the Danish guys, and there was so much blood dripping down the cobblestones that they renamed the square "Blood Square." So said Danny. But when I researched it, the Danes weren't beheaded, the Swedes were. Then the Danish king crowned himself. So Danny had it a little backward, unless it was the language barrier. Either way, blood was all over that square. Lisa loved that story because she loves murder mysteries. So we went to the square and I fell in love with those little cobblestone streets. I forgot about the blood and the rolling heads, and I had one of my "stepping into history" moments.

So then we began to search for a boutique hotel in the Old Town— the kind of place that would keep me happily adrift in a world that was split between the then and the now—a place situated on a street where, if you looked down it and squinted long enough, you could see the Vikings and a wagon or two, being led by a horse or an ox.

The hotel we decided to stay in was dedicated to the memory of the British Royal Navy and Admiral Horatio Nelson and his lover, a Lady Somebody. Lady Emma Hamilton. She was a lady, but not like a "Hey, lady!" She was much fancier than that. The hotel had letters in cases from her to him. It was a love-affair museum. We found out that the hotel was also dedicated to sea captains and seafaring men in the time of Admiral Nelson. Two boat mastheads greeted me when I walked in. One was male and the other female. They were old but newly painted with enamel paint and gold trim, which made them look new and shiny. I felt giddy every time I saw them and I would wink at them.

Even though the record company had already rented the Sheraton hotel room for me, I found that staying in the historic area where this little boutique hotel really inspired me to write, so it was worth the money. The people at the boutique hotel said they had a suite for me but they actually had an apartment, which ended up being better than a hotel room. It was at the top of a winding stairwell. The furniture in the apartment was old and the antique chairs and the wooden floors echoed my steps against the white walls, which were hung with portraits of women. I wondered if they had paced the same floors, maybe waiting or dreaming of their lover's embrace. And sometimes when I came back at night, I'd play some Marvin Gaye from my iPod on portable speakers and dance wildly around the living room as I tried to remember what I learned from some classes I took on spirit dancing. A group of women met every month on the full moon to dance in a circle, and once I was invited to join them. I howled like a wolf, and I thought it was cool that you could behave like that and still be invited back. Anyway I danced around by myself and wondered if I and the dames on the wall were in our own circle dance. (But that was after Lisa, my adventurous, hardworking, good-sport manager, went to her room.)

The bedroom I took in the place was on the second floor and overlooked a courtyard that was a restaurant in the summer. Every dawn (which isn't so early in Sweden due to the whole dark/light thing they got going on there) I'd wake up to the sound of two young women laughing and talking (in Swedish, of course). And that always made me remember where I was. Then I'd get up and order room service and write poetry in the dining room. I'd also try and do my yoga, but this new world had my head spinning. I just couldn't stay focused on it, even though rhythm, music, and yoga are kind of alike sometimes.

So even though I was away from my family, I had a great time in Sweden, immersing myself in the culture and in the dance world. And when I came back, I took a break to understand what I had just done—to look at the good, the bad, and the ugly. (Ya know, my son used to get "time-outs" for singing the theme song of that movie in kindergarten. I still can't get over how wrong it was to punish him for that. It's such a great choral arrangement for kids to learn and so much fun to sing together. But I digress.) During this break I realized that touring inspired me. Being able to watch other artists perform and be passionate about their work woke me up.

So after some time off with the two D's (Declyn and David) and Mama Grace (my mother-in-law, whom I adore), I went back to *Bring Ya to the Brink*, and eventually the music fell into place. It's an exhilarating moment when, after all my worrying about if I'll ever get the songs right or if I'm good at what I do, suddenly the material comes alive. And you know what? I've come to understand that I may never feel that my work is good enough. But I really can't let my doubt stop me from writing songs. Inspiration can strike anytime, anywhere. Every once in a while, I'll wake up, and inspiration just comes to me, and I have to write. I have to keep writing and brave out every stupid line of ridiculous poetry for one good line. Which, seemingly out of nowhere, does happen. And when it does, I send out a thank-you.

Going to Europe to write really made me grow. I returned to my voice as a writer and artist in a way that I had never done before. The funny thing was that I had always heard that travel was a great thing for a writer—that's the first time I ever traveled overseas just to write ... and without a minder, too. Of course, I did have help. I had a driver (so okay, I traveled a little like a celebrity, but only a little). But for the most part, I was just myself, without a lot of the usual brouhaha. I wasn't touring at the same time and doing press, or trying to be a mom or a wife. I wasn't trying to do anything but write. It was so peaceful and comforting to be able to write down what I felt and saw, because that's all I was doing. I felt awake for the first time in years.

Then I started to wrap up the whole album and record my vocals in the studio over my garage with William Wittman, my longtime collaborator. I also researched a great mixer who I had in mind from day one, Jeremy Wheatley from England—he had mixed a Goldfrapp CD and their single "Ride a White Horse." I absolutely loved his sonic picture for dance. And so I contacted him through the record company but in the end he had a tragedy in his family, so we wound up mixing online together. In other words, it went a little like this: We would pick a time we could be online together with the same board and speakers up, and he would send the mix over to me on iChat (which is able to send big files without compression) and I would take that file and play it. And then I'd tell him what I thought needed to be louder and lower. When I heard the first track, "High and Mighty," I started to cry, because it was such a modern record. I always try and push people to make a modern record, and finally, there it was.

Music is so subjective. The great thing now is that you can go into your garage and make a wonderful record. The bad thing is that nobody is weeding out bad songs anymore. It's like not having an editor. Which is okay—Prince works by himself, but there aren't a lot of people like Prince. I like a lot of checks and balances and having a lot of different people hear the music and contribute to it.

Even though I was really proud of *Bring Ya to the Brink* when it came out in May of 2008, it didn't do as well as I wanted. "Same Ol' Story" was number one on *Billboard's* Dance/Club Play Songs, but dance radio, I was told, would not play me because I was over thirty. Like I've said, people in the music business have a bias against older people because they operate on the myth that music is a disposable art form. It is not. I was watching Nicki Minaj the other night on *Saturday Night Live* and she ended her song in a pose, just like what I used to do in my concerts. Half her hair was pink and the other half was white, and I thought, "Give me shit all you want, but I inspired stuff like that, and they even get inspired from what I wear now."

Bring Ya to the Brink was nominated for a Grammy for Best Electronic/Dance Album. But I lost to Daft Punk. Understandably— their song was sampled in a Kanye West song and it was huge. But just when I was feeling bad about myself, I ran into Nicki Minaj at the Grammys red carpet. She came up to me and said, "People don't know how obsessed I am with you." How cool is that?

The record company and I parted ways before I went to the Grammys. I had one release left but all my allies had left the company, so

I decided I should leave, too. Look, it ultimately was a good thing because then I could do what I wanted with my albums. I could own my masters; I could be in charge. I could research how to sell it, how to promote it, and not make stupid mistakes. Anyway, I'll do another dance album. The music I wrote for the musical *Kinky Boots*, the film Harvey Fierstein and I adapted for Broadway, is mostly dance.

After I left Sony, I did a little two-week tour with Ro called "Girls' Night Out," where we asked fans to donate food to local food banks. Beforehand, I met with people from Mark Burnett Productions and said, "Why don't we film the tour? Then we can do a thing about soup kitchens, too, so it would be about entertainment but also helping people." They weren't interested in that because getting the rights from the record company to music in a film can get complicated. Mark Burnett Productions did *Survivor* and when I saw the pictures of the show on the wall of their office, I said I was worried I'd get voted out of the meeting. But I really liked them.

So I signed with Mark Burnett to do something in the future. And they introduced me to the people at Donald Trump's reality show *The Celebrity Apprentice*, which I hadn't seen. But Lisa watched it, and came back to me and said, "Why don't you do *Celebrity Apprentice?*" I said, "Um, yeah—I'm a musician, why the hell do I want to do that for?" Then they told me that I could raise money for the True Colors Fund and that if anybody knows how to work in a team, I do, because everything I did was in a team. And Lisa was like, "Come on, Cyn— you could do this." So I said okay.

We taped it in New York. At first they said it was a nine-to-five type of thing, but it was not nine to five. It was seven A.M. to eleven or twelve at night—like, an eighteen-hour-day type of thing. I'd get up at four A.M. to get my hair and makeup ready by seven, so I got no sleep. And there was no downtime at all—in fact, when you ate, you had to eat standing up. You could never stop because if you did, you'd lose. Consequently I developed really, really bad reflux. My esophagus was burning all the time, and I couldn't even swallow food. Then I'd have to do these long interviews about the show. I don't know how to talk—I know how to sing. So I lost my voice, too. Plus the set was dusty and I'm allergic to dust.

Nonsingers don't know what it takes to sing. They were all making fun of me as I did my vocal exercises. I was like, "You stupid idiots, if only you knew a few exercises yourself, your voices would be so much better." The problem is some of the other contestants were wannabes who did nothing with their lives. I could never take a backseat and not do anything. It would drive me crazy.

And pretty quickly it started to get a little like high school. I had always been an outsider, and I just had to get used to it again. When Maria, the WWE wrestler, suddenly started turning her back to me, I kept thinking, "Why don't you go fuck yourself?" Which is what the people running the show wanted me to think, so that we'd start fighting, because that stuff is compelling. Nobody wants to watch a show where everybody gets along, right? Even I got drawn in when I watched it—and I knew what was going to happen. I started watching to see what I looked like on TV, and I thought, "Jeez, I thought my hair was good, I thought my taste was good." Everything that I do is an illusion of how I'd like to look—not how I actually look. That's why I get along with drag queens, because I am one.

I had so much fun with Sharon Osbourne, who I adore, but the rest of the girls were two-faced. So I started to lose my stomach for it pretty quickly. And that Victoria's Secret model, Selita Ebanks, was really sweet to me. When I was trying to help make over that young country singer, Emily West, in one of the challenges, all the others on my team were putting their two cents in, and they didn't know what the hell they were talking about. I was like, "Do you care about this kid, or do you not care?" They didn't care—they were just interested in what came out of their own mouths. When Maria the wrestler was talking to Emily West about how to do interviews, she said, "When I do press, they want to know, do I shave there or do I not?" I looked at her and just wanted to say, "Listen, Miss Thing, if you think I'm going to sit here and tell that kid how to do an interview by talking about if her pussy is shaved or not, you are out of your freakin' mind. This is about music and integrity—not about that."

I was a little leery about Donald Trump because he had traumatized Rosie O'Donnell's kids by saying bad things about their mother. When you do that, the kids don't understand. What changed my mind about him was that not only was he nice to me, he was nice to other people, and his kids were good and hardworking. And the fact that he included them in the show was significant.

I loved performing "Just Your Fool" on the finale and dancing on the desk. There I was on national TV calling attention to the lack of civil rights in the gay community. NBC kept trying to change what I said. When I was on TV for the finale, though, I said what I wanted, and they couldn't cut it cause it was live. I thought to myself, "Go on, try and edit this out now."

Just for the record, I didn't feel like I was unfairly voted off. I kind of committed hara-kiri because looking at actress Holly Robinson Peete was so paralyzing for me. She was fighting to get funds for autism, a condition her son had. And when it's a mother and a son, it just gets me right here—I automatically think about my mom with her kids and that time when my mom sang to my brother when she was in a hopeless situation that day in the bathroom.

When we did the challenge of decorating the apartment on the episode that ended in my departure, it would have been very simple for me to beat out Holly by saying, "Yes, Holly, you chose the color red for the celebrity room of the apartment, which everyone liked, but you also chose that seafoam green, or what I would call a 'puce green,' for the master bedroom."

The situation with Bret Michaels became very comical. When he decorated that apartment, he kept bringing so much stuff that I felt like I was in a Marx Brothers movie, like *A Night at the Opera*. Every time I'd turn around, there was another big object coming into the room. I was like, "No, Bret, no, no, no." But it was interesting to watch everyone. There's no way to be graceful on that show.

When I was voted off, I wore a scarf and dark glasses and red lipstick because I wanted to look like a very old-time Hollywood movie star. As I left the building, I thought, "Walk tall, put your shoulders back, be very Grace Kelly, and walk into the car very Kim Novak."

But in the end, I made my point. I got to talk about civil rights for LGBTs on national TV—that was pretty big. And we raised $45,000 for the True Colors Fund, which is the most important thing.

That show taught me that people don't really change a lot unless life provides them with a gift of understanding, which can come through a gift of misfortune early on. And through your life you can make a better life and better choices because you got that lesson already.

And I learned something else, too—waitressing still wasn't my cup of tea.

CHAPTER SEVENTEEN

I WANTED TO DO a blues album for six years, but when I finally did, it was good timing, because it seemed to me like everywhere I looked, everybody was singing the blues. People were losing their jobs, their homes, and all over the world, hard times had hit.

This time around, the album was going to be on my own label imprint, so I could actually do what I knew was right. I met the producer Scott Bomar through Josh Deutsch, who was head of the label I partnered up with for the album. It just so happened that Josh knew a lot about the blues. Scott was making some noise with a blues revival and I could look him up online. So I did. He looked like a nice guy. He had produced the soundtrack for the Bernie Mac movie *Soul Men* and had worked with Willie Mitchell. Willie had really been the godfather of Memphis soul. He made the Al Green and Ann Peebles records in the seventies. In fact, he made all the music coming out of Memphis back then. Now I work with his stepson Archie "Hubbie" Turner in my band.

When Scott told me about some of the Memphis session musicians that could work with me on the CD, I jumped. They were all members of the original Hi Records rhythm section. So I went down to his studio in Memphis for a couple of days to see how this whole thing would work. Scott is the sweetest guy you'll meet, but he's also indirect, which is not what I am. In fact that's how most Southerners are—they're not up in your face, they have an air of politeness. So here I came, the bull in the china shop.

Before I even met Scott I had been compiling songs. Once with Rick Chertoff, then by myself, then with everyone sending me songs they loved, and then with Michael Alago, who came down with Lisa and Bill and myself to Memphis.

At that time I was still battling vocal problems. I had discovered two days before Christmas that I had a polyp. If you stop singing and speaking, the polyps will sometimes go down. Mine did not. I was really crushed because just like the first time I lost my voice, I felt like, "How can I live, or even breathe, without my voice?" I think what finished my voice was when I was on a float in the Thanksgiving Day Parade in New York, and I decided to shout "Happy Thanksgiving" to everyone from Seventy-first Street to Thirty-fourth Street before I sang on TV. (I know—I got shit for brains sometimes.)

Before I recorded the blues album, I still had to complete songs for *Kinky Boots*, so I just wrote with whatever voice I had. My dear friend Howard came with me to the doctor the day I found out about the polyp. Howard has struggled with his health, and always with courage, so I wouldn't let myself feel self-pity.

To help with the polyp, I started working with a speech therapist named Barbara Lowenfels because I had to learn how to speak without squeezing my vocals together and forgetting to breathe. That was the first step. Then when I did the MAC AIDS campaign with Lady Gaga, Barbara was right there with me, reminding me to keep my shoulders back and take pauses to breathe so I wouldn't injure myself more. It was a little out of the ordinary to have her behind the camera during an interview, coaching me. And of course this was a little weird for Lisa, my manager. She kept saying, "You're kidding, right?" But bless Barbara, she helped me and I am grateful.

After two months, I was given the okay to start singing lightly again by Dr. Peak Woo, the infamous "Dr. Wu" from the Steely Dan song. And then I went back to Katie Agresta, my vocal teacher, who has helped me back on my feet each time I've fallen down. We started from what felt like scratch. Something like this is caused by being so tired and doing so much that you develop bad habits, and sometimes you don't even realize what's happening to you till it's too late. My polyp is now gone but I still have to deal with reflux, which I'm starting to fix. Okay, that was just a backstory—now back to Memphis.

I knew I wanted to do the Memphis Slim song "Mother Earth." I thought Allen Toussaint would be great on it. I met Allen when I sang at the Hurricane Katrina benefit with him at Madison Square Garden in 2006. A ton of folks were there, from Elvis Costello to Bruce Springsteen, to the wonderful Irma "Soul Queen of New Orleans" Thomas. I got to sing with her and the Dixie Cups and it was a real thrill. The producers wanted me to sing an old song called "I Know (You Don't Love Me No More)" for the benefit. And I said, "I'm playing with Allen Toussaint—shouldn't I do one of his great songs?" I thought maybe I could do a mash-up of two songs to celebrate him, so I found his song called "Last Train" that went really well with "I Know You (Don't Love Me No More.)" I didn't want to do a medley, though; I wanted to figure out a way to play the two songs over each other. If it worked, it might be really something. I figure you gotta try for the challenge instead of the safe way all the fuckin' time. I mean, there was Allen Toussaint! And he kept saying, "I find this very adventuresome." I respect him so much. I've always thought, "If you're gonna do television, try your hardest to do something that's real." Because most stuff on TV is rehearsed to the last possible moment, so that nothing magically unpredictable can happen. Like when I did the Jools Holland show last New Year's Eve, they had all these big arrangements planned, so I said, "Can I just play with strings, and the dulcimer, and maybe that guy over there could play the tin whistle?" You want to always try something different, something where even *you* don't know what's going to happen, and then you either hear the magic or you don't. And with Allen, that night, I think it worked out. After that, we wanted to work together if we ever could, but when he did a CD, I wasn't available for it.

During the last go-around to figure out the song material I would take to Memphis, I worked with Michael Alago, my computer, and some Chinese takeout in my kitchen. Michael, who I knew for years in the industry, was a great A & R person. All the songs were chosen because of their spirit, their story, and their timeless theme of history repeating itself. Here was great American music created by people who were oppressed and who wrote music that was uplifting.

Ya know, even though it's called the blues, you feel better somehow listening to it. I wanted to take the old glamour of this music but also make it into something that could be embraced now. I am always hoping to make music that is timeless. And the blues—well, that's timeless. I remember the thing that Sony was afraid of way back when was that it was going to sound like a heritage record, which was never my intention. And I was just grateful to make this music without a lot of fuckin' grief from a company struggling to survive.

I had two songs I wanted to try first in Memphis, a Lil Green song called "Romance in the Dark" (the singer and pianist Michael Feinstein recommended I listen to it after he watched a True Colors cabaret show that I did at his club) and the Tracy Nelson song "Down So Low," which I had sung on and off in 2004. I knew I had found the right band for the project: Lester Snell on keys, Howard Grimes on drums, Leroy Hodges on bass, and Skip Pitts on guitar.

So we tried out "Down So Low" and "Romance in the Dark" with the band. When the players heard the 1930s recording of "Romance in the Dark," of course they were wondering what the arrangement might be. I said to them, "Please just learn the chords, I will arrange it as I go." It is frightening to tell this to folks who like to structure everything before the "singer" gets there. But I wanted this to be live— really live. So I kept saying to Scott that everything else would come together as we played. I just needed to sing with them for a minute first. I heard Skip, the guitarist who played that wonderful riff on the *Shaft* record, call what I was doing "head arrangements" and I thought, "Yeah, that's right."

I brought Allen Toussaint in early the first day he was at the studio, and I worked out the arrangements with the special artists as they came in. It was really the opposite from what Howard, the drummer, said Uncle Willie (Mitchell) did. Everyone in Memphis was influenced by this brilliant man. But even though I hadn't known him, or studied under him, like Scott, I knew his work. I grew up singing it and loved it. And I had some reliable ears with me who provided checks and balances, like Bill Wittman, who recorded my first album and has worked with me pretty much ever since. I also had Lisa there, who is my third eye.

When the band came in I let Allen start directing because of his venerable track record, and because I thought maybe he spoke the band's language more than I did. And Scott was cool with that, too. But Howard, who had just gotten used to taking his cues from me, got concerned and started asking why it changed. I thought the whole band would feel more comfortable with that, but I guess I was wrong.

After we did the first two songs to try the band out, Howard the drummer came up to Lisa and said, "I hear Cyndi is very popular. I heard she did a cover of a Miles Davis tune, and she had some big hits, but I'm not familiar with her music." So Lisa said, "Oh, I bet you are—did you ever hear the song 'Girls Just Want to Have Fun'?" He said no, and Lisa said, "How about 'True Colors'?" And he said, "No, I'm not familiar with those jams, but I hear she's real popular." I thought it might be good that he didn't know my work—no preconceived notions.

But everybody was very nice and generous to me. When we worked on those two songs together in that initial meeting, I knew it was going to work. We really jelled.

I think once we all felt the center of the music, we relaxed. The center of the music is the gravity of it for me. It's where I stand with the drums in the center of a song. It feels like the drums are my dance partner, and from there I listen very closely to find an interior motion within the music. I listen to hear and feel what all the instruments are creating in between and around what the drums and I are doing together.

The way I see it is that each musical phrase creates a weight on whatever side of the center of the rhythm you put it: the center of the rhythm being the drums. The bass needs to support the drums, but the best bass parts, for me, also lead the melody. Distributing the musical parts creates a balance within the song. And that's the fun part for me. It makes the song sway one way or the other, like a subtle push and pull around the drums and the singer. None of this is new, of course, even though every time I figure out how to make a song breathe like that, I feel like I've reinvented the wheel.

I learned the idea of this when I studied with a teacher named Betty Scott. She was supposed to be my introduction to studying with Lennie Tristano, the great jazz pianist. But I never got that far. I couldn't quit my rock band. I loved rock and roll too much. But what Betty taught me shaped the way I sang and constructed a song for the rest of my life.

She taught me how to listen when I sang. To work on my timing, I sang to a metronome. Then she'd blow into a pitch pipe and ask me to sing the note she played. Then she went over intervals with me by blowing a note into a pitch pipe and asking me to sing the fifth or the third of the note, to help me develop an understanding of harmony and an ear for what other instruments were playing around me. To further help me understand this, she had me study the recordings of Billie Holiday with the great saxophonist Lester Young, specifically how Billie responded to what Lester played, and how Lester responded to what Billie sang. After singing with them note for note and breath for breath for almost two years, I felt I could begin to understand how to sing in the center of a song like Billie and answer the way Lester would answer.

My whole style and arrangement approach is kind on based of the simplicity of that approach. I kept it in mind when I arranged "Time After Time" and "True Colors." That's why I made them record the track live with the electronic drum, so we could feel the center and what could sway around it.

Every once and a while, like when I recorded *At Last*, I could do it blatantly, but never in dance or pop. I always had to sneak in that stuff on those projects. But great blues has all that naturally. So when the opportunity came to sing with some of the greatest blues/soul guys in the business, I jumped. If you listen closely to the song "Mother Earth" on the *Memphis Blues* CD, you'll hear that Lester Snell and Allen Toussaint are playing back and forth to each other. You will hear "pure joy," as Lester put it once, and some fine call-and-response.

And one more thing I want to tell you about listening to call-and-response. If you are ever are up at dawn and just have a minute, listen to the birds. Sometimes if you can answer one of the whistles right, they'll kindly let you into their round. If you are open enough, your heart might break open with how sweet they are, and then you'll hear and feel their rhythm too—until you mess up. When I do they fly away and ditch me.

I have always loved mixing different styles and genres of music together. I guess it's like how we used to dress in the eighties: we mixed all the decades of fashion together at once, as my first stylist, Laura Wills, once put it. It took me most of my career to think of saying to the people I work with in the studio, "I do things a little unconventionally sometimes, so please bear with me. It might sound weird at first, but just go with me for a minute, and you'll hear what I'm hearing."

And that's what I tried to tell these much more seasoned musicians than myself while making Memphis Blues. Because for me, Memphis Blues is a soulful blues which is different from New Orleans style, which has more swing to it. Allen Toussant plays New Orleans style, but the minute he played the hypnotic opening of "Shattered Dreams" the two styles just fell into place. I didn't have to try and explain anymore to the band; they heard it—that is, until I brought in the guitarist Jonny Lang. Then suddenly, I had two lead guitarists: Jonny and Skip Pitts, whose approaches to the music were completely different. It left me in the position of having to coax them and the band into melding their styles to create this swampy feel to the rhythm that I was envisioning, one that evoked memories of Robert Johnson's early recording of "Cross Road Blues."

I kept telling them what was happening in the story of the song like we were making a movie. I told them that each part was a character. And I shared whatever visions I had while I was singing so they could feel them too. And we began to make a version of "Cross Road Blues" that felt to me like an old black-and-white movie. I guess when my mom played *Peter and the Wolf* to me way back when, it must have left a big impression.

In Memphis I had entered such a different world of musicians with a different language and culture. These were some of the greatest musicians I'd ever worked with. And I'm so glad we didn't write out music for them to play, like charts, because instead of reading we just listened to each other and fell into a natural lull by using that call-and-response approach. Everything was live, which was totally opposite from my last CD. And all the while above the little sofa in the control room was a painted portrait on velvet of Jimi Hendrix. (He always pops up no matter where I am.)

So we moved forward, and all of a sudden the harmonica master Charlie Musselwhite, the legendary B.B. King, and the wonderful Jonny Lang were on the album. Then I heard the bass player, Leroy Hodges, talking to Howard Grimes, the drummer, about "Ann this" and "Ann that." And I said, "Ann who? Ann Peebles? Oh my God— you know her? Can you call her?" It was as simple as that. I thought I'd jump out of my skin. I sang along with her for years, like I did with Aretha and Billie and Ella and Big Maybelle.

So when I recorded "Rollin and Tumblin" with Ann, I tried to tell her at first how much her music meant to me, but I became emotional and started crying. I think that scares people when you're trying to direct them so I had to leave the room. I gave myself the old scuba-diving lesson: "Why are you crying? Aren't you happy? Okay, then . . . Breathe." At Scott's studio, we recorded on an eight-track machine. How's that for analog? It made a real nice warm, thick sound. Bill Wittman knew how to work it too because he said it was the first machine he ever worked on.

It took a while to get B.B. involved. He worked all the time and really, when you mention my name to people, half don't know who I am and half don't think I can sing. When I told Scott that I would like to do a song with Allen playing on keyboards and B.B. King on guitar, he said, "Then you gotta choose a Louis Jordan song, because B.B. always talks about Louis Jordan." Louis Jordan was a hugely influential jazz and blues musician, composer, and bandleader. So I went online (I love my computer) and pulled up his music. The first song that came up was "Early in the Morning," and it was so much fun—even the cover was great, just like my aunt Gloria's old cha-cha record covers. He talks in the beginning and at the end, and there's great music and a story too. I thought Allen would shine on this song, because it has a New Orleans feel to it. I was right; Allen was wonderful and as Lester put it, "It was pure joy." The best you can hope for is to have a session that's pure joy.

When we sent that song out to B.B., his peeps got back to us and said he could do it. But the only time we could get him was when I was going to be away at a gig and then I'd be going with my family to Turks and Caicos with Lisa and her family for the kids' spring break. So B.B. recorded his parts at his studio in Las Vegas with Scott Bomar, and I didn't actually get to meet him again. But listen, I was still so thrilled that I did a track with the man I met as a student at Johnson State College, when I was so overwhelmed I couldn't talk. And B.B. not only played and sang great, but he even did some banter on that song with me, too. Wow!

In my effort to make the blues more accessible to the person who wouldn't normally listen to blues, I thought I needed to do something aesthetically pleasing with the album cover. So I thought I'd bring it back to the old days, when people like Alberta Hunter and Ma Rainey were dressed to the nines. B.B. King is *still* dressed to the nines in a suit. Then I thought, "How can we make it sexy?" So I asked Ellen Von

Unwerth if she would take the album cover pictures of me because she really took some beautiful pictures when I did the Viva Glam campaign with Lady Gaga. I thought combining the boudoir with the blues looked great together. And I knew Ellen would make a glamorous, modern image inspired by older pictures I found for reference.

I got excited to shoot the picture on the back of the album, too. I had a fake snake, and there was smoke. I wanted a masculine/feminine version of Robert Johnson, but with a tight leather suit. I thought it would add a new edge to the look (plus any fabric that has a slight sheen to it makes a better photograph). The suit wasn't a new idea, but the leather part was. And my stylist Nikki put it together. Then Nikki had the idea to make the collar asymmetrical, too. And Jutta Weiss made wild red wigs for me, and I was able to get James Kardones to do my makeup, and all of a sudden, I became an art piece.

When it came time to mix I was still in Turks and Caicos. I knew that was going to happen so I asked for a suite with a separate living room—someplace I could set up speakers. Bill and Scott were in Long Island mixing at PIE Studios. I had a little studio packed with me—talk about your luggage—with speakers, a little interface board that I could plug my speakers into, and a computer. The idea was to go online when they were ready and have them send it over iChat. Then I'd listen and give my comments; they'd make the adjustments; I'd listen and approve it; and they'd move on to the next mix. Sounds reasonable, right? In the meantime I thought that if I could contact Keith Richards to play on one of the tracks, maybe "Rollin and Tumblin," that would be great. I knew the person who cut his manager's hair so I figured, "What the heck? I'll give it a shot."

So when we arrived in Turks and Caicos, the room was not really the suite I had hoped for. Instead of a living room, there was an extra kids' room, and it was a really bad-sounding room with wood everywhere, and it was long and narrow, so it wasn't a good fit for the speakers. The master bedroom was my only option. It was bigger and wider, with fewer hard surfaces in it.

There were only two times of the day when Bill and Scott could work—around eleven A.M. and six or seven P.M. So I put a speaker on a chair on either side of the bed. Then I stood in the middle at the foot of the bed to hear what they mixed. But within a day after we arrived my son developed a virus that was going around, or food poisoning, or something. He was up all night so sick that in the morning my husband took him to the hospital, where they had to give the poor kid intravenous fluid because he was so dehydrated.

Well, within two days, my husband got the same thing. Cut to: Bill and Scott calling from Long Island with the mixes. They needed an answer. So because I couldn't put Bill and Scott off, I had to stand at the foot of the bed with David and Declyn lying in it, sick, and listen to those mixes. Now the thing about listening to a mix is that you should listen loud—not so loud you can't hear, but loud enough that you can. So there were my two guys lying in the middle of those big-ass JBL speakers, just looking at me. And it wasn't just one day like this, either. I felt so bad. I tried not to look at them. I tried to listen intently and give my instructions clearly while I just wanted to cry for them. I figured, "Yeah, this is the blues all right."

Ya know, the thing about food on an island is that everything is brought in, so it isn't always fresh. Thank God for that Diet Center pudding I brought with me. That and a probiotic, and I didn't get sick. Declyn was better in three days, and David was better three days later. Then we went home. How's that for restful?

At least we were together. And then, on the plane home before we took off, I get a call from Keith Richards. It was kind of surreal. The announcements were coming on, but I didn't want to get off the phone with Keith Richards. So I quickly said, "Hey-I'm-making-a-blues-album-you-want-to-play-on-it?" His answer, in a relaxed English drawl, was, "If you're singing blues, baby, I'm in." And I said, "I-think-you'd-be-great-on-'Rollin-and-Tumblin.'" And he said, "Sure, I think I know that one—ha ha." But in the end, when I told him the deadline, he said he didn't think he'd be back in the US in time. Because guess where he was? On vacation in Turks and Caicos. (Guess he wasn't staying at the same resort we were in.)

I decided to dedicate the album to Ma Rainey, who is the Mother of the Blues. And she was a feminist. She wore gold chains; she had gold teeth. She was gangsta before gangsta. And she was gay! Although I didn't do a Ma Rainey song (next time), her spirit was in the fashion of the clothing I wore—in the suit, in the chains.

At the end of the project Howard the drummer said to me, "All those people who heard 'Girls' have been waiting to hear what you have to say now. And when they hear this, it's going to go straight to the top. You ever think about that?" And I said, "Yeah, with every re-cording." *Memphis Blues* came out on my birthday in 2010, and it was the largest-selling blues CD that year. It was number one for thirteen weeks on the blues chart. And then it was nominated, alongside blues greats and legends including Charlie Musselwhite, for a Grammy for Best Traditional Blues Album—my fourteenth nomination.

I took my son with me to the ceremony which I had wanted to do for a long time. Well, the Grammy went to Pinetop Perkins, who was nominated for a blues album he did with Willie "Big Eyes" Smith. He was ninety-seven years old. He made a great record. He died just five weeks later.

I had so much fun with Dec at the Grammys. He was so happy because he sat right behind Akon, who turned around and said hello to us. And Dec loves Lil Wayne, so when he was nearby, Dec said, "Just call out 'Weezy,'" so I did. And Lil Wayne looked at me, and I waved and asked for his autograph. He was all excited and I said to him, "Weezy, you make great music, now be good." And he put his hand over his heart and said, "I promise." Then I walked past L.L. Cool J and he jumped up and said hello, and then I was saying hello to everybody—Kanye West, Bieber, whatever the heck that kid's name is. Then Gaga jumped up and said she missed me, and I gave her a hug. Dec got to see everybody up close.

People would ask me, "What do you think is the highlight tonight?" It really was having Dec and David out there with me. But also I got to sing with the legendary soul singers Mavis Staples and Betty Wright, and with blues singer Maria Muldaur. I can't even explain how it felt to look into their faces and sing to them. I don't know if they ever understood what they gave to me over the years through their work. And there was also the wonderful band that backed us up. The great blues guitarist Buddy Guy was in that band too. He couldn't make rehearsal, because he was traveling from a gig. So during the performance when he answered my voice with his guitar as I sang my part, I choked. I couldn't believe that it was actually him answering my voice. I am grateful to be a singer who gets to sing with so many wonderful musicians and other singers.

But with all the good that was happening, in the back of my head I had some serious concerns, specifically my upcoming tour to South America. My last South American tour, two years before was for a dance CD, which went over really well. I kept wondering how these countries would receive the blues. South American people love to dance. Their musical culture is celebratory. I thought, "Okay, what is it in their music that lights them up?" Of course, it's the rhythm. Then I starting thinking about all the different rhythms I could find in blues music. I thought about how I could present the blues to a continent in a way that they could feel connected to it and take ownership of it. Then I remembered Martin Scorsese's seven-part series *The Blues* on PBS and the fife and drum band he had in it. I remembered how I thought it sounded an awful lot like Carnival drums. The wild thing was that we were going down to play Brazil a week before Carnival. So I thought that if I could find a Carnival drummer who might understand the concept, I could connect the two different feels of this music.

I thought I might be able to place the Carnival rhythm in the middle of a shuffle blues song like "Just Your Fool" or "Down Don't Bother Me" or in "Crossroads." Anyway, the record guy in Brazil found a woman named Lan Lan who played Carnival drums. I sent her an mp3 of Otha Turner and his Rising Star Fife and Drum Corps and said, "Doesn't this sound like Carnival rhythm to you?" And she said it was because Bahia, Brazil, isnt that far from Africa. And that's why it sounds like they're connected. The enslaved people from Africa were brought to Brazil first and then sent through the Americas. And I thought, "Yeah, and with them came this wonderful rhythm that, ironically, would later free so many of us." I thought that if this approach to the music worked, it would be magical.

I met Lan Lan at sound check the day of the first show. I was traveling with this wonderful band; three guys from Memphis and two guys from NYC. (A lot of the time I also traveled with Charlie Musselwhite, but he couldn't make it to South America this time.) One of the Memphis guys is the legendary drummer, Steve Potts. He holds down a rhythm like he's driving a Corvette. But I love him even more because he is open to trying out an idea that could be great or could be crazy. When I played the Otha Turner stuff to Steve, he heard what I wanted to do and thought it could work too. And when we actually tried it, and Lan Lan played along in the center of the shuffle with that Otha Turner/Carnival drum rhythm, it not only worked, it was otherworldly. When these two distinctly separate rhythms were played together it felt like they created a vortex, one I could sing in the middle of. After that first night of the South American, "Memphis Blues" tour, the blues became profoundly deeper for me and I think for all of us in the band.

One night while I was onstage singing in São Paulo, Brazil, listening to Lan Lan and Steve Potts, I saw a native king in my mind's eye. It's funny how this vision was in Black and White. His beautiful coffee and cream skin and white feathers that surrounded his entire head and back were dazzling. As I danced and sang, I felt him say to me, "The conquerors came and conquered, but they could never conquer the rhythm. And in the rhythm is freedom."

When we toured in Europe for *Memphis Blues*, I worked to make sure the shows kicked ass. As Charlie Musselwhite says, "The donkey must fall," and I believed it did. I wanted to leave the promoters in Europe feeling like they were watching something special. And we were. We had no lighting man or staging, but we made some powerful music. I used the floor of the stage, the sides of the monitor speakers, and the audience chairs for staging, so that each song looked a little different.

ANOTHER SURREAL moment in my life was trying to put together the *Memphis Blues Live* DVD. I was getting ready for a European tour after being in Australia, and I had a one-week window to edit it. The director of photography that I hired was a fellow named Ben. He was someone I had worked with some twenty years before. He made me look beautiful, and he was also attached to a friend of mine and great producer named John, so I thought this would work fine. John would be my liaison and act as a middle man.

Okay, it didn't happen that way. Because John (an extraordinary fellow who was once in a famous plane crash in Taipei and worked himself back onto his feet without the use of a wheelchair) decided to refill a pain prescription in Juarez, Mexico, instead of near his home in Los Angeles, because it was cheaper. His mom lived in Mexico. (I guess the plan was to see her, too.) Well, when he was in Mexico, his cab driver had a fender bender, and when the police showed up and saw his American passport and an American prescription for meds, they took him in. They held him in jail for money, and when important people came to his aid, they upped the fee.

So all this was going on when I filmed and—cut to the chase—my middle man and liaison to the DP was gone. So when Ben cut the footage together, it was very static. Even though he had an elevated dolly, it was the same shot over and over. And without a middle guy, most folks revert back to what they are used to doing. To the guy's credit, there were some beautiful shots, but when I told him, "Please don't shoot me from my right side," there was a reason—I didn't look so good.

He wanted to be the editor, and everything I told him not to do, he did anyway, and I had to fix it—with more expense and I was already over budget because when you're the record company, it's your money! So I thought about the footage we had from filming our recording in Memphis, and the footage I combed through for my web site and didn't use. And of the street shot I did. I even had some stuff on my phone. So I started to put together a story with everything I had. Thank God for Arcade Films and the executive producer I'd worked with over the years, Chris. We actually put this sweet little piece together about Memphis. But I didn't finish all of it before leaving, so I worked with Ben online when I could access the internet in Europe, and Bill mixed the concert from the notes I gave him when we were home. I also worked with Sheri Lee, a brilliant art director, so the package was beautiful. All my fuss about using the Edward Hopper palette in the lighting onstage paid off. Two weeks into the European tour I actually finished and handed in the project.

THERE'S ALWAYS something happening in my life (again, God bless my manager, Lisa). Like I said, I wrote the music for *Kinky Boots*, the musical, with Harvey Fierstein. It's based on a 2005 film (in turn based on a true story) about a guy who inherits an ailing shoe factory, and he hits on the idea to make shoes for drag queens in order to save the business. The story has real heart. And it's been freeing for me as a writer, because I can write in the style that's right for the character. To get inspiration I listen to songs from Rodgers and Hammerstein, which I sang to when I was five. And writing the songs with a few collaborators, like Sammy James Jr., Stephen Oremus, Rich Morel, and Steve Gaboury, has been such fun. I feel like I'm five again sometimes. I guess Harvey must have known all along that I'd love it.

And then I've got this reality series, which is being done with Mark Burnett Productions. He's the guy that produced *The Celebrity Apprentice*, and he thought my crazy life would make a good show. It's never boring, that's for sure. We just started taping it and it's been really fun. It's focused on my work and how that affects me and my family. Nobody would believe what happens in my life. *I* don't even believe it. Here's an example: I was in the Buenos Aires airport not long ago, and all the flights were delayed. More and more people kept coming into this little airport, and everyone was sitting around wondering what was happening. I looked around me and saw people shrugging their shoulders and laughing, taking it in stride. One of my favorite things about Argentinians is their sense of humor.

All of us looked like something out of central casting—including me. Up ahead and to my right was a South American soccer team.

To my right and now leaning heavily against the side of the duty-free store was a bride-to-be with her bachelorette party, and the girl had a mask on to prevent her from seeing where she was going. They wanted to get the party started, so before long they were three sheets to the wind. Then a member of the bachelorette party grabbed the mic from an airline employee and started singing. Then the soccer players joined in. Then an airplane employee said, "By the way, Cyndi Lauper is here, and I think she should sing a song." I had sunglasses on, and I was kind of in a corner, so I thought I was being discreet.

Then everyone started getting rowdy and cheering. So I thought, "Okay, I'll go because if I don't, I don't know what will happen next." I didn't want to be carried up by the soccer players. So I sang "True Colors" and some "Girls Just Want to Have Fun." I gave my phone to one of the kids to film it, not realizing that everyone else was filming too (and that it would be on YouTube before I could blink). Then the crowd started moving in for autographs and photographs with me, which wasn't such a safe situation. I was standing next to a woman with a baby carriage, so I said, "Whoa—get her out of here." Then I said, "And get me out of here, too." So they sent me down the escalator to stand and wait by the tarmac. And there I stood, waving, as everyone passed by to catch their flight—the last photo op before they left. I know my life is crazy sometimes, but that time, I really felt like I was living in a movie. You can't make that shit up.

CHAPTER EIGHTEEN

Life continues to happen, with all its twists and turns. For instance, in March 2011 I was going to Japan and then Australia as part of the world tour to support the *Memphis Blues* CD. When we were flying into Japan all of a sudden we were going down and then we were going back up again. I thought, "It's another airport adventure, like Buenos Aires." But it wasn't—it was actually serious. It was an earthquake. We had no place to land, so we had to land on a military base. There were some young Japanese guys with their cell phones checking on their friends. They said it hit up north, but no one said anything about a tsunami; I had no idea at the time.

Finally, we were told we had to be flown to the local Tokyo airport. By that time it was ten or eleven at night and there were people everywhere. Harried airline employees were running about trying to service them. Some were lying on the floor in what looked like disposable sleeping bags. And I thought, "Disposable sleeping bags? Only in Japan." I watched as everyone in this crisis handled themselves gracefully. Everyone was calm and generous and behaving with dignity.

I have a long history with Japan, starting in 1984. When I went over then, they had changed the name of "Girls Just Want to Have Fun" to "High School Danceteria." Later, in 1986, I said, "Do you not want girls to understand that this song is about empowerment and entitlement?" I said to my promotion guy, Teri Tatsumi, "Do you think you'll be changing 'True Colors'?" and he said, "It will be 'True Colors,' and they will understand what it means." He made sure of it.

Al Arashita, whose company was Kyoto, brought me over to Japan in 1986 for my "True Colors" tour and it was very successful. We did Tokyo and Osaka, which is what everyone else did. I also played the Budokan arena for three or four sold-out shows. Before I showed up, they had me sing on a TV show and they worked it out so I'd be singing live in the studio in New York to Japan. As a result of that and other promotions, tickets for Budokan sold out in a few hours. I was kind of shocked. I kept thinking, "Who do they think is playing?" Because at that point I was still counting seats. (Actually, I still worry about empty seats.)

When I sang "True Colors" in Japan at Budokan, it was a magical moment because I sang it without my band. The original plan was to sing it just with a guitar but the guitar player we had with us, Aldo, was going through a bad time. He wasn't the secure guy I had met when he was in the studio making his own music.

So when it came time to do something sensitive and understated, I didn't feel Aldo could play intimately with me in front of a full-to-the-brim Budokan. So Dave Wolff said to sing it alone, but I wasn't alone, because the crowd sang it with me. And when I stopped and listened to them, I heard it in their wonderful accent, and it was the first time I had ever heard any audience, large or small, sing "True Colors" back to me.

Al opened Japan to me. After the shows, he would want to meet us at a restaurant so he could show us all the different foods. I was the first Westerner to tour all through Japan, and I was the first woman ever to be painted and photographed with a Kabuki artist by a Kabuki artist. I was the first Westerner to be taken to the Kobe bean-throwing ceremony and honored as the "princess of good fortune." The Japanese always took me in and always wanted to hear my music, even when my American record company thought I sucked.

In 1989, when I went over there again, another promotion guy said to me that part of why the Japanese liked me was because baby talk was very popular. I said, "What do you mean?" and he said, "Cyndi, when you speak Japanese, you speak baby talk." I had no fucking idea! I thought I knew some Japanese, because I learned it in the piano bar. Meanwhile, I sounded like an idiot. Plus my voice was higher at the time.

In 2011, when I got to our hotel in Tokyo, there were people sleeping in those sleeping bags and with blankets everywhere because the trains and buses stopped—everything stopped—so there were people in lobbies all over Tokyo. I felt so guilty about going up to my hotel room. Then I turned the TV on and that's when I understood the magnitude of what happened—the tsunami, a whole town swept away, people screaming.

Then my manager Lisa called and said, "If you want to come home, that's fine." I started thinking about it and realized there were a lot of reasons why I couldn't. The Japanese had always taken me in. How could I leave them? And we were safe.

Then I got a call from my manager saying, "Piers Morgan wants to talk to you." I had just woken up from the bed rocking back and forth and it was so comforting, I felt like a little kid. I was like, "They got toilets that are warm, and they got beds that rock . . ." Then I opened my eyes and was like, "Wait a minute—it's another fuckin' earthquake!"

And Joy Behar, whom I had known through *The View*, wanted me to call in to her show. So I did, because everybody wanted to know why I was there. I said, "What do you think I'm here for?"

When those people sang "True Colors" to me it was powerful and if I left, honestly, what the hell would "True Colors" have meant? After that country had opened its heart to me? Nothing. So I'd stay to perform for eighty or ninety minutes and we'd give them a little distraction. We'd lift them up. I thought to myself that I could use whatever I have. So I used the reiki stuff that I learned, and I had come to learn that the sound of my voice, especially the midrange was very soothing. I've become friends with some fans, and there is one named Donny who lives in Georgia. He told me about this girl he knew who had cancer, and it was toward the end. So I called to sing to her, and her mother kept trying to say, "This is Cyndi Lauper." Her hearing was going but I decided that right off the bat I would sing "True Colors" to her in that low midrange soft sound. And she quieted down. That's when I realized that there was something more to my voice than just singing hit songs. So if I stayed in Japan maybe the sound of my voice would help the Japanese, like it did that girl.

So I stayed. Because I couldn't let them down. And it wasn't just me that stayed—so did my whole band and crew, and the whole Japanese crew, and Yuki, the guy in charge of the tour whose baby had just turned one the day the tsunami hit. I did as many shows as I could on that tour with a Japanese flugelhorn player named Toku. After a while, we were the only tour in Japan—no one was left, not Japanese, not American, not anybody. But we stayed because we wanted to give people some peace.

Then, a year later, Lisa said, "They want you back in Japan for the anniversary of the tsunami, and we can add on a lot of other dates and we can do the whole South Asian region." But because I had been touring for so long, my kid and my husband needed me. I needed my family, too. I realized my kid was growing up, and I was missing everything. So I said to Lisa, "I can't go away for another couple of months—I'll do the anniversary of three-eleven. That I have to do, no question. And then I want to come home."

Lisa worked it out with Wowow, which is like Japan's HBO, that if I appeared on their post-Grammys show in Los Angeles, they would sponsor a concert for me on the anniversary of the tsunami and show it for free in movie theaters in the three prefectures affected by the tsunami. Movie theaters across the rest of the country would also play it and donate their proceeds to the Red Cross. I felt honored to be asked to be a part of that, so I did whatever they wanted.

The Grammys are a big deal in Japan. They show it live in the morning, almost like a news show. So after I attended the Grammys, I went to a separate studio across from the Staples Center to give my commentary. We thought it was funny that they were set up in the penalty box of the ESPN Zone. The night of the Grammys was a little sad because Whitney Houston died. Any time a singer dies, it shakes up the singing community. We all email and text each other. But even though I was shook up that day, I still did my job. I knew if I did this, it would allow me to do something good for the Japanese people.

The day after I arrived in Japan for the anniversart of the tsunami, I got into hair and makeup at ten A.M. and I did TV interviews from the hotel room. I met a lot of different people, including a guy named Gutch. He gave me some sake from Fukushima and he said it was a "presento" and I said, "Let's bust it out now and toast Fukushima." We did his TV shoot and had some sake for his radio show. It was not like work because he was so funny. Every interview started out with a conversation about the tsunami. It was such a hard year for them.

Then everyone started talking about all that I did for the Japanese people, and I started to feel like a fraud. First, it wasn't just me. It was all of us—the Japanese crew, too. Nobody went home. So I figured that if they're going to make me into this hero, I should really do something good. I started to think about how I could help the kids who were in the devastated areas. I had talked to Yoko Ono before I left. She had gone up to a school in the Fukushima prefecture and hugged the kids. Nobody touches the people there because they're afraid of radiation. So I called my husband, David, because I was really upset about this whole "making me out to be someone I'm not" thing. I'm not Lady Di. And I'm not Bono. My husband said that maybe they need someone to be that for them: "Don't take that away just because of how you feel about it. Why don't you go up to a school up north and bring a tree?"

Yuki, who was running my tour through Kyoto, and Nestor, who was my bodyguard, helped me make it happen. Reiko Yukawa is Yuki's mom. She is a famous rock journalist, considered to be the rock and roll sensei of Japan. She has interviewed every rocker since Elvis and the Beatles. So she kind of walked me through it. Yuki didn't want me to go to a radioactive area so we went to a devastated area that was on the other side of the mountains from Sendai called Ishinomaki, which translates to "Rock and Roll." Yuki's mom knew a fellow who was a funeral director and asked him if he might know a garden center. (I thought they must have a Home Depot, but they didn't.)

The funeral director told Reiko that he had been doing a thousand funerals a week and he had this garden center for all the funerals he was doing. He generously donated ten cherry blossom trees. I decided to bring trees because the trees could grow with the kids and the cherry blossoms would bloom around the anniversary of the tsunami. So the kids could see some blossoms instead of devastation.

When we got there the kids were gathered in the auditorium. They were like any other grade-school kids—loud, and the boys were pushing into each other. The principal looked harried, but they were all waiting and the news crews were there too. I guess us going was big news. The media asked about the devastation and why I had come. I told them I just wanted the people to know I haven't forgotten about them.

After we went to the school we drove through the town—or what was the town. We drove by a music store and decided to go inside and a little old man showed me where the waterline was. I wanted to buy something from him—it's important to keep the commerce going since people aren't buying from there. Then they took me to a school farther in. The whole hill that used to be filled with houses was completely devastated. There were no houses left. When the tsunami hit, they told me about how the kids at another school were put on the roof, but there wasn't enough room for the parents, so they stayed on the bottom and when the water came they all were drowned.

Then we went to a temple in the middle of a graveyard. The big heavy gravestones had been tossed around like they were nothing. Inside, tables were filled with shopping bags containing human remains, unclaimed bodies. I lit incense and rang a bell three times and prayed for them. I also donated what I had in my purse. The trip really was devastating. When you see devastation like that—well, it's devastating.

It had been snowing there and the snow had turned into rain. So it was cold and slushy. Then we took the bullet train back to Tokyo. I sang and did the show that we all prepared for on the eleventh. At the exact time the tsunami hit, all of Japan stopped for a minute to pray. Even the trains stopped. I wanted so much for my performance to be extra great, but I'm not even sure I breathed until the fourth song into my set. I felt a little overwhelmed, like I wished I was Superwoman, but instead I was just me. In my heart I know there are no accidents. I was supposed to be there. I think Wowow was happy with the show. I hope the people of Japan were, too. The day I called my husband, David, from Japan, he said, "There's a lot going on in the world. Sometimes the best we can do is to just be there for each other."

AFTERWORD

You may find that life goes in a circle. Sometimes the same situation comes up again and again till we get it right. I have begun to think that when this happens to me, the first time maybe I was too young, the second time too angry, but the third time? I've got to show up.

And here's a fine example: I am here at Simon & Schuster writing my life story. And as I said, I was here before for my first full-time job when I was seventeen years old as the worst gal Friday anyone had ever seen. I was fired and have since called myself a gal Friday the thirteenth. On one of the last days that I was writing this book with Jancee at Simon & Schuster, I met a security guard in the elevator. I noticed he was getting off at the same floor where they gave me an office, so I smiled at him and said, "What? Are they getting you to write your life story, too?" And he said, "No, I don't think my life story would be as interesting as yours." And I said, "Really? I bet it is if you just think about it." I wanted to tell him I was an ex-employee of the place too. But I didn't, I just smiled and told him to have a nice day. If life is for learning, then we all better get to know our book. I hope there is something in this book that will help you with your story. When one person shares their story, it might help another guy get a head start. If my story can help anyone else, then I think it's important.

And remember this: It's not what others think about you that will allow you to succeed. It's what you think about you that allows you to succeed. Because if you can picture yourself doing something, don't listen to anybody who tells you that you can't. You have to just try. Otherwise you're gonna be saying should've, could've, would've, and you don't want to be saying that in your life. And if you get to the top of the mountain, share your story.

Xx
Cyn

First band I was ever in, before I was the lead singer, 1974.

Posing with Flyer. This was my first art direction, 1976.

Blue Angel, 1978.

At Long Island club My Father's Place, with Rockin A, 1980.

In back, left to right: Gregory, me, Carol, Jon "the mayor," and not sure who that is on the right. In front left to right: Carol's husband, Carl.

Waiting at an airport with my band during the "Fun" tour, although it's questionable how much fun we're all actually having, 1985.

Also on "Fun" tour. I love that hat. I still have it.

On plane with Dave Wolfe, 1984.

At one of the
airports, 1984.

With Dave Wolfe backstage, 1984.

On tour in Canada, 1984. This was one of my favorite outfits.

With John Turi at Lone Star, NYC. Jim Gregory is behind us, 1990.

With Lisa Barbaris
in Romania, 2000.

Bad Vlad's castle,
Romania, 2000.

Sammy Merendino.

Kat Dyson, me, Allison Cornell, 2003.

Bill Wittman.

Me and Steve Gaboury.